# TOM STOPPARD
# AN ASSESSMENT

# TOM STOPPARD
# AN ASSESSMENT

Tim Brassell

St. Martin's Press　　　New York

© Tim Brassell 1985

All rights reserved. For information, write:
St. Martin's Press, Inc., 175 Fifth Avenue, New York, NY 10010
Printed in Hong Kong
Published in the United Kingdom by The Macmillan Press Ltd.
First published in the United States of America in 1985

ISBN 0–312–80888–7

**Library of Congress Cataloging in Publication Data**

Brassell, Tim, 1953–
  Tom Stoppard: an assessment.

  Bibliography: p.
  Includes index.
  1. Stoppard, Tom—Criticism and interpretation.
I. Title.
PR6069.T6Z59  1984        822′.914        83–40126
ISBN 0–312–80888–7

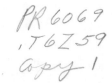

# Contents

# A Note on Punctuation

Since Stoppard himself uses three dots (. . .) regularly in his own punctuation, a line break is added to all quotations from his work where material has been omitted. Three dots *without* a line break thus means that nothing is missing. This applies to quotations from Stoppard *only*.

# Acknowledgement

Extracts from the plays: *Rosencrantz and Guildenstern are Dead*, *Enter a Free Man*, *A Separate Peace*, *If You're Glad I'll Be Frank*, *Albert's Bridge*, *The Real Inspector Hound*, *After Magritte*, *Where Are They Now?*, *Jumpers*, *Travesties*, *Artist Descending a Staircase*, *Every Good Boy Deserves Favour*, *Professional Foul*, *Night and Day*, *Dirty Linen*, *Dogg's Hamlet*, *Cahoot's Macbeth* and *On the Razzle* are reproduced by permission of Faber & Faber Ltd, London.

# Preface

'Interpretation' (as Susan Sontag has said), 'is the revenge of the intellect on art.' It's a view which I strongly suspect Tom Stoppard shares, so perhaps I'd better say at the outset that vengeance has formed no part of my conscious intentions in preparing this book. I have, on the contrary, been guided by the belief that Stoppard's work, with its characteristic marriage of humour and seriousness and its flamboyant theatricality, is a valuable and unique asset to our contemporary theatre. I hope that more people might come to share this view after reading the book, whether as students, actors, producers or theatregoers, and that this 'interpretation' may send them back where their attention rightly belongs – to the plays, and to Stoppard's art.

When I began work on this book in 1975 (originally for a research degree), there was next to nothing in print about Tom Stoppard's plays beyond a few scholarly articles and a mountain of reviews. Since then a number of short monographs have appeared in Britain and America, but not the major study which his plays demand. The more they are studied on examination syllabuses at all levels on both sides of the Atlantic, the more that absence – and the need to examine and rectify some of the misunderstandings that seem to have attached themselves to his work – has been demonstrated. It is in the hope of contributing at least a starting point in that direction that this study is therefore published.

I would like to acknowledge the invaluable encouragement and guidance given to me by Michael Quinn of University College, Cardiff, in setting this book in motion and for the fatherly eye he has kept on it since. I want also to thank Catherine Hepworth, Geoffrey Axworthy of the Sherman Theatre and Julia Steward at Macmillan for their kindness and assistance at various stages, and Joyce Bruce and Jean Shacklady for their valiant deciphering of my handwriting. My thanks are also due to Faber and Faber and the Grove Press for permission to reproduce copyright material from

Tom Stoppard's work and to Tom Stoppard and Clive Exton for permission to quote from *The Boundary*. Chapter 7 of this book was first published in a slightly different version in *Gambit* magazine, vol. 10, no. 37 (John Calder, 1981). Above all, my thanks are due to Tom Stoppard for many happy and enlightening hours of reading and theatregoing.

TJB

Newcastle upon Tyne
1983

# 1 Introduction

'Tom Stoppard . . . works with a brilliance, an intellectual agility, and a capacity of mind as well as wit that have no rival on the contemporary stage.'

(Harold Hobson)[1]

'It's time we stopped dismissing comedy as an inferior genre, and thanked Heaven for a new comic master.'

(Ronald Bryden)[2]

'As a dramatist, Stoppard is a dandy. His plays toy with difficult subjects, but they are essentially not very serious. They are pirouettes by a rather vain dancer who knows he can leap higher than anyone else but seems to have forgotten why.'

(Robert Brustein)[3]

'Stoppard's work is beloved by those for whom theatre is an end and not a means, a ramification and not a modifier of the *status quo* . . . He is the wittiest of our West End playwrights and his plays assure the reactionary that theatre was and is what they always trusted it was, anodyne and anaesthetising.'

(Philip Roberts)[4]

Tom Stoppard is unquestionably a major power in the contemporary theatre both in this country and, increasingly, in America. Ever since the first appearance of *Rosencrantz and Guildenstern are Dead* in 1966, his plays have enjoyed almost unrivalled box office success and the press reviewers have (as the first two quotations demonstrate) sung his praises to the skies. There has, however, been surprising indifference and at times outright hostility to his work in academic circles, as the second pair of quotations demonstrates. Or perhaps it is not so surprising, for Stoppard's plays continually testify to his enthusiasm for the world of theatre and showbusiness, a world with an often suspect connotation for those writing analytically about drama. When

1

asked by Benedict Nightingale what he wanted his audiences to
leave the theatre thinking and feeling after a performance of one of
his plays, Stoppard replied:

> I'm sorry to tell you that my ambitions in that direction are very
> modest and possibly shameful. I don't wish them to think very
> much more than that it was money well spent.[5]

Four years earlier, writing in the *Times Literary Supplement*, he had
gone aggressively further, making such playful but unendearing
swipes as:

> it is understandable that in seeking its own *raison d'être*, the vast
> oracular Lego set of Lit Crit with its chairs and lectureships, its
> colloquia and symposia, its presses, reprints, off-prints, mono-
> graphs, reviews, footnotes and fireside chats, should come up with
> something better than that it beats working for a living.[6]

The purpose of that article was to suggest that the analysis of
drama was irrelevant to playwrights, directors, actors and, for the
most part, audiences; that it was, in the main, aimed merely at
fellow-theoreticians and thereby lacked 'the essential touch of
reality which reassures the scientist that he is earning his keep.'[7]
   This general divergence of opinion about Stoppard between the
'theatre' world and the 'drama' world is curious in view of the
indivisibility of the two in practice: drama is, after all, written to be
performed and theatre is the act of its performance. The conflicting
reactions to his work seem to reflect the crisis in our current cultural
thinking about the theatre. As Stoppard implies, an over-literary
attitude towards drama is a contradiction since it cannot sensibly
exist in separation from the performing conditions that nurture it;
that the word 'theatre' and more especially its derivative 'theatricality' should seem in danger of becoming semi-pejorative terms is
therefore disturbing. The problem is partly an historical one.
Raymond Williams has pointed out how little heed scholarship has
generally taken of drama as a performance art and how one is
restricted in its appreciation by the common adoption of the kind of
literary approaches appropriate for poetry or novels. He stresses
that

> the drama is, or can be, both literature and theatre, not the one at
> the expense of the other, but each *because* of the other.[8]

What is wrong with much modern drama is that it is such poor theatre; a play which does not use its chosen medium well deserves to fail. Stoppard's plays, on the other hand, are brimful of theatricality and are always concerned, in the first instance, with entertaining their audiences. To believe that such an approach necessarily implies frivolity and superficiality is as unenlightened and culturally snobbish as to believe, for instance, that television drama, by definition, cannot be worth watching. What, after all, is unusual about 'playfulness' in a 'play'? I do not believe that those academics who have written about Stoppard in dismissive terms have penetrated beyond their own prejudices about theatre. Seeing only surface dazzle, self-conscious wit, verbal acrobatics and a 'toying' with ideas in his work, they have failed to recognise the unique manner in which each of his comedies is woven around a serious core. The ensuing study is an attempt to right this balance, to bring an essentially academic approach to this most theatrical of contemporary talents, to explore the controlling ideas of the plays, and to show those whose approach has been unfairly dismissive something of what they have missed. I want finally to suggest that Stoppard's comedies are a valuable reminder within a dramatic climate largely dominated by traditional, naturalistic precepts and often dour seriousness that 'theatricality' may be an essential part of a healthy, living theatre.

In the following chapters equal stress will not be given to all the plays. Most of Stoppard's shorter, early pieces have been dealt with in only cursory terms.[9] So, too, have his adaptations, with the important exception of *On the Razzle* which is based much more loosely on its original. Two introductory sections will sketch in Stoppard's background and his published non-dramatic writing – a single novel which deserves more attention than it has had, and a set of short stories. A third provides a brief introduction to some of the currents in the modern theatre most relevant to Stoppard's work. The plays are then examined in roughly chronological order, including those written for radio and television. Particular attention is paid to *Rosencrantz and Guildenstern are Dead* and the three original full-length plays which follow: *Jumpers*, *Travesties* and *Night and Day*, with a single chapter devoted to each.[10]

\* \* \*

Born on 3 July 1937, in the Czechoslovakian town of Zlin (since re-named Gottwaldov), Tomas Straussler spent his earliest years avoiding World War II. The younger of the two sons of Czech parents, Eugene and Martha Straussler, he moved with his family in 1939 to Singapore, where his father, a doctor with the Bata shoe company, had been posted. Three years later he moved again, evacuated to India with his mother and brother just before the Japanese invasion in which his father was killed. Four years were then spent in India before his mother, managing a Bata shop in Darjeeling, remarried. Tom duly took the name of his stepfather, Kenneth Stoppard, an officer in the British army, and the family came back to England, where Mr Stoppard worked in the machine tool business.

Despite this colourful-sounding background, English has been Stoppard's tongue almost from the start. His first school in Darjeeling was an English-language, American-run institution, attended by children of many different nationalities. After settling in England, he moved to Dolphin Preparatory School in Nottingham, and then to Pocklington School in Yorkshire as a boarder, leaving at the age of seventeen, after completing his 'A' levels. He returned home to Bristol (where the family had settled in 1950) and joined the *Western Daily Press* as a 'cub' reporter on a weekly wage of £2.10s. 8d. This was in 1954, and he continued full-time work as a journalist for the next six years, switching in 1958 to the group's evening paper, the *Evening World* (now defunct), where he frequently covered theatre as a second-string critic, wrote the weekly film review column for a few months and on one occasion deputised for the motoring correspondent despite the fact that he couldn't drive!

Stoppard's practical attitude to his craft is in part the legacy of this journalistic background, which also helps to account for the considerable range of reading to which his plays bear witness. (His interest in philosophy revealed in *Rosencrantz and Guildenstern are Dead* and *Jumpers* prompted many, including Arnold Hinchliffe and Robert Brustein,[11] to assume that he must be a graduate.) But, as he told Ronald Hayman:

> a lot of my reading has resulted from the sheer necessity of having something to deliver . . . You read the works of Norman Mailer in fourteen days in order to write an article of 1 200 words.[12]

In 1960, however, he decided that a professional commitment to his own creative writing was overdue. In his own words:

In July 1960, sitting gloomily in the turquoise sea, waiting for the
mainland boat to rescue me from the crush of Capri, I
remembered that it was my twenty-third birthday; twenty-three
and still unpublished, still unstaged – still, as a matter of fact,
unwriting . . . So getting back to Bristol from my annual three
weeks, I handed in my notice after six years of reporting, subbing,
reviewing and interviewing, and, having contracted to write two
weekly columns for a total of six guineas, started writing a stage
play, *A Walk on the Water*.[13]

Late in 1962, Stoppard finally moved from Bristol to Notting Hill as
the drama critic on a new London magazine called *Scene*. This
folded after eight months, but fortunately by this time his writing
was beginning to produce an income: Faber and Faber bought three
of his short stories, the publisher Anthony Blond commissioned a
novel and Rediffusion Television bought and transmitted *A Walk on
the Water*, which Stoppard had been unsuccessfully hawking since
writing it in three months flat in 1960. In the following eventful
year, 1964, the short stories appeared in a new collection called
*Introduction Two* and BBC Radio broadcast two fifteen-minute radio
plays – *The Dissolution of Dominic Boot* in February and *'M' is for
Moon Among Other Things* (adapted from a rejected short story) in
April.[14] Also in 1964, Stoppard was commissioned to write five
episodes of the Light Programme serial *The Dales* and, along with
three other promising British playwrights (another was James
Saunders), he was invited to West Berlin for a five-month
colloquium held under the auspices of the Ford Foundation. It was
here that a first, embryonic version of *Rosencrantz and Guildenstern are
Dead* was written, a version which Stoppard now hopes is buried in
eternal darkness![15] During this period a revised version of *A Walk on
the Water* was also staged in Hamburg under the title *Old Riley
Walked the Water*.

In the next year, 1965, the Royal Shakespeare Company took out
an option on a completely new draft of *Rosencrantz*, a radio version of
*A Walk on the Water* was broadcast by the BBC and *The Gamblers*, a
one-act play set in a condemned cell (written some years earlier and
never published), was staged as an extra-mural exercise by students
of the Bristol Old Vic Theatre School. Stoppard also wrote alternate
episodes for a BBC World Service series (broadcast in Arabic)
chronicling London life through the eyes of an Arab student, and
married Jose Ingle, a nurse who lived in the same block of flats when

he moved to London. (They were divorced in 1972 and he married Miriam Moore-Robinson, his present wife.) Then, in February 1966, the broadcasting of the one-act radio play *If You're Glad I'll Be Frank* heralded the start of what proved to be the decisive year in Stoppard's career.

In this play for the first time his characteristic style is heard in a mêlée of wild comedy with a small, plaintive voice at the heart of the storm. It was followed in May by *Tango*, his adaptation of Mrozek's play for the R.S.C., whose one-year option on *Rosencrantz* then ran out. Just weeks later, almost in tandem with the publication of the Blond novel, *Lord Malquist and Mr Moon*, came the first, legendary performance at the Edinburgh Fringe Festival of *Rosencrantz and Guildenstern are Dead*. After six years of hard work, success arrived with the utmost suddenness: the members of the Oxford Theatre Group who had been offered the play in a slightly shorter version than the one we know (Stoppard was still working on the third act, but time was short) could scarcely have conceived the inherent potential of their discovery or the instant acclaim it would bring its author. Ronald Bryden in *The Observer* unhesitatingly said of the play, 'It's the most brilliant debut by a young playwright since Arden's.[16] Kenneth Tynan, the literary adviser to Olivier's National Theatre regime, telegraphed the young author at once for a script and initiated the process leading to the London production of the play (complete with a revised third act) which opened at the Old Vic Theatre on 11 April 1967.[17] Thus it was that the first professional production in Britain of one of Stoppard's own plays took place on the hallowed stage of the National Theatre itself. Within a decade it had had more than 250 productions in 20 different languages[18] and grossed 'well over £300,000' for its author.[19] Such success can only be described as spectacular.

# 2 'Style' versus 'Substance'

By a strange coincidence Stoppard's first (and, to date, only) novel was published in the self-same week as the first performance of *Rosencrantz and Guildenstern are Dead* at Edinburgh. As Stoppard lightheartedly told Jon Bradshaw very much later,

> I believed my reputation would be made by the novel. I believed the play would be of little consequence.[1]

Yet whether or not his natural orientation towards the stage was ever seriously in doubt, his fiction certainly deserves to be read and studied, not least for the interesting light it sheds on his subsequent development as a playwright.

\*　　　\*　　　\*

The three short stories published in 1964 in *Introduction Two*, a showcase for new story-writing talent, bear the hallmark of Stoppard's many years as a journalist. Two of them have journalism as their explicit subject and all of them present semi-autobiographical material in a curiously remote tone, as if the author is unusually anxious to detach himself from the implications of what is being said; this results in a striking and sometimes uneasy sense of tension in the writing, as if strong feelings were deliberately being reined back. Stoppard seems to be examining himself and his subjects at a remove, testing his universe as if by refraction from a neighbouring planet, and while the men and women in these stories are sympathetically presented, they are generally powerless: their lives, in differing ways, do not seem to be properly under their control.

This is most evident in 'The Story', which relates in a bare, factual manner how the newspaper coverage of a minor court case, involving a teacher's interference with a young girl, makes headline news and leads the convicted man to commit suicide. It is the process by which this happens that concerns, and clearly worries, Stoppard. The courtroom journalist (the persona he adopts) is reluctant to use the story; it was a first offence and the fine was only £25. The defendant's solicitor, however, has been unwise enough to let slip the fact that his client is a master at 'one of the top schools'. In the light of this, and pressure from a Press Services Agency colleague whom he meets by chance in the street straight after the hearing, the journalist is eventually persuaded to phone over the details.

> He was being nice about it. If I gave him the details he would send them over and it would just be a favour I had done him in the street. With me phoning it meant I'd get paid what was going.[2]

The teacher's local paper picks up the story and it subsequently spreads to the nationals. A week later, he jumps in front of an underground train.

The narrative deliberately works at a remove from the court case and the victim, as an almost deadpan account of the journalist's thoughts and actions, and the sense of his own culpability which surfaces is all the more powerful for being implied rather than stated. But Stoppard is not merely putting some of the ethical implications of his profession to the test (as, years later, in the play *Night and Day*); like Priestley in *An Inspector Calls*, he is interested in the interlocking chains of human responsibility. Once the journalist has released the story, both he and its eventual victim seem to have little control over the unfolding train of events as Stoppard evokes a sinister sense of vast wheels turning, oiled not by men and women but by some vague metaphysical fate.

'Reunion', though on a smaller scale, is cast in a similar mould. It presents a single conversation resulting from the brief return of a spurned male to the woman he still loves, an encounter full of tension and awkwardness. Since her mind is made up, their wills can only clash and the man becomes uncomfortably conscious of his powerlessness. Stoppard's dialogue, though not entirely convincing, is characteristic in its pathos and understated emotion:

> 'You said you wouldn't come.'
> 'It was true then.'

'You're all right.'
'No,' he said. 'Are you?'
'Fine.'
'Different?'
'You can't expect it to be the same.'
'I mean, better?'
'Different.'
'Is that better?'
'Oh, please. There's no point.'   (p. 122)

The awkwardness of the situation for both parties is neatly conveyed, but one gains the distinct impression that Stoppard's own sense of awkwardness is equally present, as he wrestles to be serious without being excessively self-conscious. There are very few examples in his subsequent work where he is prepared to confront emotional crises of this nature without recourse to parody or humorous deflection in some form or another.

More successful here is the handling of the man's wry attempts to deflect the painful implications of his situation, and these increasingly dominate the story. Finding nothing in the woman to which he can appeal, he grows ever more desperate:

'There is a certain word,' he said very carefully, 'which if shouted at the right pitch and in a silence worthy of it, would nudge the universe into gear . . .

All the things which just miss will just click right.' (p. 123)

By making us identify specifically with the man's intensity in this way, rather than confronting the two characters head-on, Stoppard strikes a note that becomes increasingly characteristic of his earlier style. This dislocated feeling that things are terribly out of joint and that the power to rectify them must be somewhere close at hand becomes a recurrent obsession of his characters. In *Lord Malquist and Mr Moon*, in particular, Moon shares this unnamed man's neurotic desire to nudge the universe back into gear – his remedy being a home-made bomb. Just as Malquist, his opposite, is less sympathetically presented in the novel, so too is the woman here, capable of adjusting and adapting as the man is not:

'Oh, shut up,' the woman said, finally, and the hollow ballooned, shaking emptily, his body disconnecting. . .

and it took a long time, stairs and streets later, before he got a hold
on it again. (p. 125)

Comedy is conspicuous by its absence from these two short stories,
but is firmly in control of the other, 'Life, Times: Fragments', which,
as its mildly punning title announces, also has journalism as its
subject, or, to be precise, a journalist-would-be-writer who feels he
has become 'too good for journalism' (p. 126), and behind whom,
fairly clearly, lurks Stoppard's own shadow. A sharp, humorous
vein of irony runs through these fragments, a rather unrelated mêlée
of incidents from a writer's working life which reads rather like
every thousandth page of someone's diary, and gives a strong hint of
the wit and ingenuity of Stoppard's later writing. In particular, the
cynical tone recalls that of Stoppard's witty article in *Author* about
the indefinite postponements that strike whenever publication or
performance are imminent.[3] At its best though, particularly
towards the end, this episodic assortment contains very much the
best writing in any of the three short stories.

In the first of the fragments, the writer mistakenly kills off a
woman as he writes a report on a road accident, and undergoes deep
remorse – until she dies properly the next day, which somehow
obliterates the error. The second relates his failure to get a job on the
*Evening Standard* by not knowing the name of the Foreign Secretary,
which confirms one's scent of autobiographical content in the
stories; this is precisely what once happened to Stoppard![4] The
writer then ages progressively – watching his age slip by from
twenty-six to twenty-seven while waist-deep in the sea,[5] then
dismissing every figure in the front ranks of world literature at the
age of thirty-four and declaring that he himself feels seminal – at
which his wife quickly importunes, 'No, do you mind if we don't
tonight; I've run out of the stuff.' (p. 128)

When he reaches fifty, 'the oldest sub in London', he turns to
religion:

the further he got from publication the closer he got to God, until
the two seemed to present themselves as alternatives. He tried to
resist the direction, because on the whole he would rather have
been accepted by a publisher and as he was not sure he believed in
God, and for a long time he compromised by praying at his
typewriter. (p. 129)

Finally, after the writer has received 127 rejection slips, he concedes
that God has won:

> 'I cast off my wordly aspirations, and offer myself, Dear Lord,
> wholly to your eternal service.' And the Lord heard him and He
> sent an angel to the writer as he knelt, and the angel said, 'The
> Lord thanks you for your contribution but regrets that it is not
> quite suitable for the Kingdom of Heaven.' (p. 129).

The writer subsequently dies of despair, but a fell stroke of irony,
beautifully capping the comedy, contrives to ensure that his suicide
note is found by a critic sensitive to its literary worth. Posthumously,
the writer is at last 'discovered'.

No one would claim that these stories are among Stoppard's
strongest work. They are fascinating evidence, however, of the way
in which his mind and ideas were shaping themselves at this early
point in his writing career. The autobiographical resonances
disappear almost entirely after this time (at least until *The Real
Thing*), but the stories nevertheless provide some clear pointers to
what is in store: the stylistic economy (the longest of them is a mere
six pages), the detachment and poise of some of the narrative, and
the running theme of human powerlessness – the man in 'Reunion'
unable to win back the woman he has lost, the journalist in 'The
Story' unable to control the spiralling news-spreading process and
the writer in 'Life, Times: Fragments' unable to find the fame and
fortune he considers to be his due. A recurrent and disturbing
concern that the human race is not wholly in control can thus be
discerned as all three stories touch on what becomes a central
concern throughout Stoppard's writing: that experience ought to
make sense but the formula for making it do so lies mockingly,
infuriatingly out of reach.

\*              \*              \*

*Lord Malquist and Mr Moon*[6] is difficult to classify. It gives the
immediate impression of a bizarre comic novel bustling with
eccentric characters and events, many of them seemingly introduced to further the ostentatious display of authorial style.
Stoppard's chameleon-like presentation gaily arranges his colour-
fully far-fetched characters within a narrative by turns playful and
subdued, and there is a general air of detached understatement
faintly reminiscent of Nabokov as he charts a series of strange events

taking place on two far-from-ordinary January days. Yet as one reads on, it becomes increasingly clear that Stoppard is, at least intermittently, giving serious treatment to a number of poignant human problems. Like so much of his later work, strands of serious writing are continually woven into the comic fabric and it is ultimately these which are most impressive; while the novel's humour is uneven, the switches into a more serious mood have considerable power, like the sudden darkenings of a brilliantly lit room.

Attempting to summarise the 'storyline' of *Lord Malquist and Mr Moon*, especially in its initial stages, is rather like trying to wind up a ball of wool meticulously entangled by a cat. Stoppard introduces five initial scenarios, each written in a quite different style – a horse-drawn coach running amok after mowing down a stout female pedestrian, a tense encounter between two cowboys, a woman parched with thirst watched by a predatory lion, a berobed man entering a city on the back of a donkey, and the romantic ecstasy of a young beauty seated, it transpires, on the lavatory – and then, with considerable dexterity and even greater ingenuity, assembles them all into a coherent, if eccentric frame, within the space of a few pages. We are not in the Wild West, the desert or the eighteenth century after all, but in the cosmopolitan metropolis of modern-day London, and we are chiefly in the bizarre company of Lord Malquist, a twentieth-century earl seeking to sustain all the anachronistic refinement of his eighteenth-century forebears (it is his coach) and his hired diarist, Mr Moon, the Boswell to his Johnson, an obsessively insecure little man perpetually nursing a home-made bomb. As the action develops, the earl becomes increasingly involved with Moon's wife Jane (the young beauty), who is already the darling of the two rival cowboys, and Moon completes the pattern by duly landing up in Lady Malquist's bed. By the end it is as though Moon's neurosis has encompassed the whole novel, such is its increasing madness: the cowboys' feud turns nasty when their live bullets begin to claim real victims; Malquist, living vastly above his limited means, is evicted from his home, and Moon's bomb explodes in the middle of Trafalgar Square just as the funeral procession of a national hero (clearly Churchill) is entering it, fortuitously releasing not a vicious shower of shrapnel but a huge balloon with an obscene message written across it. Finally, with heavy irony, the husband of the fat lady run down by Malquist at the start of the novel throws a real bomb at his coach in revenge – only to kill Moon, who has borrowed it to take himself home.

The five-string opening of the novel is a collage of considerable virtuosity in which Stoppard exploits the confusion he engenders with comic relish, using a device subsequently employed in many of the plays. This is to baffle his readers or audiences by presenting an apparently absurd situation, then to argue himself out of it by supplying an ingenious and plausible (though often far-fetched) solution. The play *After Magritte* is sustained almost solely on the basis of this device.[7] Here the cowboys eventually turn out to be involved in a promotion stunt for Western Trail Pork'n'Beans, while the 'white woman' suffering from drought and watched by a lion is duly revealed to be Malquist's wife, Lady Laura Malquist, drunkenly staggering into Green Park and chancing upon her husband's missing pet lion, Rollo. The originality of this device is apt to wear rather thin after a while, but the ingenuity of the explanations remains spirited.

What increasingly sustains the novel is, however, the inter-relations Stoppard develops between his characters' many playworlds. His approach is generally to present them with complete narrative detachment in the terms in which they are prone to imagine themselves. He thereby creates liberal opportunities for parodying stereotyped roles from the cinema and pulp fiction while simultaneously exposing the crass, ready-made realities in which his characters will themselves to believe. At the same time, the novel is wired up to itself at several points by the interplay between these different perspectives. The cowboys' duel, for instance, is described three times from three quite separate points of view: first the cowboys' own (a Hollywood Western parody), then Jane's, then Moon's. In the second, Jane is out with Lord Malquist in his coach, and is therefore given the full romantic treatment:

A shadow passed over her exquisite features, and her soft ripe bosom heaved.
'Too late, too late!' a voice cried within her. 'Ah, would that we had met when we were free!' For him she would have gladly turned her back on Society and escaped with him to some perfect spot away from all this, but she knew deep down in her heart that this would not bring them happiness. They were duty bound to live out their rôles in this hollow masquerade, even as they recoiled from the hypocritical conventions that kept them apart. No, all they could do was to snatch a few precious moments together. (p. 160)

Here, and elsewhere with Jane, the heavily mannered style of light romantic fiction is entirely geared to her immature and romantic conception of herself, which is not even interrupted by the sight of the cowboys' fatal shoot-out right before her eyes; more romantically disturbing is Moon's equally abrupt appearance beside the coach:

> At that moment the door was flung open and her hand flew to her mouth.
> 'My husband!' she cried.   (p. 161)

The blatant inappropriateness of the parodic tone makes it highly amusing, but it also provides a telling and ironic commentary on Jane's fondly delusive notions of her own nature.

The recurrent and major theme of the novel is thus of the games people play, and of the fantasies with which they distract themselves from the everyday business of living. Moon alone sees acutely what is wrong:

> 'The thing about people is,' said Moon, 'that hardly anyone behaves naturally any more, they all behave the way they think they are supposed to be, as if they'd read about themselves or seen themselves at the pictures. The whole of life is like that now . . . .
>
> Originality has been used up.'   (p. 53)

There are evident difficulties in welding such disparate characters and styles into a cohesive storyline, but Stoppard skilfully capitalises upon this irreconcilability by organising the characters' self-created, solipsistic worlds on a *principle* of collision. The dialogues and encounters between them thereby reveal a degree of non-communication which is both comic and unsettling. As Moon discovers when he finds Long John Slaughter on his doorstep, mutual understanding can barely travel above the lowest common denominator:

> 'Your horse outside?'
> 'Mare,' said Slaughter. 'It's a mare.'
> 'I didn't see her outside.'
> 'No, I just climbed off her in the end and she just went on walking. As if she had been wound up. I don't think it was a real horse, or mare. I think it was a wind-up one. God knows where the damn

thing is now. Probably walked into the sea.'
Moon asked, 'Are you making a film?'
'Wish I was. Now that's something I could do.'
'Yes. I'm sorry, I can't remember your name.'
'L. J. Slaughter. I should be in films all right.'
'You couldn't have real bullets in a film,' Moon said.
'In a film you wouldn't need them,' said Slaughter.
Moon felt as if the conversation was a weight he had to drag along
on the end of a rope.   (p. 114)

In this way the insubstantiality of each character's status is
intensified, their individual realities exposed as affected mas-
querades. The cowboys understand each other because they are
playing the same game – a game, incidentally, which finally gets
them both killed. But Moon has no meeting-point with them, nor,
indeed, with his wife, Jane, whose immersion in romantic fantasy
excludes actual contact, even with her own husband. Her game is
equally dangerous, too, since it eventually leads her into the sexual
clutches of Malquist, whose 'game' with her turns out to be
deceptively serious.

Lord Malquist demonstrates the way in which non-
communication can be sought. There is an implicit evasiveness
about his superficially cultivated manner; in fact, he cultivates the
superficial:

My dear lady, I am already somewhat uneasy about going
punting dressed for the gaming tables. I think to drink *crème de
menthe* in a pale blue cravat would be the abandonment of
everything I stand for.   (p. 62)

Stoppard captures the style he seeks for Malquist perfectly, with a
mannered, epithetical address strongly reminiscent of the likes of
Sir Henry Wooton, the liberal dandy in Oscar Wilde's novel *The
Picture of Dorian Gray* – much more genteel Victorian, in fact, than
eighteenth-century. Just as the constant stylistic adventurousness of
*Lord Malquist and Mr Moon* suggests a general Joycean influence, so
the earl's verbal brilliance can be partially attributed to Wilde, and
it is no coincidence that these literary masters are assembled
together, eight years later, in Stoppard's eclectic *Travesties*. And, as
with Wooton, the shortcomings of such delightful verbal cleverness
are exposed. Malquist uses his 'style' as a defensive weapon, a thing

of superficial brilliance which glosses over his outright irresponsibility and enables him to close his eyes to those aspects of reality he prefers not to contemplate, as, for example, when the valuers move into his house:

> 'My lord! I have the gravest news – the situation is quite beyond reprieve. An injunction has been served and Sir Mortimer asks me to say that only liquidization of the property – '
> The ninth earl went up two steps and addressed Fitch severely.
> 'You may instruct Sir Mortimer that I let them have Petfinch but I'm damned if I can be expected to exist without a house in town.'
> 'I'm sorry, my lord, but if you had cut your coat to suit your cloth – '
> 'You are not my tailor, Fitch, thank God.'
> 'I mean your conduct – '
> 'My conduct has been one of modesty and self-denial. May I refer you to Sir George Verney who went about everywhere in a coach-and-six flanked by two six-foot Negroes blowing on silver horns.'
> And the ninth earl moved Fitch aside with his stick and went into the house. (pp. 173–4)

Such games are conscious, and are adopted as a shield, though Malquist's panache and sheer poise very nearly succeed in concealing the fact. With his falcon and lion in Hyde Park, he displays all the possible anachronisms of an eighteenth-century aristocrat's existence in the heart of twentieth-century London bustle.

There is plenty of comedy as a result. Yet, unlike the two cowboys or the Irish tramp-like figure of the Risen Christ (the man on the donkey at the start of the novel), who seem thinly drawn in comparison, Malquist does not exist merely for the sake of the parody which presents him, to illustrate the theme of the games people play. He is created to extol the virtue of style, and what he comes to represent within the play's moral world is ultimately more important than the details of his character. He is drawn to Moon's Boswell by the flattering lure of immortalising himself as a second Doctor Johnson. Were Moon successful, he would merely immortalise his own superficiality; in practice, he cannot even achieve this. For the style which he cultivates is as empty as the Malquist family coffers (even his cheque to his faithful diarist bounces) and its superficial lustre cannot paper over his callous indifference when Rollo attacks (and possibly kills) a park-keeper, or when his coach runs the woman down at the beginning of the novel:

> 'Breeding,' he remarked with approval. 'As Lord Curzon said to
> the actress, a lady does not move.'   (p. 12)

Indeed, the earl practically admits to his moral indifference by
declaring, in a memorable epigram: 'Since we cannot hope for
order let us withdraw with style from the chaos.' (p. 21) Such
withdrawal is not only impossible but, as Stoppard is progressively
concerned to reveal, implies a complete lack of concern with all
human and social values. Elsewhere the earl declares to Moon that
he stands for 'Style, dear boy . . . Style. There is nothing else.'
(p. 63) And indeed with Malquist there is nothing behind the style
he pursues with such precision and singularity; hence it is the stark
contrast between his glazed wit and Moon's over-desperate concern
which stands at the heart of the novel.

Moon tries to tell himself that he stands for 'substance' as opposed
to 'style', but cannot justify the idea to himself and sinks back into
his habitual confusion (p. 63). This contrast is nevertheless of the
utmost importance. In Malquist's sense, 'style' is an emphatic focus
upon the way that things are done, while 'substance', to Moon, is
about the human values he believes are being squeezed out by the
pressures of modern life, wherever he looks. Each characteristic is
not only crystallised but carried to wild excess by the respective
exponents so that, despite our inevitable admiration for the surface
impressiveness of Malquist and our considerable sympathy drawn to
the horribly muddled concern of Moon, the contrast between them
is handled very critically by Stoppard. Right at the start of the
novel, for instance, the implications of the contrast are sharply
recorded in the two men's reactions to the crowds assembling to pay
their respects to the dead statesman. Malquist, full of contemptuous
cynicism, remarks:

> I long to impose some aesthetic discipline on them, rearrange
> them into art. It would give a point to their existence   (p. 10)

while Moon experiences a panic-striken sense of involvement with
such great masses of people:

> He tried to empty his mind but when he closed his eyes the crowd
> multiplied and began to pile up against the walls until it filled the

city to its brim, a mass pressed wall to wall, blind prisoners
packed into the city's hold.  (p. 10)

Where Malquist sets out to impress, from as great a distance and
with as little involvement as possible, Moon struggles despairingly
to live in harmony with his environment. Neither succeeds. At the
end of the novel Malquist enters into a sexual relationship with Jane
which must be an abnegation of the philosophy of appearances;
stylishness depends on a certain aesthetic distance which the
intimacy of sex makes impossible.

Moon's failure is of a different kind: a failure to keep a balanced
perspective. He is as obsessive and neurotic as Malquist is aloof and
unemotional, a lonely, frightened and desperately insecure figure
clutching for values in a disintegrating universe. He feels his identity
and the whole quality of human life menaced by the outward-
spiralling, apparently uncontrolled processes of modern life:

> It's all got too huge, disproportionate to the human scale, it's all
> gone rotten because life – I feel it about to burst at the seams
> because the sheer volume and numbers of the things we're filling
> it up with, and people, it's all multiplying madly and no-one is
> controlling it because it's all got too *big*.  (p. 18)

This fearful neurosis runs much deeper than a sense of claustro-
phobia. Moon is quite alienated from the modern environment he
inhabits and, where Malquist retreats, Moon constantly allows
muddle and chaos to close in upon him. Believing that a public
act of violence could 'stop the slide', he reassures himself with
the bomb that has been made by his eccentric Uncle
Jackson and although Jane tells him that 'Uncle Jackson couldn't
make a bomb' (p. 32) and 'Uncle Jackson was cuckoo' (p. 33) he
insists on keeping it on a twelve-hour fuse, ready for use at the
chosen moment. As he tells one of the cowboys:

> we require an explosion. It is not simply a matter of retribution, it
> is a matter of shocking people into a moment of recognition –
> *bang!* – so that they might make a total reassessment, recognise
> that life has gone badly wrong somewhere.  (p. 116)

Here the parallel with the spurned lover in 'Reunion' becomes
explicit.

Within the novel, Moon's position is unique. With Malquist, Stoppard has only to provide the words and the gestures to present the 'style'. With Moon, he has to penetrate the character's thoughts and consciousness to create his 'substance', which has the effect of drawing the reader into a uniquely close relationship with him. Rather strangely, this sympathy is able to survive the fact that Moon actually commits murder at one point, in the context of a powerful, compulsive scene – the novel's most vivid – towards the end of the long chapter 'A Couple of Deaths and Exits'. With his head already bleeding from an assault of Jane's bedroom paraphernalia and his hand from tins he has opened to feed the tiresome Irishman who declares himself to be the Risen Christ, Moon accidentally falls into the bath he is running for Jane; then, wrapped up in a large towel, manages to cut his foot on a piece of broken mirror on the floor. At this point of exasperation, weariness and pain, he then discovers a gentleman known as 'The General' in his dining-room, twisting the maid's body into an obscene position in order to photograph it (she has been killed by a ricochet from one of the cowboys' guns). Moon smashes a bottle over the General's head, then turns on all the gas taps, water taps and electricity switches in the entire house in a neurotic, destructive urge against the energy sources that sustain city life:

> He could hear water rushing around the house and the geyser roaring on the edge of eruption, and the music swelled and fought under the lights. He felt all the power stations throb, strain against their rivets and begin to glow and beat like hearts, compressing matter into energy that escaped at once, pumping through the body of the world. . .
>
> He tried to think himself loose from all the rest but the barriers knocked each other over; the key to the equation between himself and the world was now beyond reason, comfort beyond ritual. He had no answers any more, only a bomb which correctly placed might blow a hole for him to fall through.     (p. 88)

It is at this point, with this startling vision of a spiralling, all-powerful and inhuman universe closing in upon him, that Moon detonates his bomb.

Moon's naïve faith in the bomb is pathetic and yet, however misguided his ideas, his underlying motives are humane. The

constant presence of his bomb on his person recalls the Professor in
Conrad's *The Secret Agent*, but there is no strain of the anarchist-
terrorist about Moon. On the contrary, he bears a strong resemblance to Prufrock, a fact emphasised by the whirling fragments of
Eliot's poem which continually echo inside his head. Like Prufrock,
he is a man disabled in the face of direct experience; where Prufrock
ventures to ask, on the verge of 'the room':

> Do I dare
> Disturb the universe?[8]

Moon wonders if he dare presume to release his bomb, to set in
motion his personal apocalypse. The title of the long chapter
'Spectator as Hero' suggests a further debt to Eliot's conception of
his 'hero'. Stoppard even uses Prufrock-like sea imagery in order to
relate Moon's eventual sexual encounter with Lady Malquist
(p. 143), the first full experience he has had. His marriage is
unconsummated, and remains so, although Jane apparently loses
her virginity at about the same time – to Lord Malquist. Jane's
frigidity is one of Moon's special burdens, though he strives to
remain tender and patient whatever the provocation, even when
she throws half the contents of her bedroom at him. 'She only likes to
play' (p. 142) he confesses to Lady Malquist, and the remark,
designed to excuse his own virginity, provides an acute incidental
summary of Jane's whole character. Their marital life, like so much
else in the novel, is a series of games, a relationship that has never
progressed beyond its childhood origins. Jane's playfulness keeps
her from real communication; she resembles her namesake, the
daily comic-strip sex symbol of the *Daily Mirror*, a girl loved and
desired by all but touched by none in the pre-permissive era of Fleet
Street in the 1950s. It is particularly ironic that the cowboys call her
'Fertility' (after 'Calamity') Jane, for one of the most conspicuous
absences from the novel is children. The empty nursery in the
Malquists' house is a poignant symbol of their barrenness, and sex,
where it takes place at all, is a loveless adventure rather than a
relationship.

Yet Moon loves Jane desperately, and Stoppard keeps allowing
his character's emotion to break through the surface as an
intermittent reminder that this aspect of his subject is *not* comic:

> Moon plunged without faith.
> 'Who the hell is he and why is he wearing those clothes? – and

what was he doing with you – oh *Jane*, why do you – ?'
Jane bit her lip to keep back the tears that trembled on the
edge of memory.   (p. 31)

As Jane constantly runs into games to protect herself from deep
emotion, so Moon constantly buries himself in it. His deep and
turbulent feelings can find no home with his wife, and finally,
despite his love for Jane, he succumbs to the suspect charms of Lady
Malquist. Even here, it is because he believes that he has at last
discovered in her a person who shares his humanitarian concerns, a
belief prompted by her response to the mowing down of Mrs Cuttle
by her husband's coach:

> He heard the change in Lady Malquist's voice.
> 'Was she all right?'
> 'I'm afraid she was killed, my lady.'
> Pause. Moon looked at her face and the real emotion on it
> shocked him. It seemed so long since he had been exposed to
> anything so real.   (p. 131)

It is this apparent sincerity which draws Moon into a relationship of
consummation with the earl's wife. Yet her 'real emotion' also
extends the contrast between 'style' and 'substance'. Previously we
have encountered shades of 'style': the cowboys, the Risen Christ,
Jane and her romantic games and, above all, Malquist himself; now
we learn that there are shades of 'substance' too, as Moon discovers
that Lady Malquist's warmth is, in its way, just as mercenary as her
husband's coldness: the Risen Christ follows fast upon his heels into
her four-poster bed.

His sense of betrayal is redoubled by what follows between Jane
and Lord Malquist. She has been flirting with the ninth earl ever
since their first meeting and Moon regularly discovers them in
compromising positions – an idea that Stoppard returns to in
*Jumpers*.[9] First Malquist is 'reading' her navel, then examining her
breast (for cancer, she explains), then trapping her in a Yoga-like
embrace 'of Laocoon complexity' (p. 180), which, as Malquist
reassures him, is 'the third contemplative position', from which she
is presently unable to extricate herself. However, the sharp change
of mood at the end takes us a long distance from any comedy, into a
bare factual vein which, as the short stories suggested, can contain
torrents of unstated emotion:

> Lord Malquist's clothes were draped over the towel rail. Jane's clothes were on the floor. He tried the door to the dressing-room but it was locked so he went out again into Laura's room and tried the other door, and then knocked. There was a pause.
> 'Who is it?' Jane called.
> 'Me,' said Moon.
> 'What do you want?' Her voice puzzled him.
> 'My shoes. And my coat.'
> 'Why?'
> 'It's raining,' he said. 'I want to go home.'
> 'Well, you can't come in. Go *away*.'
> He stood listening.  (p. 191)

Jane, like Moon, believes she has found a kindred spirit, with whom (in her case) she imagines she can *evade* the implications of a deep relationship. Her choice is likely to prove equally disastrous. Meanwhile, Moon retires in distress, and takes Malquist's coach home – the last journey he ever makes, thanks to Mr Cuttle's rather more effective bomb.

While Jane and Malquist only play they are safe in the protective world each has built. Yet while she is only playing with the cowboys, they fight a fatal duel over her. Stoppard asks where all these games end – even with a minor character such as The General his pornographic games lead to his death – and suggests that with Malquist and Jane the pose is finally dropped. The actors leave the stage and resort to their own devices. What they will discover, stripped, Stoppard will not tell. For Moon, however, there is only a disastrously ironic death: he has no stage to leave.

What most affects us about Moon's death is that there is a kind of heroic insight behind his ineptitude. He is the prototype for a number of Stoppard's dramatic creations, some of whom even share his name, with its appropriate quality of luminous, wistful insight. Malquist is a prototype of a very different kind: breezily and superficially clever, often very funny, but selfish and ruthless. In opposition to him, Moon's voice, however confused, however flailing, will not got away – and we hear it again, the voice of Rosencrantz and Guildenstern against the Player, of George against Archie in *Jumpers*, even of Professor Anderson against the totalitarian mentality of the Soviet block in *Professional Foul*. In *Lord Malquist and Mr Moon* it is not only Moon's bomb that creates echoes of Conrad's *The Secret Agent*: Winnie Verloc's famous dictum that 'things do not stand much looking into'[10] is a variation of Malquist's essential maxim. And Moon, with perhaps a passing resemblance to Conrad's Stevie, is determinedly set upon the path of looking into things as deeply as possible. Between these extremities, neatly divided here into 'style' and 'substance', Stoppard's characters continue to vaccilate throughout his subsequent plays. And for those who may incline towards the dismissive blanket suggestion that 'style' is the essential hallmark of Stoppard's work, one can scarcely do better than refer them to the sharp, humorous and decidedly critical treatment of the idea here, in 1966, in *Lord Malquist and Mr Moon*. Stoppard has not written a novel since, and once admitted to an interviewer:

> I'm not terribly attracted to writing novels, because their impact is dispersed over the time someone takes to read them. And could I trust any readers to lock the doors and take the telephone off the hook? I could not . . . [but] in the theatre one has the full attention of one's audience.[11]

Yet, for all that, his own novel remains in many respects an impressive achievement, both in its own right and as a precursor of subsequent dramatic triumphs.

# 3 Post-War Theatre: Some Contemporary Currents

Before turning to Stoppard's plays, and in particular to his first major achievement, *Rosencrantz and Guildenstern are Dead*, it is important to establish, in broad terms, the nature of the theatre which he entered with such a flourish. According to the critical orthodoxy established by John Russell Taylor, the London opening of *Rosencrantz* in April 1967 came some eleven years after the revolutionary impact of Osborne's *Look Back in Anger*, but the West End bill of fare at that time shows scant evidence of this new theatrical age, offering a wide array of musicals (*Hello Dolly, Fiddler on the Roof, Oliver, Charlie Girl*, etc.), two 'classics' (*The Rivals* with Ralph Richardson at the Haymarket, *The Three Sisters* at the Royal Court), two twentieth-century British revivals (Shaw's *Getting Married* and Coward's *Fallen Angels*) and just three new plays: John Mortimer's *The Judge* at the Cambridge, Joe Orton's second great success, *Loot*, at the Criterion (*Entertaining Mr Sloane* was his first, in 1964) and *Relatively Speaking*, Alan Ayckbourn's West End debut, at the Duke of York's. Although the prime goal of many of the new writers since the late 1950s has no longer been the performance of their plays on the stages of the West End, this unquestionably represents a poor showing. Only the mild outrageousness of subject matter of *Loot* (in its satirical treatment of death) and *The Judge* (a discreet tale of prostitution) distinguishes the list from what might have been found in the early '50s. Furthermore, it is barely different from a typical West End billing of the early '80s!

The West End, then, may have launched most of Stoppard's successes but has in general become an increasingly unreliable barometer of the post-war British theatre. For as we look back from the '80s, it is clear that Taylor's broad premises in *Anger and After*

24

were correct and that since the advent of the English Stage Company and the arrival of Osborne our theatre, if not transformed, has been remarkably rejuvenated. It was especially ironic, therefore, that Arthur Miller should have declared in 1956: 'I sense that the British theatre is hermetically sealed against the way society moves,'[1] for since then British playwrights have advanced on several fronts: taking a more direct approach to social and political issues; bringing the language of their characters much closer to ordinary speech (partially as a result of the removal of theatre censorship in 1968) and driving out that tone of polite propriety so characteristic of the theatre of Rattigan and his contemporaries; above all, perhaps, in reaching new audiences through the work of the 'fringe' and community theatre groups which have sprouted up across the country. During the same period, too, a large network of influential regional theatres has arrived, and an Arts Council with sufficient financial muscle to support them. Few connections thus seem to remain with that almost exclusively West End-centred theatre of the late '40s and early '50s which, as if to sustain the illusion that the pre-war values had been 'saved', was dominated by the same '30s writers (Terence Rattigan, Noel Coward, J. B. Priestley, N. C. Hunter, Agatha Christie) and by the same prevalent forms – thrillers, comedies of manners, Broadway musicals, Shakespearean revivals, lightweight romances and only those more serious plays which dealt with domestic or marital upheavals or with moral principles of fidelity, honesty and conscience. As Kenneth Tynan cuttingly declared in 1954, the new playwrights who did emerge were all

> writing the same play . . . whose inhabitants belong to a social class derived partly from romantic novels and partly from the playwright's vision of the leisured life he will lead after the play is a success.[2]

The contrast with, say, Arnold Wesker in the late '50s, Edward Bond in the '60s, or David Edgar in the '70s could scarcely be keener.

Yet within this substantially changed picture, stagecraft – outside the work of a few small experimental groups – has seemingly changed least of all, with many of the techniques of playwriting and staging conventions established long before Osborne's arrival proving surprisingly durable. It is true that most of the new post-war theatre buildings have open or thrust stages in preference to the traditional proscenium arch, but the prevalence of realistic box sets is still astonishing. For writers, too, it is not only the naturalistic mode in general which has survived, but often the specific construction techniques of the 'well-made' play, however much its language and characters may have moved with the times[3] – a point which Terence Rattigan made in a newspaper interview shortly before his death:

> It's a bit of a joke to think of the writers whose names were used to belabour me. John Osborne and Harold Pinter, for example. Two superb craftsmen, both writers of exceptionally well-made plays. They'd be annoyed if anyone suggested otherwise.[4]

This fact was clearly emphasised by a 1979 revival of Osborne's *Look Back in Anger* at the Young Vic, which prompted Francis King in the *Sunday Telegraph* to remark

> There is still pleasure to be derived from a paradoxical combination of traditional craftsmanship and youthful invective, but after two decades one asks oneself in amazement: 'What on earth was all the fuss about?' In the year of Suez and the Hungarian Rising, could this firing of a popgun into the face of the theatre-going public have really provoked so much reactionary terror from the old and so much revolutionary fervour from the young? Admittedly, Terence Rattigan was never capable of Mr. Osborne's clamorous eloquence; but how did a play otherwise so little different in technique from his own, have the effect of virtually sweeping him and his like out of the theatre?[5]

Despite its novel contemporaneity (at the time of its appearance), *Look Back in Anger* is entirely methodical in creating its illusory 'natural-ness', employing an old-fashioned pattern of exposition, confrontation and *dénouement*, placing its characters within the same, familiar picture-frame and directing their words and actions towards the voyeuristic audience in the 'fourth wall'. And although this pattern has been considerably refined during the 1960s and '70s it is still recognisable behind the domestic naturalism which has remained the dominant mode in our theatres and has become the dominant mode on our television screens.

There is a beautiful parody of the idea of this 'fourth wall' in

Buñuel's film *The Discreet Charm of the Bourgeoisie* (1972), in which the ambassador and his rich friends are feasting in an unfamiliar dining-room; suddenly the far wall collapses downwards and an auditorium crowded with spectators is revealed, watching the diners who, quite predictably, cower and flee! This is not merely a witty surrealist touch: Buñuel is drawing on a long and rich European tradition of subverting, in differing ways, the naturalism to which the British theatre has so steadfastly clung. The critic Michael Billington admitted in 1980 at an international theatre conference on new approaches to naturalism that his contribution 'was to point out that we in Britain cannot have a return to naturalism since we've never got that far away from it'.[6] Yet as early as 1887, Strindberg complained in his Author's Preface to *Miss Julie* that 'we have not succeeded in adapting the old form to the new content, so that the new wine has burst the old bottles'.[7] Since then, with a variety of successes and failures, the tides of Expressionism, Surrealism, Existentialism and Marxism (to name only the main ones) have washed through the European theatre. Prior to 1955 and 1956, the accumulated weight of these movements had scarcely been felt in Britain; during those two years, however, an unprecedented number of plays by Brecht, Genet, Ionesco and Beckett came to the London stage for the first time. Their immediate impact on the native tradition was slight. Miller and Williams were also arriving at the same time and it is their influence, pushing the naturalistic tradition into a new contemporaneity, which is readily discerned in the work of Osborne, Wesker, Delaney, Bolt and the others in the first wave of post-*Anger* playwrights. (Miller also left his mark on Stoppard, as we shall see in discussing *Enter a Free Man* in Chapter 5.) With hindsight, however, it is now clear that the European authors, with their bolder approach to stagecraft, to character, to theatricality, to the whole treatment of ideas on the stage, did, in time, have a radical effect on the developing consciousness of an important number of our more original, more formally adventurous British playwrights of the '60s and '70s, including Arden, Bond, Pinter and Stoppard.

Within the European Theatre's attacks on naturalism two very different and, in some respects, opposing points of departure stand out. The first, the Brechtian world-view, stressed man's rôle as an integral part of society, and the second, the Theatre of the Absurd, stressed man's rôle as a psychological outcast from society. In each case, their target was not just a set of theatrical conventions, but the nineteenth-century world-view which nurtured them and which had now become utterly redundant, whether from social, philosophical, religious or political standpoints: that of the individual exercising his free will and conscience against the determining pressures of his environment or his past. It is this fundamental concept which was so well served by the 'fourth wall' convention of naturalism, with its characters grouped in an ideal social microcosm, 'the room', in which dynamic forces impinging from without could provoke the kind of limited moral crisis which could be powerfully represented on the stage. What the room excludes, however, is just as important as what it makes possible: the playwright's conscious rapport with his audience, the formal explorations of multi-dimensional viewpoints, the presentation of ideas other than through formal characterisation, and other more openly theatrical approaches. Such restrictions, which were keenly felt and resisted in the European mainland theatre throughout the first half of the twentieth century, seemed a matter of gentle quiescence to British playwrights (in marked contrast to their fellow-novelists, whose more fluid and protean medium continued to adapt itself successfully to the endless stream of socio-cultural change, from Hardy to Forster to Woolf to Joyce to Beckett to Fowles). It was, therefore, on the room and all that it stood for, that the European attack centred, rejecting its moral assumptions, its rounded, fully knowable characters and its 'well-made' plots in order to locate, in Strindberg's phrase, the new bottles for the new wine. The Absurdist theatre, heavily existential and predominantly French, shrank the room to a prison, a cell or a cage, seeing man as a powerless creature divorced from all purposeful orientation. And the Brechtian theatre (which we shall look at first) dispensed with the room altogether, in favour of the more panoramic conception of series of shortish scenes linked to social or historical themes – the so-called 'epic' theatre. Where the first undermined the naturalistic conventions to the point of inward collapse, the second physically rejected them.

While the influence of Brecht in this country has generally been more apparent in terms of lip-service than stagecraft, it has undoubtedly helped to break the primacy of the domestic focus *per se* in serious drama. The first, momentous visit of the Berliner Ensemble to London was in 1956, and in its wake came a succession of plays with epic structures of sorts, such as Bolt's *A Man For All Seasons*, Osborne's *Luther* and Whiting's *The Devils*. But in these and most other cases the debt is largely superficial; they are costume dramas rather than history plays in Brecht's sense, with sympathetic heroes moulded in the traditional English manner. Indeed, the closer we come to the true spirit of Brecht, as in the scene with the knight in *Luther*, which generates genuine dialectical tension, the more the plays creak. None of these authors comes close to creating the kind of genuinely open-ended structure at which Brecht aimed, where the spectator remains critical and detached and where his moral biases and sympathies are not pre-conditioned by the presentation. None breaks with naturalistic illusion as decisively as Brecht's 'verfremdung' technique dictates and all rely quite heavily on traditional precepts for producing dramatic tension. It is, of course, a commonly held view that Brecht's own plays do not stand the test of these theories either; as Martin Esslin suggests, 'Brecht's success lies in his partial failure to realize his own intentions'.[8] What is undeniable, however, is that his own plays realise them to a far greater extent than those of his many imitators. In *Mother Courage and her Children*, for example, one of the works brought to London in 1956, he creates a powerful anti-war play in which no single character articulates pacifist sentiments. Each scene is a largely self-contained illustration of one more contradictory strand in the web of the giant contradiction of values and principles that war must represent and Mother Courage herself is 'as much a willing accessory as a helpless victim'.[9] Only a handful of British plays have come anywhere close to objectivity of this kind, among them the Theatre Workshop's *Oh, What a Lovely War* (1963), in which the World War I soldiers were dressed as clowns to inhibit a stock, sympathetic response and Adrian Mitchell's adaptation for Peter Brook of Peter Weiss's *The Persecution and Assassination of Marat as Performed by the Inmates of the Asylum of Charenton under the Direction of the Marquis de Sade* (1964), where the 'play within a play' structure creates separate and contradictory layers of response to Sade and to the inmates playing out the rôles in his drama. This is compounded by the narrative function of the Herald and of four grotesque singers who provide a further commentary on the unfolding action. As a result the audience is, to an unusual extent, forced to determine its own response to the whole spectacle. This is similarly true of *Serjeant Musgrave's Dance*, first staged in 1959, John Arden's radical and unusually free marriage of realism with song, ballad and verse. Here, and in several of his other plays, the deliberate ambiguity and contrariness of his characters suggests a debt to Brechtian notions of objectivity. Arden's formalism and austerity are matched only by Edward Bond, Brecht's closest disciple in our contemporary theatre, whose plays frequently resort to alien settings, such as Oriental or Shakespearean parables in *The Narrow Road to the Deep North* (1966) or *Lear* (1971), in order to create their savage indictments of the animalism of human nature in the modern capitalist world.

In general, however, it has been as the intellectual champion of a politically committed drama rather than as a revolutionary theatre practitioner that Brecht's influence has been most discernible during the 1960s and 1970s, as the native tradition of anti-establishment naturalism produced in the first wave of post-*Anger* playwrights has progressively re-shaped itself into a new, hard-edged school of social (often social*ist*) realism. The 'school' does not by any means share a united political front but it includes such writers as David Hare, Trevor Griffiths, John McGrath, Howard Brenton, Stephen Poliakoff and David Edgar, many of whom first emerged in the 'fringe' theatre groups of the late '6os before reaching their wider contemporary audiences. As Edgar has suggested,

> most of the new playwrights of the 1970s came into the theatre at a time when there was a consensus between play-makers and their audiences that British society was rotten at the root, and that it was the proper business of the theatre to anatomise its rottenness and point the way to radical change.[10]

Much of that consensus (as he admits) seems to have disappeared from the theatre of the '8os, but not the influence of these writers or of their work, where well-rounded characterisation is typically employed within structures that suggest some of the breadth of Brecht's political vision. Among the best examples one might cite are Brenton and Hare's *Brassneck* (1973), an ambitious panorama of post-war corruption, Griffiths' *Comedians* ((1975), a neat social microcosm in a night-school for stand-up comics, Brenton's *Weapons of Happiness* (1976), in which workers occupy a crisps factory threatened with closure, or Edgar's *Destiny* (1977), on the rise of a crypto-Fascist party. As Laurence Kitchin observed more than twenty years ago:

> Brecht's subject-matter, more even than his technical influence,

has an international appeal because it touches at so many points on the conflicts of a divided world.[11]

It is, then, this kind of Brechtian influence, together with the quite separate influence from the filled-out naturalism of the television world (the kind of 'illusion' Brecht shunned so vehemently) which has been successfully welded together by these writers, who now form (if anyone does) the mainstream of our present-day theatre. In her introduction to *Revolutions in Modern English Drama*, Katharine Worth suggested that

> The English theatre in 1972 looks as though it might be about to move out of the orbit of realism which has held it throughout the century and into another for which there is as yet no name.[12]

A decade later, as so often before, the breakthrough has not arrived, a further testimony (if one was needed) to the remarkable endurance of the perpetually self-refining naturalistic tradition within the British theatre.

The Marxist, Brechtian dramatists believe that man can remake the world by countering its alienating, dehumanising influences. The Absurd dramatists believe he cannot. Loss of human control (the predominant theme in Stoppard's fiction) is their essential credo, the product of a grim and hostile determinism carried through into their visually powerful stage icons. Their 'compressionism', as Laurence Kitchin labels it[13], has enjoyed only limited currency, partly because you can only shrink a room and its inhabitants so far. Sartre in *Huis Clos* (1944) reduces it to an existential hell with a handle-less door and no windows, using naturalistic characters and settings against themselves. Vian goes further in *The Empire Builders* (1959), where the members of a family are pursued upwards through their apartment block by a mysterious and hideous noise which progressively reduces their numbers. They are accompanied by, and frequently beat up, a silent, heavily bandaged creature called a *schmürz*, who seems to crystallise an implied analogy with French colonial oppression and whose fellow-creatures take over at the end of the play. In Ionesco's *Rhinoceros* (1959), the hero, Berenger, watches with horror as his friends turn into conformist rhinos and is finally reduced to one himself, while in Beckett's own case a similar reductive process takes his characters into the dustbins of *Endgame* (1958), the enveloping earth of *Happy Days* (1961) and the urns of *Play* (1964). This inherent logic then culminates in the mere sound of breathing emanating from a heap of garbage and naked bodies in *Breath* (1971) and in the frantic, disembodied, gabbling mouth of *Not I* (1973). Eventually, in Beckett's work in particular and that of other Absurdists in general, the fundamentally anti-dramatic impulses and restricted dynamic possibilities of the movement have become increasingly plain. As Hinchliffe says, the Absurd

> entered a dramatic cul-de-sac whose essential limitations would finally triumph over the desire to write plays[14]

and by 1970 Beckett was continuing in virtual isolation.

What the influence of the Absurd, like that of Brecht, brought into the British theatre was a keen sense of liberation. The dazzling imaginative quality of the finest work in this tradition and the sheer bravado and innovation of its stagecraft could not fail to impress itself on the younger playwrights of the later 1950s and the 1960s. Again, though, genuine imitators were few and far between and, as Kitchin rightly suggests, the Absurd's pervasively comic tone in the midst of intellectual seriousness is a combination which 'something in the English character . . . deeply mistrusts'.[15] There are, nevertheless, some clear examples of assimilated influence, catalytic rather than direct, such as David Campton's menacing fantasy playlets, *The Lunatic View* (1957) and *A View from the Brink* (1960). James Saunders's early one-acter *Alas, Poor Fred* is subtitled 'a duologue in the style of Ionesco' and a rather more elusive influence continues to inform his later successes, *Next Time I'll Sing to You* (1963) and *A Scent of Flowers* (1965). N. F. Simpson's comedies *A Resounding Tinkle* (1957) and *One Way Pendulum* (1959) offer, as their titles suggest, heavily eccentric and paradoxical visions of everyday boredom with more than a whisper of Absurdity. Since then, this influence has not so much disappeared as gone underground, according to Martin Esslin (writing in 1968):

> far from being finished or spent . . . (it) is being absorbed into the mainstream of the tradition . . . The underlying explicit or implicit assumptions which we have labelled the Theatre of the Absurd continue, and continue vigorously.[16]

The passage of time has, I think, belied at least part of this proposition. The 'mainstream' is held, with an undiminished grip, by the regrouped forces of realism. But there are a number of important British writers, mostly working in relative isolation from one another, who have taken the imaginative boldness of the Absurdists and something, perhaps, of their philosophy to heart in pursuing their own paths of formal experimentation along non-naturalistic lines. They have a largely instinctive grasp of theatrical tension and imagery, a studied awareness of what language can and cannot do (recognising that it is our major index on reality) and, on occasions, a sense of the nightmarish abyss that underlies our precarious existence. The two most important are Tom Stoppard (as the rest of this book is intended to show) and Harold Pinter, who, though working in an idiom which seems to owe little if anything to Genet or Ionesco, continually subverts the seeming ordinariness of his characters' lives by showing the almost subliminal currents of violence glinting beneath the apparently safe waves. His characters are constantly suspect as, combining menace with mendacity, they make us fearfully aware that, as in real life, other people can never be wholly known. Like the Absurdists, Pinter is set on violating the sanctity of the individual which naturalism so resolutely upholds.

Across the Atlantic, too, several important dramatists have shown clear signs of a debt to the Absurd in pursuit of their own bold paths. Albee in *The American Dream* (1962) shows parents butchering the adopted child they have taken in and in *The Sandbox* (1962) a character called the Angel of Death hovers in the background. *Seascape* (1975) crystallises the influence of Beckett as two characters waiting on a sand-dune encounter two talking lizards. Jules Feiffer in *Little Murders* (1967) and the work of Sam Shepard show comparable imaginative daring, directed in each case towards a biting satire of contemporary American society. Where these writers differ so fundamentally from the mainstream realistic tradition is, in essence, in their theatricality. This can take many forms, from, say, the flamboyance of Stoppard's *Travesties* (1974), to the ruthless territorial exchanges of Pinter's *The Homecoming* (1965) or, in more extreme forms, to the linguistic warfare and deliberate provocation of Peter Handke's *Offending the Audience* (1966) and his other *sprechenstücken*.[17] What connects them, however, to each other and to the Theatre of the Absurd, is their refusal to minimise the audience's awareness that what they are watching is a *performance*, a gathering and collusion of author, actor and audience, in which the audience's rôle extends beyond a simple passive voyeurism. This

revived insistence on the theatricality of the theatre (which Brecht
also fought for) can be usefully related to the ostentatious self-
consciousness of a great many contemporary novelists – the stylistic
experimentation, the authorial unreliability, the persistent, quest-
ing self-reference, the general trickery employed with the reader's
necessary connivance. In an influential essay, the Post-modernist
critic John Barth has, for instance, referred to parody and travesty
(albeit somewhat disparagingly) as two of the manifestations of the
new approach which he sees as dominating the post-war literary
vanguard, in which

> artistic conventions are likely to be re-tried, subverted, trans-
> cended, transformed, or even deployed against themselves to
> generate new and lively work.[18]

For Barth, this search to revive new versions of traditional forms is
what separates Post-modernism from Modernism. The relevance of
these comments to Stoppard's work may already be apparent from
our consideration of his novel which, though uneven, contains many
of Barth's Post-modernist characteristics. They are still more
relevant to Stoppard's plays, especially *Rosencrantz and Guildenstern
are Dead*. And since Barth places Beckett (whose work first appeared
during the 1930s) firmly at the tail-end of Modernism, a question
that may usefully arise – without delving into the complex realms of
contemporary critical theory – is whether Stoppard's plays might,
in their own unique way, represent a step past Beckett into the
vanguard of our Post-modern theatre.

# 4 In the Off-Stage World

The response to the London opening of *Rosencrantz and Guildenstern are Dead* (in a new, longer version) at the Old Vic in April 1967 showed that the acclaim which had greeted its appearance at Edinburgh's Cranston Street Hall the previous August was no fluke, that it did, indeed, break new ground in the British theatre. Harold Hobson described the opening as 'the most important event in the British professional theatre in the last nine years'.[1] Ronald Bryden reasserted his view of the play as 'the most brilliant dramatic debut of the 'Sixties'[2] and Irving Wardle saluted its originality by declaring, 'I know of no theatrical precedent for it'.[3] Derek Goldby's production, with John Stride and Edward Petherbridge (respectively) in the title rôles, continued in repertoire for an unprecedented three-and-a-half years. Stoppard was voted Most Promising Playwright in the 1967 *Evening Standard* theatre awards, won the John Whiting Award and took, on the play's Broadway opening, the 1968 'Tony' and Drama Critics' Circle Best Play awards – a remarkable set of accolades for any author's first professional stage play. Yet success, as we have seen, only came after six years of struggle, and even the genesis of this play can be traced back to 1964, as Stoppard related in the magazine *Author*:

My agent picked up my interest in Rosencrantz and Guildenstern and suggested a comedy about what happened to them in England. For good measure, he added that the king of England might be Lear. The possibility appealed to me and I began working on a burlesque Shakespeare farce. By the autumn of 1964 I had written a bad one, but had got interested in the characters as existential immortals. I scrapped the play and in October 1964 started *Rosencrantz and Guildenstern are Dead*, set not in England but within the framework of *Hamlet*. Jeremy Brooks at the Royal Shakespeare Company heard about it and asked for it, and I sent him two completed acts in April 1965. A few weeks

later, amid much reported enthusiasm, the RSC commissioned
the third act.[4]

This, more or less, is the version of the play which eventually
reached the Edinburgh Fringe and later the National Theatre, but
the earlier stages of its development have more than a curiosity
value and offer a useful yardstick for gauging the scale of Stoppard's
final achievement.

The 'burlesque Shakespeare farce' which Stoppard describes as
'bad' was, in fact, given a single performance by English amateurs
in a Berlin Theatre as part of his Ford Foundation residency.[5] The
subsequent version in fact was probably started prior to October,
since in that month it was performed in a one-act embryonic version
called *Guildenstern and Rosencrantz* at the Questors Theatre in Ealing,
directed by Stoppard himself on his return from Germany. This
draft, according to a letter from Alfred Emmet of the Questors to
*Theatre Quarterly*,

> is set on 'A plain in Denmark' and takes place during Act IV,
> Scene 4 of *Hamlet*. It is certainly not a mere 'Shakespearean
> pastiche' as Stoppard suggested in your interview – perhaps he
> wrote more than one version in Germany – but is clearly the seed
> from which the full version grew. Rosencrantz and Guildenstern
> are shown as suspended in a moment of time, not knowing the
> what or why of their existence. . . . Much of the dialogue,
> including several substantial speeches, was incorporated ver-
> batim in the final play, mostly in the last act.[6]

It appears, then, that there were two early try-outs in 1964, the first
in verse incorporating King Lear, the second in prose dialogue
incorporating part of what became the final version, and that
*Rosencrantz and Guildenstern are Dead* developed out of the minor
tradition of Shakespearean burlesque. At least one Shakespearean
burlesque had taken the same characters for its heroes: W. S.
Gilbert's playlet *Rosencrantz and Guildenstern*, sub-titled 'A Tragic
Episode, In Three Tableaux, founded on an Old Danish Legend'
and first performed at the Vaudeville Theatre, London, in 1891. It
has almost no specific connections with Stoppard's play, but the
contrast is nevertheless revealing: unlike Stoppard, Gilbert inverts
the plot of *Hamlet* so that Rosencrantz, his hero, outsmarts the
prince and wins Ophelia, his secret childhood sweetheart, at the

final curtain! The crucial catalyst in this achievement is Rosencrantz and Guildenstern's discovery of a dire five-act tragedy called 'Gonzago', penned by Claudius in his youth. Knowing that even to mention it in his presence constitutes a capital offence, they so manipulate affairs that Hamlet unwittingly performs it, with the players, before his outraged uncle. They lay hands on a copy through the connivance of Ophelia, whose father Polonius, as Lord Chamberlain, has a copy of every play published in the kingdom, and her terrified account of how she stole the play at midnight typifies Gilbert's style:

> Last night I stole down from my room alone
> And sought my father's den. I entered it!
> The clock struck twelve, and then – oh, horrible! –
> From chest and cabinet there issued forth
> The mouldy spectres of five thousand plays,
> All dead and gone – and many of them damned!
> I shook with horror! They encompassed me,
> Chattering forth the scenes and parts of scenes
> Which my poor father wisely had cut out.
> Oh, horrible – oh, 'twas most horrible!
> (*Covering her face*)[7]

There are a number of similarly topical references beneath the mock-Elizabethan surface of Gilbert's playful and brief diversion, which is typical of burlesque writing of this kind.

Stoppard's *Rosencrantz and Guildenstern are Dead* is, however, a very much more elaborate piece of writing and construction. As a complete piece of dramatic composition in its own right, it far exceeds the usual terms of reference of a burlesque and if, as the evidence suggests, it began as a Shakespearean pastiche of this kind, then the comparison with Gilbert's playlet shows just how far it has transcended these origins. For, while retaining the broad context given by Shakespeare, Stoppard develops his 'borrowed' characters into his own creations speculating philosophically upon the 'reality' of a dramatic situation – the plot of *Hamlet* – which they cannot understand. This obliges Stoppard to adopt a critical view of the way in which his 'heroes' are handled by Shakespeare.

In *Hamlet* Rosencrantz and Guildenstern are summoned to the Danish court by Claudius in order to probe the enigmatic behaviour of Hamlet, whose fellow-scholars they have, until recently, been.

The prince perceives that their former friendship with him has given way to a new mercenary allegiance to Claudius, and although he makes this uncomfortably obvious to them, Rosencrantz and Guildenstern are nevertheless chosen to accompany him to England. During the crossing Hamlet manages to escape from the ship, following a fortuitous attack by a pirate vessel, but not before he discovers in his companions' possession a letter to the English king commanding his execution. On his return he recounts to Horatio how he substituted for it another commanding *their* deaths.

> *Horatio:*   So Guildenstern and Rosencrantz go to't.
> *Hamlet*:    Why, man, they did make love to this employment,
>              They are not near my conscience, their defeat
>              Does by their own insinuation grow.
>              'Tis dangerous when the baser nature comes
>              Between the pass and fell incensed points
>              Of mighty opposites.[8]

This disclaimer makes clear the direction of sympathies intended by Shakespeare, and in *Hamlet* itself it is never suggested that Rosencrantz and Guildenstern become aware of their fate. Indeed, it does not much matter either way, for when the English ambassadors arrive at the end of the play to inform the king that the instructions of the letter have been carried out, and that 'Rosencrantz and Guildenstern are dead', their news is hustled into insignificance by the tragic tableau of royal corpses that confronts them.

In an interview in 1968, Stoppard expressed his firm opinion that

> Hamlet's assumption that they (Rosencrantz and Guildenstern) were privy to Claudius' plot is entirely gratuitous. As far as their involvement in Shakespeare's text is concerned they are told very little about what is going on and much of what they are told isn't true. So I see them much more clearly as a couple of bewildered innocents rather than a couple of henchmen, which is the usual way they are depicted in productions of *Hamlet*.[9]

In *Rosencrantz and Guildenstern are Dead* Stoppard therefore presents his heroes as two likeable but utterly confused characters, engaged in a perpetual struggle to comprehend the complex manoeuvrings that are taking place around them as the plot of *Hamlet* unfolds. As Ronald Bryden has said, 'They are frightened strangers in a world somebody else seems to have made.'[10] The absurdity of their position becomes increasingly pronounced, culminating in their journey to England without the prince they are supposed to be escorting and carrying a letter which demands their own deaths! Where Shakespeare implicitly defends Hamlet's action in substituting the letters, Stoppard calls attention to the possibility of seeing it, certainly from at least two points of view (Rosencrantz and Guildenstern's), as unnecessarily vicious. The sympathies of a *Hamlet* audience lie firmly with the prince and for them his survival from the potential peril of the ship is clearly imperative; Stoppard's concern, however, is to redress this balance of sympathies in favour of Rosencrantz and Guildenstern. Seizing on a nuance of sympathy for the pair that Shakespeare's overall intentions militate firmly against, he turns them into objects both of compassion and of ironic humour.

All three acts of *Rosencrantz and Guildenstern are Dead* alternate between the characters' 'on-stage' and 'off-stage' selves. The 'on-stage' sections are provided by incorporating pertinent passages of *Hamlet* directly into the play: the much longer 'off-stage' sections show Rosencrantz and Guildenstern left to their own devices, generally trying to make sense of the 'on-stage' episodes and of their own relationship to them. In creating these 'off-stage' realities, however, Stoppard does nothing to make Shakespeare's minor characters major, refusing them the complex and lavish attention that 'heroes' traditionally receive. Instead, his objective is to explore the undeveloped nature of the perpetual minion, the man constantly relegated to the furthest recesses of the stage, without the faintest understanding of the action unfolding around him:

*Guil:* Why is he mad?!
*Ros:* *I* don't know!
*Player:* The old man thinks he's in love with his daughter.
*Ros (appalled):* Good God! We're out of our depth here.
*Player:* No, no, no – *he* hasn't got a daughter – the old man thinks he's in love with *his* daughter.
*Ros:* The old man is?
*Player:* Hamlet, in love with the old man's daughter, the old man thinks.
*Ros:* Ha! It's beginning to make sense.[11]

Such exchanges are riddled with hilarious confusion. At other times the pair merely pass time in their 'off-stage' realm by playing games, and it is with one of these that the first act opens: a game of coin-spinning in which Rosencrantz wins those that land 'heads', Guildenstern those that land 'tails'. Rosencrantz has won sixty-nine times in a row as the play begins, and the coins continue to land 'heads' every time. Behind the ironic comedy here – we know that the pair are to lose their heads – is a more sinister implication, subsequently developed in a number of other ways: Rosencrantz and Guildenstern exist in a world in which the normal rules of probability and expectation are simply not operating. (When the coin finally lands 'tails', the court sweeps in for the first 'on-stage' section and the game is over.) Their other main pastime, a game of questions, is also deeply ironic: as they string lines of them together, trying to avoid statements, *non-sequiturs*, repetitions and rhetoric, and to 'answer' every question with another question, they little realise how the game is mirroring their predicament, which is to inhabit a world full of questions which, for them, have no answers.

The 'off-stage' coin-spinning game is interrupted by the first of their encounters with the only other characters of significance, the group of tragedians who perform at Elsinore at the prince's behest in *Hamlet* (III, ii). In *Rosencrantz and Guildenstern are Dead* they have clearly fallen on hard times and readily perform anything that people will pay to watch, which usually involves Alfred, the troupe's transvestite specialist:

> *Guil:* No enigma, no dignity, nothing classical, portentous, only this – a comic pornographer and a rabble of prostitutes. . . .
> *Player:* You should have caught us in better times. We were purists then. (p. 19)

This first meeting with the players takes place (it seems) on the road to Elsinore. They agree to present a special wayside performance for the courtiers, but before this happens Rosencrantz and Guildenstern find they have suddenly reached the court, leaving the players by the roadside. This time-jump is one of many indications that natural forces are not in control of the action and there is some sympathy for the Player when, reappearing in the second act, he rebukes them for walking off. As the tragedians' leader (and their sole spokesman throughout) he explains, with some exasperation, that the actors were half-way through their performance before they realised they had no audience. Later in the same act, Rosencrantz and Guildenstern come upon the players once again, this time as they are holding the dress rehearsal for 'The Murder of Gonzago', shortly to be performed before the court. The rehearsal contains a noteworthy addition to the version in *Hamlet*, a scene in which two spies (clearly Rosencrantz and Guildenstern, though they do not recognise themselves) are put to death. This interpolation evidently suggests that the players have some knowledge of the intended direction of events. Finally the players turn up again in the third act, which takes place aboard the ship bound for England. They are stowaways, having made a fast escape from the court after their play offended the king. Hamlet then duly escapes, leaving Rosencrantz and Guildenstern to discover the letter which seals their fates and brings home to them most completely the full implications of their powerlessness.

What the players seem to have grasped is a truth which eludes Rosencrantz and Guildenstern to the very end: that the 'on-stage' encounters hold the key to their existence. They are hovering on the edge of a great drama that every so often sweeps them up in its wake as Stoppard works passages of *Hamlet* into the play, but their only response is baffled incomprehension:

> As soon as we make a move they'll come pouring in from every side, shouting obscure instructions, confusing us with ridiculous remarks, messing us about from here to breakfast and getting our names wrong.  (p. 62)

In the wake of these bewildering machinations, Stoppard's heroes flounder hopelessly out of their depth. When not playing games, they spend the time deliberating on their almost total disorientation towards the seemingly chaotic affairs of the court, unable to remember their 'instructions' or even how they arrived:

*Guil:* What's the first thing you remember?
*Ros:* Oh, let's see . . . The first thing that comes into my head, you mean?
*Guil:* No – the first thing you remember.
*Ros:* Ah. (*Pause*) No, it's no good, it's gone. It was a long time ago.

> *Guil* (*patient but edged*): You don't get my meaning. What is the
>    first thing after all the things you've forgotten?
> *Ros:* Oh I see. (*Pause*) I've forgotten the question.   (p. 11)

They never get significantly further than this – at times, indeed, they
do not even seem completely sure which one of them is Rosencrantz
and which is Guildenstern – because they never become aware that
they themselves are actually participating in this perplexing drama.
The inscrutability of their entire surroundings in the face of this
basic ignorance is the core of Stoppard's play.

*          *          *

The crucial factor in exploring Rosencrantz and Guildenstern's
strange predicament is the use to which Stoppard puts *Hamlet* within
his own play – in other words, the relationship he creates between his
two levels of dramatic 'reality'. Technically, the manner in which he
dovetails Shakespeare's lithe Elizabethan verse and prose into his
own colloquial modern English is ingenious and often hilarious.
When, for example, the king has ordered the courtiers to search for
Hamlet, an idle, frivolous suggestion from Rosencrantz propels
them into a scene from *Hamlet* before they have had time to collect
themselves:

> *Ros:*        Give him a shout.
> *Guil:*       I thought we'd been into all that.
> *Ros(shouts):* **Hamlet!**
> *Guil:*       Don't be absurd!
> *Ros(shouts):* **Lord Hamlet!**
>               (*Hamlet enters. Rosencrantz is a little dismayed.*)
>               **What have you done, my lord, with the dead
>               body?**
> *Hamlet:* **Compounded it with dust, whereto 'tis
>           kin.**   (pp. 65–6)

And Act IV, sc. ii of *Hamlet* duly continues. The insertion of the line
'Don't be absurd!' between Rosencrantz's authentic off-stage shouts
from *Hamlet* (marked in the text as 'calling without' [IV.ii.2] and
in bold type above) fuses the two kinds of language with great panache.
In such a transition, the most unexpected moments or remarks can
become springboards into this strange other world. This epitomises
Stoppard's technique, both here and in his novel, of establishing two

linguistically remote styles and yoking them with considerable dexterity into a structure with this kind of non-communication at its core. The two worlds whose dialogue creates the play's formal structure are thus conceived in deliberate incongruity as a means of intensifying the bewilderment of Rosencrantz and Guildenstern which is Stoppard's central theme; as we share the modern speech idiom of his heroes, so too, in a manner reminiscent of Moon's sense of estrangement, we share in their sense of foreignness in the hostile *Hamlet* world with its remote, alien language.

The courtiers' bafflement is intensified by the fact that Hamlet appears to be outsmarting them at every step. His aggressive posturing in the second act of *Hamlet*, when they first come to probe him (sent, of course, by the king and queen), befuddles and humiliates them. They cannot glean his motives or intentions, and his insight into the duality (at best) of their allegiances makes their position all the more uncomfortable. This is equally true in *Hamlet* and *Rosencrantz and Guildenstern are Dead*, but it is exacerbated in the latter by the fact that Stoppard 'chops' most of Shakespeare's dialogue, incorporating only a few lines from the opening and closing sections of this lengthy encounter on each side of his first act interval! The first five lines provide no more than the prince's initial welcome before the curtain is down and the houselights up; and when the curtain rises again, the final thirteen lines of Shakespeare's scene offer only a series of almost cryptic exchanges that culminate in Hamlet's deliberately oblique

> I am but mad north-north-west; when the wind is southerly, I know a hawk from a handsaw.   (II.ii.382–3)

The most obvious reason for excluding practically all of the conversation between the prince and his schoolfellows in this scene is that to do so intensifies their bewilderment, which is central to Stoppard's intentions. Seen in this light, it is an amusing theatrical device that eclipses the characters at the very point at which they might be, for the first time, on the verge of some enlightenment, and, as such, it is one of a great many jokes at his heroes' expense that Stoppard incorporates into the play. In dramatic terms, the exclusion of most of the scene also prevents an excessively long extract of Shakespeare's play – 158 lines – from destroying the momentum of *Rosencrantz and Guildenstern are Dead*. But, most fundamentally, it enables him to leave out a number of exchanges which cut across the grain of his interpretation of Rosencrantz and Guildenstern as essentially innocent. His motive for doing so, and the question of whether it is justified, deserves some scrutiny.

From a total of nine significant encounters in *Hamlet* between Rosencrantz and Guildenstern and either Hamlet or the king and queen, Stoppard incorporates six in full and omits two entirely – the other being the 'chopped' scene just referred to (II. ii). In addition, Shakespeare has the pair present at the players' performance of 'The Murder of Gonzago', a scene that Stoppard also omits, though he does engineer the king's abrupt exit so that it passes through the 'off-stage' territory of the uncomprehending courtiers. In the case of the 'chopped' scene, there are several exchanges that he excludes which show the courtiers making clear attempts to control the direction of their conversation with the prince:

> *Hamlet:* O God! I could be bounded in a nut-shell, and count myself a king of infinite space; were it not that I have bad dreams.
> *Guil:*  Which dreams, indeed, are ambition . . . (II.ii.257–60)

This attempt at manipulating Hamlet is clumsy and obvious, and Stoppard's heroes are often both, but it further suggests an insinuating and probing side of Guildenstern's nature which falls precisely within Shakespeare's intentions but which Stoppard's cannot easily embrace. Another omitted exchange finds Guildenstern even admitting, under pressure from Hamlet, 'My lord we were sent for' (II.ii.296) – a hesitant confession which probably seals Hamlet's mistrust of his old acquaintances. The impression is clearly conveyed that, in the face of contradictory pressures from the text of *Hamlet*, Stoppard is simply omitting those sections which do not suit his purposes.

This view is strongly reinforced by the evidence of the two scenes wholly omitted (Act III, sc. ii and iii) which immediately follow the performance of 'The Murder of Gonzago'. For here Shakespeare depicts the pair at their most dutifully servile. In the first, for instance, after the courtiers have left the play at the king's side, they hasten back to the prince with messages that 'The king . . . Is in his retirement marvellously distempered' (III.ii.299–301) and 'The queen your mother, in most great affliction of spirit, hath sent me to you.' (III.ii.312–13) Clearer evidence of their allegiance is hard to imagine and, in terms of *Hamlet*, the prince's famous, high-spirited antagonism in response to it is entirely appropriate:

*Hamlet:* Will you play upon this pipe?
*Guil:*　My lord, I cannot.
*Hamlet:* I pray you.
*Guil:*　Believe me, I cannot.
*Hamlet:* I do beseech you.
*Guil:*　I know no touch of it, my lord.
*Hamlet:* It is as easy as lying; govern these ventages with your fingers and thumb, give it breath with your mouth, and it will discourse most eloquent music – look you, these are the stops.
*Guil:*　But these I cannot command to any utt'rance of harmony, I have not the skill.
*Hamlet:* Why, look you now, how unworthy a thing you make of me! you would play upon me, you would seem to know my stops, you would pluck out the heart of my mystery, you would sound me from my lowest note to the top of my compass – and there is much music, excellent voice, in this little organ, yet cannot you make it speak. 'Sblood, do you think I am easier to be played on than a pipe? call me what instrument you will, though you can fret me, you cannot play upon me. (III. ii.353–74)

This, like the scene that follows, is of major importance in establishing Rosencrantz and Guildenstern's rôles as minions and spies. The problem for Stoppard is not Hamlet's aggression and humiliation of the courtiers – which, in itself, does not threaten his premise that they never know what they are supposed to be doing or what is going on around them – but the depiction of them as virtual messenger-boys of the court. Similarly Act III, sc. iii, which takes place between the courtiers and king and queen, clearly demonstrates that they have entered the sanctum of the king's confidence. Their flattery in this scene does the pair little credit and, more importantly, suggests that they know which side of the bread the butter is on. Furthermore, the scene contains the starkest expression that Shakespeare provides of Rosencrantz and Guildenstern's possible complicity in Hamlet's proposed fate, as Claudius unequivocally declares in their presence:

I like him not, nor stands it safe with us

> To let his madness range. Therefore prepare you . . .
>     we will fetters put about this fear,
> Which now goes too free-footed   (III.iii.1–2, 25–6)

and despatches them as Hamlet's escort to England. Depending on
the precise interpretation of the word 'fetters', this can be seen as the
most glaring rebuttal of all of Stoppard's view of Rosencrantz and
Guildenstern as 'bewildered innocents'.

Whether Stoppard is entitled to exclude what Shakespeare makes
fairly clear depends crucially on how we view the relationship
between his Rosencrantz and Guildenstern and Shakespeare's
originals. There are a number of possible positions. John
Weightman, for instance, complains:

> I worry about the fact that Mr Stoppard's heroes are not properly
> connected up to *Hamlet*, because *Hamlet* is, after all, where they
> come from.[12]

In a similar vein, the critic Robert Brustein considers that the
omission of the recorder scene, and others, violates 'the integrity of
Shakespeare's original conception'.[13] Yet it is clear that Stoppard is,
above all, acting to protect the integrity of his *own* conception and
while *Hamlet* is indeed where his characters come from, the liberties
which he is entitled to take with them once they have been extracted
must become a matter for his own judgement. The question – as
with Gilbert's *Rosencrantz and Guildenstern*, which quite deliberately
twists Shakespeare's characters and plot into a new comic setting –
is whether the play works on its own terms. Stoppard's play is not
written as a critique of centuries of Shakespearean interpretation of
these two characters; if it were, our judgement might indeed be
harsh. Neither is he attempting a simple expansion, or revaluation,
of Shakespeare's materials and characters. What he *has* done is to
take a fledgling nuance from Shakespeare's play and develop it with
his own dramatic creations. Their characters and fates may be
anchored in *Hamlet*, but they spend far less time 'in' it than 'out' of it
and, within it, have very much less comprehensible relationships
with Cladius, with Gertrude and with Hamlet. It is, therefore,
somewhat misconceived to judge the success of Stoppard's play by
the precision of its relationship with *Hamlet* – just as it
would be to judge the success of his own later play *Travesties* by the
completeness of its intermittent parody of *The Importance of Being*

*Earnest.* In studying what Stoppard has *not* done with his characters from *Hamlet*, many of his critics have taken insufficient note of what he *has* achieved with them within his own serious, complex and beautifully patterned comedy.

*       *       *

Primarily, as his comments suggest, Stoppard is interested in Rosencrantz and Guildenstern as victims – victims of Hamlet the prince, as we have seen, and, in a wider sense, of *Hamlet* the play. For the world which the courtiers inhabit in *Rosencrantz* is not only incoherent but hostile – a world in which coins mysteriously land 'heads' every time, with even the natural laws of physics suspended. The philosophical implications here are highly disturbing, but their own attempts to explore them produce only comically chaotic reasoning. Guildenstern, the philosopher of the pair, only grows more and more confused as he tests out premises that never make sense, whereas Rosencrantz, the more excitable character, is only capable of questioning their predicament in a fumbling, alarmed way. A more coherent analysis has, however, been provided by Jonathan Bennett in his essay on both *Jumpers* and *Rosencrantz* which, from a philosopher's viewpoint, studies the nature of the courtiers' baffling sense of 'reality'. He concludes that

> Stoppard works intensively at a small cluster of intimately connected concepts . . . identity, memory, activity and death.[14]

As Bennett says, Rosencrantz and Guildenstern cannot begin to relate themselves to their world without a firmer grasp of their identities than they appear to possess, especially as they spend most of the play unsure which of them is Rosencrantz and which Guildenstern. But it is perhaps their absence of memory which is most disabling:

> *Ros:* We're his *friends.*
> *Guil:* How do you know?
> *Ros:* From our young days brought up with him.
> *Guil:* You've only got their word for it.
> *Ros:* But that's what we depend on. (p. 79)

It is on the sinister aspects of this dependence that Stoppard's ironic humour is given greatest rein. Rosencrantz and Guildenstern can remember nothing before a vague recollection of a man on horseback banging on the shutter to summon them to the Danish court. All of their pertinent history is contained in the cues they manage to pick up from Gertrude and Claudius:

> *Ros:* What have we got to go on?
> *Guil:* We have been briefed. Hamlet's transformation. What do you recollect?
> *Ros:* Well he's changed, hasn't he? The exterior and inward man fails to resemble –
> *Guil:* Draw him on to pleasures – glean what afflicts him.
> *Ros:* Something more than his father's death –
> *Guil:* He's always talking about us – there aren't two people living whom he dotes on more than us. (p. 29)
> *Ros:* We cheer him up – find out what's the matter –
> *Guil:* Exactly, it's a matter of asking the right questions and giving away as little as we can. (p. 29)

The manner in which their phraseology in this exchange confusedly repeats the speeches which the king and queen have just delivered is a measure of the insubstantiality and vulnerability of their whole characters. They therefore have no option but to rely on the little they *are* told. As Guildenstern says:

> There's a logic at work – it's all done for you, don't worry. Enjoy it. Relax. To be taken in hand and led, like being a child again, even without the innocence. (p. 29)

But this course leads smoothly to disaster: the disturbing implications of the 'logic at work' in their corner of the universe are clear from the impossible run of 'heads' at the start of the play. As Bennett says, they are 'epistemically empty':

> they are in touch with no past, and so they can neither construe the present nor direct themselves purposefully towards the future.[15]

Finally, therefore, having lived in blank incomprehension of their identities, their pasts and their possible and probable actions, they die in equal unenlightenment, capable only of abandoning their failed struggle for understanding and returning to the non-being from which they came.

Bennett's article is useful in demonstrating how thoroughly Stoppard's characters are deprived of meaningful orientation and how their plight exposes the fragility of the conventions on which we all rely in our lives. But it must be recognised from the start that their plight is dramatic and their existence wholly circumscribed by the fact that they are characters in a play. For *Rosencrantz and Guildenstern are Dead* is a modern development of the age-old analogue of the playworld with the real world:

> All the world's a stage
> And all the men and women merely players:
> They have their exits and their entrances.[16]

Rosencrantz and Guildenstern's world is a stage, and the production being staged is *Hamlet*. They exist within its parameters, not only in the brief 'on-stage' sections from Shakespeare's play, but in the 'off-stage' sections of Stoppard's own creation. This novel application of the playworld analogue is thus not employed in order to focus upon the ambivalence of a real world and a playworld. Instead, it is two playworlds that collide, that of *Hamlet* and, inextricably reined to it, Rosencrantz and Guildenstern's own. Ignorant of the fact that their world is a playworld, in turn dependent upon yet another playworld, they are constantly amazed at the failure of all their assumptions about probability and the operation of natural laws. Stoppard ensures, however, that the audience is never allowed to forget this playworld 'reality'; the fulcrum of his play is our ironic awareness of the presence of Shakespeare's text as the controlling and determining force behind it.

This irony is chiefly directed towards the connecting links between the two plays as the plot of *Hamlet* insidiously penetrates Rosencrantz and Guildenstern's 'off-stage' world. There is, for instance, the players' dumbshow, the prelude to 'the Murder of Gonzago', in which two spies, wearing cloaks identical to Rosencrantz and Guildenstern's, present a letter to the English king and are promptly executed:

> (*Ros. approaches 'his' Spy doubtfully. He does not quite understand why the coats are familiar. Ros. stands close, touches the coat, thoughtfully . . .* )
> *Ros:* Well, if it isn't –! No, wait a minute, don't tell me – it's a long time since – where was it? (p. 60)

Just as Hamlet uses 'The Murder of Gonzago' to confront Claudius with his past, so Stoppard stretches the playlet's fabric to confront his heroes with their future; as they contemplate 'themselves', the crisis of their circumscribed existence is imaginatively evoked. The audience's familiarity with *Hamlet* is obviously crucial to this irony, making nonsense of Stoppard's professed belief that it is not essential to an understanding of his play. It is only this knowledge which lends a wry humour to lines such as Guildenstern's hopeful thought: 'There may be something in the letter to keep us going a bit' (p. 76) and the irony even extends to the players when Rosencrantz and Guildenstern find that they too are on the ship to England:

> *Guil:* What are you doing here?
>
> *Player:* . . . Our play offended the king.
> *Guil:* Yes.
> *Player:* Well, he's a second husband himself. Tactless really. (p. 83)

The chief importance of this is again that it emphasises the distinct nature of the actor–audience relationship which *Rosencrantz and Guildenstern are Dead* exploits. Dramatic irony is generally created through the exclusion of one or more relevant characters from scenes involving their close interests, a technique masterfully epitomised in *Othello*. Here, however, the key to the irony lies in another play altogether. *Hamlet* dogs the confounded courtiers to their deaths and when they apprehend the final direction of their fates, their horrified questions have an answer equally horrifying in its sheer simplicity:

> *Guil:* But why? Was it all for this? Who are we that so much should converge on our little deaths? (*In anguish to the Player.*) Who are *we*?
> *Player:* You are Rosencrantz and Guildenstern. That's enough. (p. 89)

It is 'enough' to identify Rosencrantz and Guildenstern (it is not even necessary to identify them from each other!) in order to define the nature and purpose of their existence: they exist for and in terms of *Hamlet*: to enter the Danish court, to go to England with the prince, to arrive without him and to die.

A second level of dramatic irony in *Rosencrantz and Guildenstern are Dead* derives from the nature of the courtiers' own 'off-stage' playworld which, again, they cannot recognise as such. The exchange:

> *Guil:* See anyone?
> *Ros:* No. You?
> *Guil:* No. (*At footlights.*) What a fine persecution – to be kept intrigued without ever quite being enlightened.    (p. 30)

serves a dual purpose. It emphasises the mystification that the pair feel in the hostile environment of *Hamlet*,[17] but also suggests that the first key to their enlightenment must stem from an awareness of their audience at the other side of the footlights, from a recognition that their world is lived out on the boards of a stage. Rosencrantz says at one point:

> I feel like a spectator – an appalling prospect. The only thing that makes it bearable is the irrational belief that somebody interesting will come on in a minute.    (p. 30)

But such interest is maintained only fleetingly, continually over-whelmed by bafflement. In a passage strangely appropriate to *Rosencrantz and Guildenstern are Dead* (and to Moon in Stoppard's novel), Elizabeth Burns has written:

> The theatrical quality of life, taken for granted by nearly everyone, seems to be experienced most concretely by those who feel themselves on the margin of events either because they have adopted the rôle of spectator, or because, though present, they have not yet been offered a part or have not learnt it sufficiently well to enable them to join the actors.[18]

Stoppard's heroes are conscious of the theatricality of the *Hamlet* world, yet what they fail to understand is that they too are an integral part of that bizarre and incomprehensible world with all its theatricality, with all its predetermined plotting and rôle-playing. Their roles are indeed marginal, but, as C. W. E. Bigsby says, marginality 'is a matter of focus. In this play, Hamlet is marginal.'[19] And, as events prove, Rosencrantz and Guildenstern are very much more than the spectators 'on the margin of events' which they imagine themselves to be.

Yet although they do not perceive the nature of their playworld, the players do – a contrast which is fundamental to the exploration of the concept of 'reality' in the play. As the dress rehearsal of 'The Murder of Gonzago' and a series of cryptic remarks reveal, the tragedians know the context and the direction of their existence:

*Player:* Are you familiar with this play?
*Guil:* No.
*Player:* A slaughterhouse – eight corpses all told. It brings out the best in us.   (p. 60)

Unlike the players, Rosencrantz and Guildenstern are not actors by profession; they can understand neither their rôles nor the fact that they have rôles and their search for their *raison d'être* is futile without this enlightenment. In contrast, Stoppard implies that the players' wholehearted acceptance of acting as a mode of living frees them from this kind of existential uncertainty. They create their own reality by acting, by improvisation and by performance, accepting or at least resigning themselves to the shifting reality they are given, within the confines of *Hamlet* – though they enjoy a relatively happy ending. The difference of attitude between them and Rosencrantz and Guildenstern recalls the central contrast in Stoppard's novel between Moon and Malquist; the players, like Malquist, survive on the philosophy that 'things don't stand much looking into.' [20] Indeed, their extrovert leader revels in the unreality of the world of acting – 'We transport you into a world of intrigue and illusion' (p. 16) – while Rosencrantz and Guildenstern, unaware of their own confinement in this world, pass the play's three acts in a bewildered search for clues and connections which is, at a deeper level, a quest for identity and meaning:

*Player:* Uncertainty is the normal state. You're nobody special.
*Guil:* But for God's sake what are we supposed to *do*?!
*Player:* Relax. Respond. That's what people do. You can't go through life questioning your situation at every turn.
*Guil:* But we don't know what's going on, or what to do with ourselves. We don't know how to *act*.   (pp. 47–8)

In place of the actor's adaptability, Rosencrantz and Guildenstern insist on certainty and understanding, and (on Stoppard's tenets) *Hamlet* offers them neither. John Weightman has described the pair as 'comparable to actors who haven't yet been adequately briefed about their parts'[21] but, more accurately, they are not aware that they *are* actors, and it is neither their profession nor inclination to be so. William Babula's suggestion that they find their rôles 'baffling'[22] is similarly imprecise; though their world is certainly a baffling one, they never grasp the essential fact that they have been assigned rôles within it.

This concern with the nature of character in *Rosencrantz and Guildenstern are Dead* invites comparison of the play with a number of similar studies of rôle-playing. Chief among these is Pirandello's self-conscious exploration of inescapably defined rôles in *Six Characters in Search of an Author*. For him such 'bound' rôles are at least real to their own truth and by pitting his group of characters against a group of actors, he produces a brilliant juxtaposition of the 'reality' of the illusion (as offered by the Six Characters) against the 'illusion' of reality (which is all the actors can offer). The Producer who attempts to stage the family's tragedy in his theatre echoes Stoppard's Player in declaring

> But what's the truth got to do with it? Acting's what we're here for! Truth's all very fine . . . but only up to a point.[23]

He has not understood that the 'acting' of the Six Characters is their only possible 'truth'; they have to seek the theatre in order to establish their 'reality'. In a similar vein, Dennis Potter's stimulating novel *Hide and Seek* offers us a central character (who is only slowly revealed as such) struggling to liberate himself from the obsessive and unpleasant mind of his authorial creator. Constantly manipulated and intimidated, like the creations of Stoppard and Pirandello, he is faced with an impossible, doomed struggle to assert his independence.

The common underlying theme in these various studies of characters visibly controlled from without is that of determinism. The ideas of rôle and fate expressed in *Rosencrantz and Guildenstern are Dead* do not operate merely to further the playfully theatrical comedy inherent in the courtiers' struggle to understand the meaning of their predicament; they invoke the inability of all mankind to understand those forces ultimately in control of their lives and fates. Yet precisely because Rosencrantz and Guildenstern's fate is determined by *Hamlet*, and not by random forces, Stoppard further suggests that there is some method behind the seeming madness of their lives. This madness may be inscrutable to those it most nearly concerns, but, as the Player says, menacingly,

> There's a design at work in all art – surely you know that? (p. 57)

Like the players, the audience can see the design where Rosencrantz and Guildenstern cannot, and there is some reassurance to be gained from this over-view. At the same time, what tempers our recognition of the courtiers' amusingly ironic plight is a latent awareness that, like them, we cannot see the 'design' behind our own lives. Our sympathies are thus directed towards these two men groping in an existential void which, to varying degrees, may mirror our own. When, for instance, Guildenstern says

> There must have been a moment, at the beginning, where we could have said – no. But somehow we missed it  (p. 91)

the irony, which depends on our knowledge that there could not have been any such moment, also embraces a poignant intuition that such moments are notoriously hard to recognise within one's own experience. Here, and intermittently throughout the play, Rosencrantz and Guildenstern transcend the narrow confines of their predicament, appealing to us not merely as dramatic creations trapped in theatrical melodrama but as human beings trapped in a world which does not make sense, which refuses to follow the expected rules.

In a passage towards the end of the second act, where the courtiers are about to board the ship for England (which is, unknown to them, to be the beginning of their end), this tentative empathy between Stoppard's bewildered heroes and his audience is caught in a curiously poignant resonance in Guildenstern's vague apprehension of things drawing to a close:

> *Guil:* It's autumnal.
> *Ros (examining the ground):* No leaves.
> *Guil:* Autumnal – nothing to do with leaves. It is to do with a
> certain brownness at the edges of the day . . . Brown is
> creeping up on us, take my word for it . . . Russets and
> tangerine shades of old gold flushing the very outside edge
> of the senses . . . deep shining ochres, burnt umber and
> parchments of baked earth – reflecting on itself and

through itself, filtering the light. At such times, perhaps, coincidentally, the leaves might fall somewhere, by repute. Yesterday was blue, like smoke.   (p. 68)

The phrase 'flushing the very outside edge of the senses' is peculiarly appropriate to this pair of half-aware minds whose experience and substance are so ruthlessly circumscribed, while the last image implies both the haziness of the courtiers' powers of recollection and the bright blue skies of summer, which, as Guildenstern so vaguely apprehends, have already begun to give way to the browns of autumn. Struggling to articulate how his experience *feels*, Guildenstern creates a complex image which captures almost poetically their imminent fate. Drawn from a range of natural experience (the passing of the seasons) which lies beyond their orbit, it also illustrates their sensory deprivation. A few lines earlier, Rosencrantz said breezily, with unconscious irony, 'The spring can't last forever' (p. 68). The summer of their lives, by implication, never arrived at all and Guildenstern's elusive apprehension of a leafless autumn existing only 'at the edges of the day' extends the metaphor towards its inevitable conclusion. This hovering on the perpetual edge of awareness and of 'real' experience, recalls Eliot's poem 'Marina':

What seas what shores what grey rocks and what islands
What water lapping the bow
And scent of pine and woodthrush singing through the fog
What images return
O my daughter.[24]

Pericles hovers on the borders of recognition, hearing the song of the woodthrush, but blinded by the fog, unable to give full meaning to his sensory experiences. Despite the obvious differences of technique, Stoppard, like Eliot, calls attention to what is present but cannot be perceived. Rosencrantz and Guildenstern cannot wait for the fog to clear, for by then they will be dead, but Stoppard invests them with just sufficient humanity to glean, intermittently, an elusive sense of a world of meaning and value to which they cannot relate – a world, in this instance, of nature's seasons.

A second strain of imagery is aural: there are repeated references to musical sounds on the air and wherever these are heard, they foreshadow the imminent arrival of the players. For Guildenstern, the music acts as a vague pointer to the unnaturalness of their position:

> Ninety-two coins spun consecutively have come down heads ninety-two consecutive times . . . and for the last three minutes on the wind of a windless day I have heard the sound of drum and flute. (p. 12)

The eeriness of this phenomenon is not alleviated by its eventual association with the players' approach, which, since they clearly know the pattern of events in *Hamlet* and the fate awaiting the pair, is never an auspicious omen. At the end of the second act the sinister implication of the sound is confirmed when it is heard faintly in the distance but no one appears. It is heard again in Act Three and Guildenstern, in a bored but expectant state, responds with eagerness: 'Out of the void, finally a sound'. (p. 81) But as the players slowly emerge from the ship's barrels where they have stowed themselves away (which apparently explains their failure to follow the music onto the stage at the previous juncture), Rosencrantz and Guildenstern's void remains unfulfilled, and the sounds they cannot comprehend become an image of the mystifying power of events within the boundaries of their awareness but outside the boundaries of their understanding.

The tentative sympathy that Stoppard seeks to establish for his 'victims' of *Hamlet* thus works in ways quite unconnected with *Hamlet* itself, and this is demonstrated with most clarity by his treatment of the theme of death. While the comedy is never abandoned, it becomes increasingly wry and sombre as the theme of mortality is developed in the third act of the play. The introducing of death into comedy usually succeeds in shattering the humour altogether, as in the quintessential example of *Love's Labour Lost*:

> To move wild laughter in the throat of death?
> It cannot be; it is impossible:
> Mirth cannot move a soul in agony.[25]

As soon as the Princess receives the news of her father's death, the play moves into a different register; the game-playing has to come to an abrupt end. The gay princess becomes a serious woman, the high-spirited Berowne becomes down-cast and petulant. Stoppard's characters, however, have a peculiar ability to move us at the same time as amusing us, as Moon clearly demonstrates in *Lord Malquist and Mr Moon*. Here too, Guildenstern's speculations upon death achieve this dual effect: they have a human edge that his idle philosophising and time-passing banter decidedly lack. When, for example, he and Rosencrantz re-read the letter which now commands their deaths instead of Hamlet's, he reacts with an unmistakable, passionate sense of shock:

> Death is not anything . . . death is not . . . . It's the absence of presence, nothing more . . . the endless time of never coming back . . . a gap you can't see, and when the wind blows through it, it makes no sound.   (pp. 90–91)

As Guildenstern gropes almost inarticulately for the right words,[26] Stoppard makes us acutely conscious of the unwritten tragic possibilities of his characters' lives. The manner in which they learn of their fates, in the contents of the mysteriously altered letter, sums up their total inability to control their lives and though they may hardly have lived, death (as Bennett establishes) is the stern ultimate 'reality' which cannot be acted or shammed. Guildenstern's sharp awareness of this truth brings the audience to its closest point of contact with Stoppard's frail heroes.

The sympathy which is deliberately engendered in this manner is emphasised with particular force by the contrast which Stoppard again pursues between the tragedians and the two courtiers as the Player displays an exasperating indifference to the news of his colleagues' impending doom:

> *Player:* In our experience, most things end in death.
> *Guil(fear, vengeance, scorn):* Your experience! *Actors!* (*He snatches a dagger from the Player's belt and holds the point at the Player's throat: the Player backs and Guildenstern advances, speaking more quietly.*) I'm talking about death – and you've never experienced *that.* And you cannot *act* it. You die a thousand casual deaths – with none of that intensity which squeezes out life . . . and no blood runs cold anywhere. Because even as you die you know that you will come back in a different hat. But no one gets up after *death* – there is no applause – there is only silence and some second-hand clothes, and that's – *death* – (*And he pushes the blade in up to the hilt. The Player stands with huge, terrible eyes,*

> *clutches at the wound as the blade withdraws: he makes small weeping sounds and falls to his knees, and then right down . . .*
>
> *The Player finally lies still. A short moment of silence. Then the tragedians start to applaud with genuine admiration. The Player stands up, brushing himself down.)*
> Player *(modestly):* Oh come, come, gentlemen – no flattery – it was merely competent. (pp. 89–90)

The marked contrast between the actor's feigned performance and Guildenstern's murderous passion (he, like the audience, believes he has really killed the Player) epitomises Stoppard's different approaches to these two distinct kinds of character. For the players nothing, not even death, is 'real': the Player's knife has a retractable blade. Rosencrantz and Guildenstern's 'reality', on the other hand, is finally established *only* by their deaths.

Yet at one point the play does provide an insight into the actor's true death, as opposed to the histrionics that the Player's exhibition largely comprises. This 'death' takes place when Rosencrantz and Guildenstern abandon the players by the roadside after 'hiring' them to give a performance:

> We pledged our identities, secure in the conventions of our trade; that someone would be watching. And then, gradually, no one was. We were caught, high and dry. It was not until the murderer's long soliloquy that we were able to look around; frozen as we were in profile, our eyes searched you out, first confidently, then hesitantly, then desperately as each patch of turf, each log, every exposed corner in every direction proved uninhabited, and all the while the murderous King addressed the horizon with his dreary interminable guilt . . .
>
> No one came forward. No one shouted at us. The silence was unbreakable, it imposed itself on us; it was obscene. We took off our crowns and swords and cloth of gold and moved silent on the road to Elsinore. (p. 46)

As the Player's passionate rebuke makes clear, it is performing without an audience which represents 'death' for the actor; not something hammed and rumbustuous, but something much quieter and much more insidiously real, as the actor's reality, his assumed identity, is taken from him. Since acting is his life, this is his death.

For having placed his own identity in abeyance in order to act, the abandoned player, stripped of 'the single assumption which makes our existence viable' (p. 45) is alone in his universe, with no self at all, pacing idly in the void to meet a fate which provides the true parallel to Rosencrantz and Guildenstern's.

When their final reckoning arrives, the courtiers realise that only submissive self-abandonment is possible:

> *Ros:* All right then. I don't care. I've had enough. To tell you the truth, I'm relieved. (*And he disappears from view.*)
> *Guil:* Well, we'll know better next time. Now you see me, now you – (*And disappears.*)  (p. 91)

The play then ends swiftly with the players' series of histrionically mimed deaths creating a tableau which mirrors, and is then transformed into, the final tableau of death from *Hamlet*. Following the 'deaths' of Rosencrantz and Guildenstern, however, these tableaux, like the Player's mimed death, seem a hollow sham; they recall Guildenstern's line:

> no one gets up after *death* – there is no applause – there is only silence.  (p. 89)

For Rosencrantz and Guildenstern there *is* only silence, and the entry of the English ambassador with the news that 'Rosencrantz and Guildenstern are dead'. The text, in the second edition, then indicates that the lights should fade out in the course of Horatio's speech 'Not from his mouth . . .', which immediately follows the ambassador's announcement. This ending, however, is considerably truncated from the original, and the two prints of the first edition, both in May 1967 (which indicates, incidentally, how successful the early sales of the playtext were), run on for a further page or so (cut from the National Theatre production late in the day), including Fortinbras's tribute to Hamlet and a conversation between the English ambassador and a second ambassador. (The original ending of the play is reproduced in Appendix One.) Their dialogue is of the 'off-stage' variety and is purposely designed to echo the insubstantiality and puzzlement of Rosencrantz and Guildenstern. Stoppard's first pair arrive in England with a note commanding their own deaths; he now creates a second pair who arrive to confirm that this execution has taken place, only to find, with practically the entire court of Elsinore lying dead at their feet, that they have no one

to whom they can deliver their message. Thus Stoppard suggests a
recurring pattern of incomprehension and apparent motivelessness
for all those living on the fringe of events, and he further emphasises
the intended parallel between his two pairs of attendant lords when
the play ends with a knocking sound and the indistinct shouting of
two names to the accompaniment (again emphasising its sinister
implications) of the tragedians' music. The ambassadors are
therefore summoned in just the same manner as Rosencrantz and
Guildenstern, according to their earliest memories.

Where the revised, contracted ending seems to me to gain on the
original is in the clearer contrast it suggests between the negativity of
Rosencrantz and Guildenstern's resignation at the end and the
tragic bravery and victory over self of Hamlet's 'resignation':

> There is special providence in the fall of a sparrow. If it be now,
> 'tis not to come – if it be not to come, it will be now – if it be not
> now, yet it will come – the readiness is all. Since no man, of aught
> he leaves, know what is't to leave betimes, let be.   (V.ii.217–22)

For Hamlet, placing himself in the hands of Providence and the
powers of his own resolution, there is the glory of a noble and tragic
death. For Rosencrantz and Guildenstern, mutely disappearing into
non-existence, there is only a vacuum of ignorance and despair. The
inevitability of their deaths proves, ironically, to be the single surest
aspect of their lives and for explanation they have only the cold and
passive inscrutability of the Player's declaration 'It is written.'
(p. 58) The fates of Rosencrantz and Guildenstern are indeed
written, written in *Hamlet*, and that finally is all that needs to be said.

\*           \*           \*

Kenneth Tynan has rightly said of the play that 'despite its multiple
sources, *Rosencrantz* is a genuine original, one of a kind'[27] and it is
certainly what the play represented – the arrival of an important
new writer with a rare sense of theatrical daring and comic
innovation – that is most important. It is, however, worth taking a
final glance at some of Stoppard's definite and possible sources, since
a few critics, some motivated by a desire to belittle his originality,
have sought to enumerate all those they can detect.[28] For instance,
Arnold Hinchliffe's almost scathing dismissal of the play:

> what we see is a clever author manipulating rather than

exploring, a parasite feeding off Shakespeare, Pirandello and Beckett[29]

invokes the usual triad and Stoppard generously added a fourth name when he declared

> It would be very difficult to write a play which was totally unlike Beckett, Pirandello and Kafka.[30]

The case of Pirandello, whose treatment of the interplay between illusory playworlds or mirror-worlds offers passing points of contrast rather than resemblance to *Rosencrantz*, has been discussed briefly above, while the analogy with Kafka (which Tynan also makes[31]) does not extend beyond a vague shared sense of imprisonment in an incomprehensible world. Stoppard is utterly unlike both these authors in the way in which he presents his material as a light, if philosophically inclined comedy which only slowly and tentatively turns to face the dark. Only with Beckett is any substantial comparison tenable. Other critics, notably Victor L. Cahn and Jill Levenson, extend the debt to Beckett to infer a debt to the Theatre of the Absurd in general, only to retreat from the full implications of such an awkward conclusion. Thus Cahn suggests that in *Rosencrantz*:

> Stoppard confronts absurdity head-on and at the same time takes the initial steps towards moving beyond absurdity.[32]

It would be more accurate, I think, to see Stoppard as *starting* 'beyond absurdity', having digested the movement's bold, dramatic adventurousness and turned it to his own, unique advantage. Jim Hunter seems nearer the mark when he suggests that it is not so much the Absurd as one play that needed confronting:

> Stoppard both celebrated *Waiting for Godot*, and largely got it out of his system, in *Rosencrantz*.[33]

A sense of wide-ranging cultural allusion is a constant feature of Stoppard's work, as his novel demonstrates, as the use of *Hamlet* shows here and as the later plays manifest ever more plainly. The echoes of *Godot* which run throughout *Rosencrantz* are therefore present neither in a spirit of plagiarism, nor even parody, but (as

Hunter suggests) in a spirit of celebration, as Stoppard pays his own,
idiosyncratic tribute to the play which provided the most dramatic
rejection of realism in the theatre's history. Yet at the same time, it is
vital that the marked differences between the two plays and the way
Stoppard *uses* Beckett's should be fully noted.

Talking of *Rosencrantz* in an interview on Thames Television in
1976, Stoppard suggested:

> One of the reasons that the play turned out to work so well, I
> think, is that the predicament of the characters coincides with the
> predicament of the playwright. In other words I have these two
> guys in there and there's no plot until somebody comes in three
> pages later and they have to fill three pages and I have to fill three
> pages, and there's nothing. So they end up playing word games,
> spinning coins, speculating on eternals as well as the immediate
> situation, getting nowhere, and one finds that there becomes a
> sort of empathy, a circular one, between an audience watching
> somebody killing time watching somebody killing time, sur-
> rounded by somebody killing time.[34]

This too is Beckett's evident starting point for *Waiting for Godot*, in
which two tramps wait for a man who never comes but who appears
to hold the solution to all their problems. But Didi and Gogo differ
from Rosencrantz and Guildenstern in two vital respects. First,
where Stoppard locates meaning elsewhere, in the identifiable
context of *Hamlet*, Beckett offers none: there is no comforting
dramatic irony behind his characters' bleak metaphysical plights
and the mysteries which they cannot fathom remain equally
mysterious to his audiences:

> *Vladimir:*  . . . why do you always come crawling back?
> *Estragon:*  I don't know.
> *Vladimir:*  No, but I do. It's because you don't know how to
>              defend yourself. I wouldn't have let them beat you.
> *Estragon:*  You couldn't have stopped them.
> *Vladimir:*  Why not?
> *Estragon:*  There were ten of them.
> *Vladimir:*  No, I mean before they beat you. I would have
>              stopped you from doing whatever it was you were
>              doing.
> *Estragon:*  I wasn't doing anything.

> *Vladimir:* Then why did they beat you?
> *Estragon:* I don't know.[35]

The enemy is undefined and therefore deeply sinister, whereas we know throughout *Rosencrantz and Guildenstern are Dead* that their 'enemies', indeed their whole predicament, can be seen in quite different terms in *Hamlet*. There is no possible alternative viewpoint in *Godot*, however, and the tramps' despair and squalor remains unrelieved:

> *Vladimir:* Do you not recognise the place?
> *Estragon (suddenly furious):* Recognise! What is there to recognise? All my lousy life I've crawled about in the mud! And you talk to me about scenery! (*Looking wildly about him.*) Look at this muckheap! I've never stirred from it![36]

Unlike Stoppard's audiences, Beckett's are forced to remain independent, facing the oppressive weight of his characters' experiences and failures.

The tone of these exchanges illuminates the second striking difference between Stoppard and Beckett: the nature of the characters themselves, and their relationship to the play's humour. Vladimir and Estragon are clowns as well as tramps, but their humour is constantly laced with dark echoes that are more suggestive of the Fool in *Lear* than of Rosencrantz and Guildenstern. Beckett's buffoonery works in the opposite direction from Stoppard's – darkening and intensifying rather than humanising the mood of the play. Vladimir and Estragon are most like Rosencrantz and Guildenstern (though they are never *very* like them) in such flippant exchanges as:

> *Vladimir:* That passed the time.
> *Estragon:* It would have passed in any case.
> *Vladimir:* Yes, but not so rapidly.[37]

and:

> *Estragon (laughing noisily):* He wants to know if we are friends!
> *Vladimir:* No, he means friends of *his*.
> *Estragon:* Well?

*Vladimir:* We've proved we are, by helping him.
*Estragon:* Exactly. Would we have helped him if we weren't his friends?
*Vladimir:* Possibly.[38]

The second of these, with the characters talking at cross-purposes with strong tautological undercurrents, creates the kind of conversation that has, with *Rosencrantz* and subsequent plays, become almost a hallmark of Stoppard's style. In the first, it is noticeable how the comedy veers relentlessly back to the empty passing of time, which is Beckett's prime concern in *Waiting for Godot*. In each example the quick-fire two-man patter, as in *Rosencrantz*, suggests a strain of music hall-style theatricality. This is reinforced in both plays by the use of pantomime-like stage business and theatrical routines of a visual or physical kind. In *Waiting for Godot* Beckett has his characters collapsing in a heap, losing their trousers and exchanging their hats in ostentatious pantomime style, and there is a surprising amount of similar stage business in *Rosencrantz and Guildenstern are Dead*. On page 65 Rosencrantz's trousers fall down. On pages 19 and 20 the players' boy, Alfred, struggles in and out of a skirt several times. On page 70 Rosencrantz's 'dead' leg turns out to be Guildenstern's very alive one when he pinches it. On page 63 Stoppard gives us a pantomimic 'you go that way' routine. On page 37 Hamlet walks onto the stage backwards, which is comic as a purely visual joke in its own right as well as a parody of the lines he is about to address to Polonius ('if like a crab you could go backward'). And the first manifestation of the slapstick elements occurs in the climax to the coin-tossing at the start of the play:

> *Guil. takes a third coin, spins it, catches it in his right hand, turns it over onto his left wrist, lobs it in the air, catches it with his left hand, raises his left leg, throws the coin up under it, catches it and turns it over on the top of his head, where it sits. Ros. comes, looks at it, puts it in his bag.* (p. 10)

Here perhaps, in these well-worn tricks and stage devices, Stoppard reveals his clearest debt to Beckett's pioneering stagecraft in *Godot*, and it is again intensely ironic that Rosencrantz and Guildenstern, unconscious of their own theatricality, should be the agents of most of these patently theatrical routines.

Alfred Emmet of the Questors Theatre, Ealing, has suggested

another important influence upon *Rosencrantz and Guildenstern are Dead*:

> it always forcibly struck me that in some respects the style of Stoppard's play was reminiscent of that of James Saunders' *Next Time I'll Sing To You*. Could this have been an influence attributable to their time together in Berlin?[39]

In view of Stoppard's own declaration

> I think *Next Time I'll Sing To You* is one of the best plays written since the war, simply because it's written like music. It's a most beautiful and brilliant use of language[40]

the comparison certainly merits consideration. In Saunders's play a group of actors are searching to discover some logic or purpose behind the solitary existence of a Norfolkshire hermit who, with apparent equanimity, withdrew entirely from all human contact for the greater part of his life. The circularity of their non-progress is commented upon by one of their number, Dust:

> Night after night the same circular dialogue, round and round we go . . . does he really think one night we'll reach a conclusion? Doesn't he realize that it's always the same, that it can't be otherwise?[41]

His friend, Meff, adds

> Just three things it all boils down to . . . making an entrance, making an exit, and filling in the time between.[42]

Earlier, Lizzie, the single actress involved in the proceedings, threatens revolt:

> *Lizzie:* I'm not staying if it gets unpleasant.
> *Dust:*   You'll stay until you're written out, my girl.[43]

All these pieces of dialogue have an obvious correspondence with *Rosencrantz and Guildenstern are Dead*, but beyond a certain similarity of style, dependent upon a combination of verbal quippery, philosophical introspection, and the strong awareness of the play as play, there seems no basis for an extensive comparison. Beckett, indeed, seems to have influenced both writers far more than they have influenced each other. While on a surface level Saunders's play appears to explore its subject with rather greater seriousness, its remoteness from that subject, the real Hermit, makes it no more than a search; it exists only as an enlarged and enacted discussion. Stoppard's play, on the other hand, succeeds in dramatically recreating the actual experience that is its theme – of living a narrow, pre-determined life in ignorance of the forces controlling it.

I have suggested that what first drew Stoppard to Rosencrantz and Guildenstern was the aspect of victims, bewildered and innocent victims, that he felt to lie between the lines of Shakespeare's intention. The minions of *Hamlet* become his heroes, with the nature of their resignation to their fates so strikingly different in quality and tone from the prince's own. And yet the play is not, I think, an attempt to produce *Hamlet* with a new pair of tragic heroes. The fates of Rosencrantz and Guildenstern are not tragic in *either* play. Indeed, in common with a great many contemporary writers, Stoppard appears to question whether the concept of tragedy is not obsolete in the modern age. George Steiner writes, in *The Death of Tragedy*:

> Tragedy is a deliberate advance to the edge of life, where the mind must look on blackness at the risk of vertigo.[44]

For Rosencrantz and Guildenstern there is no vertigo, and blackness has given way to blankness. They have not advanced to the edge of life – they have merely and wilfully been dumped there, to be manipulated and finally disposed of in a grimly patterned world of kings and princes in which, ultimately, they do not matter. Eliot's Prufrock sees himself in strikingly similar terms:

> No! I am not Prince Hamlet nor was meant to be;
> Am an attendant lord, one that will do
> To swell a progress, start a scene or two,
> Advise the prince, no doubt an easy tool.[45]

As already seen in discussing *Lord Malquist and Mr Moon*,[46] and in comparing Pericles' dim, fog-bound awareness in 'Marina' with Rosencrantz and Guildenstern's baffled apprehensions, Eliot seems to exert a special hold on Stoppard's imagination, and the greatest influence derives from Prufrock, the character and the poem.[47] Throughout Stoppard's writing characters struggle to orientate themselves properly to their puzzling or disturbing worlds. He is constantly fascinated by the problems of the victim, the second-rate, the also-ran, and Prufrock is an archetype of sorts for these people. It is quite probable indeed, that Eliot's poem, and especially the lines quoted above, rather than the writings of Pirandello, Kafka, Saunders, Beckett or even perhaps *Hamlet* itself, provides the real genesis of *Rosencrantz and Guildenstern are Dead*.

# 5 Escape Routes

In 1968 Stoppard said that *Rosencrantz and Guildenstern are Dead* was 'about the twelfth' play that he had written.[1] His count may not have been accurate or even serious, but a number of his relatively early plays have survived. Indeed, as this book went to press, Faber & Faber announced, somewhat surprisingly, that five of his previously unpublished early pieces for radio and television were being collected with Stoppard's 1982 radio play *The Dog It Was That Died*.[2] These include the two short radio sketches broadcast in the 1964 series *Just Before Midnight*, '*M*' *is for Moon Among Other Things*, a sad duologue centred on Marilyn Monroe's death, and *The Dissolution of Dominic Boot*, a comically fraught picaresque taxi ride through London (subsequently enlarged into a 50-minute screenplay for NBC Television in the United States). Also collected are three television pieces written between 1964 and 1966, the thriller *Neutral Ground*, a deft reworking of the Philoctetes myth eventually broadcast by Granada Television in December 1968, and two comedies for BBC 2's *Thirty-Minute Theatre*, broadcast in 1967. The first, *Teeth*, tells of a dentist (played by John Wood) who gets his wife's lover (John Stride) into his clutches in his chair; the second, *Another Moon Called Earth*, is chiefly of interest as the genesis of some of the strands of *Jumpers*: its heroine's balance is so disturbed by man's conquest of the moon that she takes to her bed, where she receives suspiciously close treatment from a man whom she claims to be her doctor. Two other early works which have remained unpublished are *The Gamblers*[3] and an unperformed screenplay called *This Way Out With Samuel Boot*, now mainly remembered as the indirect source of Stoppard's eventual fame; travelling home in a taxi after a TV company had rejected it, he and his agent Kenneth Ewing gave birth to the idea that became *Rosencrantz!*[4]

Best known of the plays which pre-date *Rosencrantz*, however, are *Enter a Free Man*, first staged in this country in 1968 and published in the same year by Faber and Faber; *A Separate Peace*, televised by the

BBC in 1966, after *Rosencrantz* stormed Edinburgh, and published by Hutchinson in 1969 (also republished in *The Dog It Was That Died* collection); and *If You're Glad I'll Be Frank*, broadcast by the Third Programme in 1966 and published with *Albert's Bridge* (another Third Programme broadcast) by Faber and Faber in 1969. *Albert's Bridge*, which won the Prix Italia in 1968 may also most usefully be considered in this chapter; although written a little later, it has much in common with these three other works, all of which provide valuable evidence of Stoppard's development as a playwright, as he explores his own strengths and weaknesses, evolves an individual comic style and experiments, at times very boldly, with dramatic form.

As we have seen, Stoppard wrote his first play in 1960 immediately after ceasing full-time journalism. This play was broadcast by Rediffusion Television in 1963 and BBC Radio in 1965, each time under the title *A Walk on the Water*, then received a stage performance at the Thalia-Theatre, Hamburg, on 30th June 1964 (during Stoppard's stay in West Berlin) as *Old Riley geht über'n Ozean* (Old Riley Walked the Water),[5] another in Vienna's Theater der Courage in February 1966 as *Der Spleen des George Riley*, and was finally staged in Britain at the St Martin's Theatre in March 1968, after the success of *Rosencrantz*, this time under its final title, *Enter a Free Man*. The production was directed by Frith Banbury and starred Michael Hordern and Megs Jenkins as George and Persephone Riley. By this time the play was almost eight years old and despite making some further revisions for this production, Stoppard evidently felt that he had left it well behind him. In 1974 he said that he felt towards the play

> a great deal of gratitude and affection, and a certain amount of embarrassment. I don't think it's a very true play, in the sense that I feel no intimacy with the people I was writing about. It works pretty well as a play, but actually it's phoney because it's a play written about other people's characters.[6]

This last phrase sheds some interesting light on Stoppard's dramatic development, for although he regards such borrowing as having been 'phoney' here, his later plays incorporate characters (and plots) borrowed from other sources with such frequency that this becomes almost a trademark of his work.

*Enter a Free Man* is built around one character, the effervescent

George Riley, a talker, a dreamer and, as Ronald Bryden declared on the play's West End debut, 'a splendid full-fledged comic creation, a dynamo of theatrical energy spraying his fantasies and paranoias over the stage like rainbow carnival streamers'.[7] Constantly imagining that he is on the verge of success as an inventor, Riley keeps convincing himself that his home life with his wife Persephone[8] and daughter Linda is stifling his creativity, whereupon he shuttles from his dining-room (one half of the stage) to his local pub (the other), boasting of his latest idea to anyone who will listen. There Harry, a total stranger, encourages his dreams:

> You're practically unique. The last of a breed. Think of all the inventors you know and see if they aren't all dead.[9]

He enthuses convivially about George's latest idea – to patent double-gummed, re-usable envelopes – and promises him capital and a business partnership; but while he is only playing up to Riley's fond image of himself, George takes everything he says seriously – until Harry shatters the illusion on the following day. Similarly, George's conviction that Florence (who has also humoured him in the pub) is prepared to elope with him is revealed to be an equally wild fantasy – she is, in fact, Harry's own girl-friend. Thus doubly humiliated, George returns to his domestic setting, no longer a prison but a necessary haven and support.

Stoppard has compared *Enter a Free Man* with *Death of a Salesman* and *Flowering Cherry*[10] and like Miller's protagonist Willy Loman and Bolt's Jim Cherry, Riley is a man whose existence is largely sustained by self-deception and illusion. But the comparison is both flattering (to Stoppard) and misleading. Unlike Miller's master-piece, *Enter a Free Man* is not concerned with the moral or social dissection of its central character; on the contrary, it capitalises heavily upon George's failings to produce much of the comedy, and when Stoppard introduces scenes in which the family's good-humoured tolerance of him is really stretched, the new tone seems alien, obtrusively imported from the contemporary post-*Anger* theatrical climate. Linda and Persephone, for instance, are initially presented as little more than stereotypes: the restless, spirited daughter, providing some opposition for her father, and the tidy, servile wife, providing none. Mrs Riley is portrayed in particularly flat and unindividualised terms as a model of forebearance with more than a touch of stupidity:

| | |
|---|---|
| *Riley:* | It came to me in a flash – just this morning. I'm home. |
| *Persephone:* | Of course you are. |
| *Riley*: | I mean home and dry. I can't see any snags. (*Waving the bigger envelope.*) It's all here! |
| *Persephone.* | It's quite small, isn't it? |
| *Riley:* | Some of the biggest things in our line are very small to look at. Think, there's the match. |
| *Persephone:* | A match? |
| *Riley:* | Yes. |
| *Persephone:* | What kind of match? |
| *Riley:* | Eh? No, no – what I've done is the *envelope*. |
| *Persephone:* | An envelope for matches? |
| *Riley:* | Who's talking about matches? |
| *Persephone:* | You were, love. |
| *Riley:* | No, I damn well wasn't! |
| *Persephone:* | As you like, George. Now, I really must get on. |
| | (p. 37) |

Linda's teenage stereotype is no less familiar:

> I'm going to make myself look a knockout tonight – I'm going to wash my hair and do my nails and stick Blue Grass up my jumper!
> (p. 53)

However, her tolerance of her father has very clear boundaries, especially where inventions such as his bizarre plant-watering system for the living-room (fuelled by rainwater from the roof) are concerned. In contrast to Persephone's placidity, Linda (like Miller's Biff) tries to reform her father by barracking him into common sense and attempting to direct his steps towards the local Employment Office. She, after all, is the family's sole breadwinner and it is her attitude, stirring up hostile undercurrents, that produces the mini-crisis in the second act. At this stage George has apparently left his wife and daughter, and Linda, on the point of eloping with her new boyfriend on a motorcycle, permits herself this unchecked outburst:

> He may be a lovely feller to stand a drink in the pub, great value for money, I'm sure – but as the family joke he's wearing a bit

thin. We're lumbered, and we'll go on being lumbered till he's
dead, and that may be *years* – (*she catches herself, contrite.*) Oh God, I
didn't mean that – I just meant –   (p. 67)

Now Persephone, who has spent the first act saying 'Whatever you
think is right, dear' (p. 47) and 'Well of course, dear. Don't fret
yourself' (p. 39) suddenly has to launch into tirade in reply:

You don't ask yourself why – you don't ask yourself what it costs
him to keep his belief in himself – to come back each time and start
again – and it's worth keeping, it's the last thing he's got . . .

You treat him like a crank lodger we've got living upstairs who
reads fairy tales and probably wishes he lived in one, but he's ours
and we're his, and don't you ever talk about him like that again.
(pp. 67–8)

At this point the 'imported' tone becomes all too apparent. There is,
for a start, a crude indebtedness to Linda Loman's stance in *Death of
a Salesman*:

I don't say he's a great man. Willy Loman never made a lot of
money. His name was never in the paper. He's not the finest
character that ever lived. But he's a human being and a terrible
thing is happening to him. So attention must be paid. . . . He's
just a big stupid man to you, but I tell you there's more good in
him than in many other people.[11]

The crucial difference is that Linda is a fully rounded character with
her strengths – resilience, love, forebearance – at one with her
limitations. In Stoppard's play, Persephone's new attitude rings
hollow and inconsistent because he has previously established her as
a comic butt. In attempting to reconcile his serious and comic
intentions within this single character, he overplays the kind of
switches of mood that are so effective at times in *Lord Malquist and Mr
Moon*.[12] Stage creations realised by human actors and actresses
cannot be so easily manipulated; it is as if a character from an N. F.
Simpson play (and Persephone has a certain amount in common
with Mrs Groomkirby in *One Way Pendulum*) were abruptly plunged
into one of Osborne's or Miller's. At such points Stoppard's
creations are most recognisibly 'someone else's characters', and at

this stage of his writing career he has not mastered the art of using them *entirely* on such terms.

This kind of critical scrutiny of domestic and suburban pressures does not fit comfortably into the kind of comedy towards which Stoppard's strongest instincts seem to draw him, and it is ground to which he never really returns. The scenes in the pub, where Riley's irrepressible comic energy is given full rein, are far more successful. Almost all of the play's amusement and vitality derive from these scenes (reminiscent at times of the style of comedian Tony Hancock), where George's exuberance, hope and delusion mingle hopelessly out of control:

> Florence, look at me. You see a man standing on the brink of great things. Below me, a vast flat plain stretches like an ocean, waiting to receive my footprints, footprints that will never be erased, and in years to come, people will see this once uncharted, untrod path and say . . . George Riley walked this way. (p. 32)

This faith in himself can be infectious and an impressionable man like the naïve young sailor Able is drawn into sharing it, though others are much less willingly conscripted into the conspiracy of fantasy. Brown is a man minding his own business, having a quiet drink in the pub, when Riley accuses him of being an industrial spy on the track of his latest invention. With Riley as interrogator and Brown as the uncomfortable victim, the conversation then veers steadily away from the subject:

> *Brown:* Edison didn't invent the lighthouse, you know. You probably got mixed up with Eddystone.
> *Riley:* What?
> *Brown* (*bashfully half-singing, smiling hopefully, explaining*): My-father-was-the-keeper-of-the-Eddystone-light-and-he-met-a-mermaid-one-fine-night . . . . (*A terrible silence.*)
> *Riley:* Your father was what?
> *Brown:* Not my father.
> *Riley:* Whose father?
> *Able:* You can bet it wasn't a real mermaid.
> *Riley:* Shut up. (*To Brown.*) Whose father was a mermaid?
> *Brown:* He wasn't a mermaid. He *met* a mermaid.
> *Riley:* Who did?
> *Brown:* This man's father.

*Riley:*    Which man's father?
*Brown*   *(testily):* I don't know.
*Riley:*    I don't believe you, Jones.
*Brown:*  Brown.
*Riley:*    This is just sailors' talk, the mythology of the seas. There
            are no such things as mermaids. I'm surprised at a grown
            man like you believing all that superstitious rubbish.
            What your father saw was a sea lion.
*Brown:*  My father didn't see a sea lion!
*Riley (topping him):* So it was your father!   (pp. 26–7)

These quotations illustrate the kind of man George Riley is:
outgoing, headstrong and optimistic, and at the same time naïve
and almost boyish in his enthusiasms – characteristics which also
expose his vulnerability. He is, for instance, quite unable to
appreciate the irony behind Harry's 'admiration':

We're common. I mean, what have we got to give the world?
Nothing. But you're – well, you're a genius! An inventor! You're a
clever bloke, sitting there in your workshop, pioneering you might
say, from your blood and your sweat for the lot of your fellow
man.   (p.16)

Part of George's attraction as a character is his total lack of guile;
with this, unfortunately, runs a complete inability to recognise it in
others.

Because George is in his element in the pub, it is particularly cruel
that this, the scene of his imagined glory, should be the place of his
public humiliation as Harry demonstrates that double-gummed
envelopes *cannot* be used twice because they have to be torn open the
first time. (Riley's other inventions are equally flawed: the plant
watering system, which cannot be turned off, is about to deluge the
living-room at the end of the play.) Even the incessant admiration of
Able deserts him:

*Riley:*    Well, never mind, never mind – I've got a few shots left in
            my locker, oh my goodness, yes – let's see there's my,
            er . . . my . . . (*Able's laugh starts coming through loud and
            clear.*)
*Able (laughing):* You didn't even know his name . . . (*Riley is hurt to
            anguish, turns and leaves.*)   (p. 78)

The stage direction speaks for itself as the aesthetic distance between George and the audience, established by his earlier clowning, shrinks to introduce Stoppard's familiar resort to pathos:

> I sat in the bus station for a while. And the park. It's very nice in the park . . .
>
> I was thinking . . . sitting there . . . in the park . . . I mean I was thinking I wouldn't mind a change, I'm not that old . . . I was thinking perhaps I'd go down to the Labour Exchange and see . . . see what the situation is.   (p. 83)

Linda's common sense begins to hold sway with her father, while some of her own naïve enthusiasm has been similarly kerbed by the discovery that her new boyfriend and fellow-eloper is married. Just as George did not know Harry's surname, so she did not know his, and with the new tone of melancholy self-appraisal, father and daughter are brought simultaneously down to earth and the family restored to a state of at least temporary harmony.

The linear direction of the plot which this dual momentum suggests emphasises the play's broadly naturalistic base: the audience is carried from a position of relative detachment into involvement with the characters' human frailties, and the characters themselves are presented in more realistic detail than in any subsequent Stoppard play until *Professional Foul* in 1977. In addition, Persephone's domestic realm provides, to some degree, a conditioning environment against which, in their different ways, George and Linda rebel. Yet at the same time Stoppard circumscribes and resists these naturalistic tendencies in two distinct ways. At a very early stage we are invited, by means of a superficially expressionistic cross-fading technique, to see the play in terms which contradict its apparently linear direction. Thus Riley enters the pub and addresses Brown and Able *before* the short opening scene – between Linda and Persephone at home – has come to an end. This overlapping technique is taken a stage further at the end of the first long pub scene which follows, when, in a soliloquy, Riley starts to recount the monotonous events of this and every morning of his life – waking to cold water, breakfasting in the kitchen, trying to work against the drone of the vacuum cleaner. During his speech these events are duly re-created on the adjacent set as if conjured from his memory: while the pub gradually fades into darkness, Persephone enters, waters the plants and greets her husband newly risen from his bed as he crosses from one setting to the other. The play's seemingly linear direction is thereby studiously undermined as the characters' words and actions are caught up within a broader cyclic pattern. As John Russell Taylor says, Stoppard 'keeps us perfectly aware that his play is built like a goldfish bowl'[13] – with Riley swimming around inside. This, of course, qualifies the domestic reconciliation at the play's apparent climax: there is no more likelihood that George will *really* cease his attempts at new inventions than that Linda will cease to fall in love.

The naturalism is further undermined by the comic patterns woven into the pub scenes, where the conversations frequently take flight into improbable, highly theatrical patter that moves well beyond the bounds of plausible 'situation comedy' and more closely resembles music-hall comedians playing off each other:

| | |
|---|---|
| *Harry:* | Country's going to the dogs. What happened to our greatness? |
| *Riley:* | Look at the Japanese! |
| *Harry:* | Look at the Japanese! |
| *Riley:* | The Japanese look after the small inventor! |
| *Harry:* | All Japanese inventors are small. |
| *Carmen:* | They're a small people. |
| *Harry:* | Very small. Short. |
| *Riley:* | The little man! |
| *Harry:* | The little people! |
| *Riley:* | Look at the transistor! |
| *Harry:* | Very small. |
| *Riley:* | Japanese! |
| *Carmen:* | Gurkhas are short. |
| *Harry:* | But exceedingly brave for their size. |
| *Carmen:* | Fearless. |
| *Riley (furiously):* | What are you talking about!   (p. 15) |

As in *Rosencrantz and Guildenstern are Dead*, there is wordplay here of a very high order, organised with the kind of highly structured dexterity that continually characterises Stoppard's work. In consequence the pub scenes are quite distinct, stylistically, from the more naturalistically handled living-room scenes; so much so, in fact, that to a contemporary reader *Enter A Free Man* often has the feel of a play travelling in two different directions. And it is the anarchic humour of George Riley rather than the limited domestic 'truth' of his family which represents the continuing stream in Stoppard's work.

*       *       *

*A Separate Peace* was televised by the BBC in August 1966, featuring Peter Jeffrey and Hannah Gordon and directed (like *Teeth* and *Another Moon* the following year) by Alan Gibson. In this short piece, one of a series of interlinked plays and documentaries on 'the Pursuit of Happiness', Stoppard cultivates a mood of pathos reminiscent of the tone in the closing scenes of *Enter a Free Man* and the last act of *Rosencrantz*, but employs it in a dramatic context which otherwise provides only scant comic amusement. It is one of the least successful early plays, a melancholy little piece based rather too obviously upon a single idea. John Brown, a would-be recluse, enters a private nursing home seeking a secure, comfortable refuge. The trouble is that there is nothing wrong with him. The staff, convinced that he must have a sinister, criminal or insane background, set about investigating his past. In vain Brown assures them that he seeks refuge only from the world: 'It's the privacy I'm after – that and the clean linen.'[14] This occasions a number of jokes on the theme of not being ill, for instance:

| | |
|---|---|
| *Matron:* | Now what's your problem, Mr. Brown? |
| *Brown:* | I have no problems. |
| *Matron:* | Your complaint. |
| *Brown:* | I have no complaints either. Full marks. |
| *Matron:* | Most people who come here have something the *matter* with them. |
| *Brown:* | That must give you a lot of extra work.   (p. 116) |

or

| | |
|---|---|
| *Matron:* | Have you been in hospital quite a lot? |
| *Brown:* | No, I've been saving up for it.   (p. 118) |

Brown's instincts are, in fact, so lethargic that he admits that the happiest days of his life were spent as a prisoner-of-war:

The camp was like breathing for the first time in months. I couldn't believe it. It was like winning, being captured. Well, it gets different people in different ways. Some couldn't stand it and some went by the book – yes, it's a duty to escape. They were digging like ferrets. They had a hole out of my hut right into the pines. There were twenty in the hut and I watched all nineteen of them go off. They were all back in a week except one who was dead. I didn't care what they called me, I'd won. They gave us food, life was regulated, in a box of earth and wire and sky, and sometimes you'd hear an aeroplane miles up, but it couldn't touch you.   (p. 132)

Such novel eccentricity typifies, to varying degrees, all of the central characters in the plays under consideration in this chapter. But there is little else here: a slender idea, drawn out for as long as possible, with a 'downbeat' simplicity that works against Stoppard's flair for energetic, stylish comedy. Such a patently untheatrical subject makes, in the main, for an untheatrical play. Its psychological exploration of its subject is also fairly negligible and the way in which Brown's character constantly reverses our expectations becomes increasingly monotonous.

Brown's remarkable passivity, is however, worth comparing with the considerably more ambitious treatment of a similar theme in David Mercer's television play *And Did Those Feet?*, first shown by the BBC in 1965. This documents the life story of twins – one very fat and one very thin – who, like Brown, lack ordinary powers of motivation. Exchanges in Stoppard's play such as:

*Matron:*  You mustn't lose interest in life.
*Brown:*   I was never very interested in the first place   (p. 121)

are strongly reminiscent of Mercer's characteristically wry dialogue style and specifically of the mood of *And Did Those Feet?*, in which the twins' behaviour closely resembles Brown's:

*Lord Fountain:*  They're not real. Not human. They're spiritually
                  deformed.
*Doctor:*         In what way?
*Lord Fountain:*  They don't *do* anything.[15]

After innumerable failures to cope with ordinary life, the twins escape from civilisation into the jungle in the company of Ishaki, the

Japanese 'enemy' with whom they spent *their* war. Brown, fond of his material comforts and of being provided for, makes his escape to a rather less adventurous nursery-like existence:

> The meals come in on trays, on the dot – the dust never settles before it's wiped, clean laundry at the appointed time – the matron does her round and temperatures are taken; pulses too, taken in pure conditions, not affected by anything outside. You need never know anything.   (p. 129)

Infantilism is a theme of both plays, and Brown seems to be hinting that his particular malaise may stem from a desire to return to a child-like state of dependence on his mother, although Stoppard never makes this explicit. Mercer, on the other hand, is if anything over-explicit in his vehemently Freudian analysis, creating for the twins the womb-like refuge of a disused swimming pool and for one of them, Timothy, distant recollections of a far more secure past:

> I have . . . a kind of memory. There we were. Floating between mother's hips with our arms round each other.[16]

*And Did Those Feet?* is a powerful and haunting play, in which the twins' failure to conform leads to an examination of conventional social *mores* and behaviour patterns. The extraordinary exposes the ordinary, and the individual psychology which is Mercer's central concern is framed within a broad social context. In Stoppard's play, the extraordinary is merely a source of quirky humour and only the idea of having Brown commence a giant mural in his hospital room (an idea that is never really developed) shows equal daring and enterprise.

The play nevertheless indicates an important change in Stoppard's method of constructing dialogue. The naturalistic authenticity, which persists in all but the more high-flown exchanges in *Enter a Free Man*, gives way to a more compact, mannered and individual style, with all the exchanges between Brown and the other characters remaining on a minimal level throughout, with none of the incidental trappings of ordinary casual conversation. Here he is talking to the one sympathetic nurse:

*Maggie:* Where do you live?
*Brown:* I've never lived. Only stayed.

*Maggie:* You should settle down somewhere.
*Brown:* Yes, I've been promising myself this.
*Maggie:* Have you got a family?
*Brown:* I expect so.
*Maggie:* Where are they?
*Brown:* I lost touch.
*Maggie:* You should find them.
*Brown (smiles):* Their name's Brown.  (pp. 115–16)

In order to maintain the sense of mystery around Brown, Stoppard pares back the realism of his dialogue and produces a new tone of subdued, unemotional detachment which specifically prefigures the two radio plays, *If You're Glad I'll Be Frank* and *Albert's Bridge.* Here the technique makes for a rather flat and one-paced characterisation, but in these subsequent successes Stoppard frees his characters far more decisively from the fetters of realistic dialogue-making by attempting to marshall them around the controlling consciousness of a single eccentric character. What emerges as a result is a centrifugal interplay of ideas – often within one character's head – at the expense of a traditional, naturalistic approach to character, and in this respect at least, *A Separate Peace* heralds a decisive advance.

*          *          *

The fruits of this breakthrough are plainly revealed in *If You're Glad I'll Be Frank*, first broadcast in February 1966 in a production by John Tydeman with Timothy West as Frank and Patsy Rowlands as Gladys. It is in this play, as John Russell Taylor also suggests, [17] that Stoppard first establishes a successful style wholly his own. (Indeed, though broadcast six months earlier than *A Separate Peace*, it has the ring of a later, more mature work, and is indisputably the more significant of the two pieces.) Commissioned to contribute to a Third Programme series about people in nonsensical jobs, he takes the recorded voice of the G.P.O. speaking clock and creates from it his central character, Gladys Jenkins, a woman trapped in her job by the impossibility of letting time stop. Her husband, named Frank (hence the pun in the title), is a bus driver who recognises the voice of his long-lost wife when ringing up for a time-check one day. Every time his bus subsequently passes the G.P.O. building, he leaps from his cab in a frantic attempt to locate her whereabouts without falling behind his timetable.

The idea of characterising the G.P.O. speaking clock sounds absurd and Simpson-esque, but what character in a Simpson play would have lines like these?

> Ad infinitum.
> I used to say ad nauseum
> but it goes on long after you feel sick.
> And I feel sick.
> When you look down from a great height
> you become dizzy. Such depth, such distance,
> such disappearing tininess so far away,
> rushing away,
> reducing the life-size to nothing –
> it upsets the scale you live by.
> Your eyes go first, followed by the head,
> and if you can't look away you feel sick.
> And that's my view of time;
> and I can't look away.
> Dizziness spirals up between
> my stomach and my head
> corkscrewing out the stopper.
> But I'm empty anyway.
> I was emptied long ago.[18]   (p. 12)

This is the stream of Gladys's thoughts which Stoppard alternates with the scenes charting Frank's progress, in monologues of rich comic writing shot through with the kind of plaintiveness of tone observed elsewhere. This stream-of-consciousness free verse demonstrates the boldness with which he is experimenting with dramatic form, both in the striking contrast it makes to the regulated, mechanical counting which provides its constant background and in the sharp, poetical insights it offers. It is difficult to resist the conclusion that this fuller break with naturalism, and the consequent advance in craft, largely results from the greater freedom of imaginative expression which the radio medium offers.

Since rather more than half of the play is taken up by Gladys's thoughts, she is its only developed character. Most of the comedy, however, centres upon the character of Frank, whose conscientious determination to keep to his bus schedules (even when his wife's life could be at stake!) is part of the same satire on society's obsession with timekeeping that Stoppard also incorporates into the wryer

moments of Gladys's monologues; and it is also pilloried by means of
the ludicrous G.P.O. organisation whose officials enter at 9 a.m.
each morning in a strict hierarchical order, lowest first, on the
alternate strikes of Big Ben! Not that this makes for efficiency,
though; Frank finds the road to Gladys littered with bureaucratic
and even facetious obstacles:

> *Frank:* Hey, you – who's in charge here?
> *Porter:* I am. Is that your bus?
> *Frank:* Who's the top man – quick!
> *Porter:* You can't park there after seven if the month's got an 'R'
> in it or before nine if it hasn't except on Christmas and the
> Chairman's birthday should it fall in Lent.
> *Frank:* I have an appointment with the Chairman.
> *Porter (to the sound of horns):* Seems to be a bit of a traffic jam out
> there.
> *Frank:* What floor's he on?
> *Porter:* He's not on the floor this early.   (p. 20)

Finally, in the rush hour, with his bus conveniently stuck in the
traffic, Frank succeeds in reaching the top man, only to be convinced
that his efforts have been in vain:

> *1st Lord:* My dear fellow – there's no Gladys – we wouldn't trust
> your wife with the *time* – it's a machine, I thought
> everyone knew that.   (p. 30)

This beautifully double-edged reply crushes Frank and puts an end
to his search, without in the least undermining our belief in Gladys
who becomes, as a result of his failure, more firmly imprisoned than
ever.

Gladys's plight provides the core of the play and, like the half-
existence of the courtiers from *Hamlet*, it is absurd. Her (literally)
awful job both imprisons and liberates her and it is on the axis of this
paradox that the play is suspended. Like John Brown, she has sought
a haven from the rough and tumble of life[19] only to find an
unexpected kind of imprisonment, trapped by the belief that she is
playing a vital part in keeping society and civilisation moving. In
this almost unbearable, subhuman role, and despite constant nausea
and dizziness, she has nevertheless managed to master a degree of

philosophical detachment towards a world full of people racing
blindly along their myriad of timed courses:

> . . . they count for nothing measured against
> the moment in which a glacier forms and melts.
> Which does not stop them from trying
> to compete.  (p. 16)

But when Frank recognises her voice, and begins to telephone her
regularly, an inner crisis threatens her painfully won detachment:

> Oh, Frank, you knew my voice,
> but how can I reply?
> I'd bring the whole thing down with a cough,
> stun them with a sigh.  (p. 23)

Frank resurrects in her the awareness of how the human scale of her
own life has been overwhelmed by her rôle and, despite the
terrifying scale of responsibility that she has assumed to be hers,
Gladys nurtures a course of defiant rebellion:

> At the third stroke
> I'm going to give it up,
> yes, yes . . . it's asking too much,
> for one person to be in the know
> of so much, for so many . . .
> and at the third stroke
> Frank will come
> . . . Frank . . .
> I'm going to drop it now,
> it can go on without me,
> and it will,
> time doesn't need me –
> they think I'm time, but I'm not –
> I'm Gladys Jenkins.  (p. 27)

Her revolt, however, is short-lived. Frank, having failed in his rescue
bid, returns to his timetabled buses, Gladys's sobbing subsides
beneath her proficient repetition of the passing hours and the world
continues with its mad reliance on time. Stoppard's satirising of this

obsession represents an important strand which runs throughout the play, but it is the complex nature of Gladys's reaction to it and the paradoxes, the humorous potential and, indeed, the horror of her perspective on life that seems to have fascinated him most, for he returns with a vengeance to a very similar theme in his next play for radio, *Albert's Bridge*.

\* \* \*

*Albert's Bridge* was first broadcast in July 1967, in a production by Charles Lefeaux in which John Hurt played Albert. Although this was shortly after the London opening of *Rosencrantz*, it is important (as well as convenient) to include it here because it is a virtual companion piece to *If You're Glad*. For Gladys, man becomes insignificant measured against the vistas of eternity. For Albert, man becomes insignificant measured from the height of the Clufton Bay Bridge on which he is employed as a painter. Gladys's growing anguish at her unnatural situation is countered by Albert's joy in his; he quickly learns to prefer his life on the bridge to his family life at home.

At the start of the play Albert is part of a four-man team painting the bridge with two-year paint. As it takes them two years to do so, it is a continuous operation. However, the local council's Bridge Sub-Committee learns of a new paint which lasts eight years, and promptly sacks the other three painters. This delights Albert, who is spending more and more of his time up on the bridge, away from his newly married wife Kate and their baby. He starts to work on Saturdays, spends most of the family's holiday in Paris at the top of the Eiffel Tower and finally takes to sleeping on the bridge. Then, two years after Albert has started to use the eight-year paint, the Sub-Committee realises, with a start, that three-quarters of it is still painted with two-year paint and is in immediate need of repainting. The remedy they propose, however, has disastrous results.

Albert derives a sense of reassurance and security from seeing men as ant-like dots hundreds of feet below him; at such a distance, he can take them comfortably in his stride. 'Is it a fact that all the dots have names?' (p. 25)[20] he asks, with bland curiosity, as if endorsing Cocteau's lines from *La Machine Infernale*:

> Oui, mon enfant, mon petit enfant, les choses qui
> paraissent abominable aux humains, si tu savais, de
> l'endroit où j'habite, elles ont peu d'importance.[21]

His continual work on the bridge progressively undermines the importance of ordinary things; he is bewitched by the lure of such a beguiling perspective:

> Dots, bricks and beetles.
> I could drown them in my spit.  (p. 24)

Like Gladys, there is something of the poet in Albert, but just as his is a movement into solipsistic detachment (as opposed to her revolt from such detachment), so his utterances throughout have a coolly distanced tone:

> Listen . . .
> The hot sun makes you think of insects,
> but this insect hum is the whole city
> caught in a seashell . . .
> All conversation is hidden there,
> among motors, coughing fits, applause,
> screams, laughter, feet on the stairs,
> secretaries typing to dictation,
> radios delivering the cricket scores,
> tapes running, wheels turning, mills grinding,
> chips frying, lavatories flushing, lovers sighing,
> the mayor blowing his nose.
> All audible life in the vibration
> of a hairdryer in the room below.  (p. 25)

Albert's detachment becomes far more complete than either Gladys's or John Brown's. Brown wants cossetting in the nursing home and Gladys's heart leaps at the sound of Frank's voice. But the bridge sets the seal on Albert's alienation; his brave new world leaves no room at all for other people. In his glorious isolation, there is room only for his ditties, as he twists the words of popular songs and even Shakespearean sonnets into hymns of self-love (thereby affording Stoppard a welcome opportunity for pastiche):

> Night and day, I am the one . . .
> day and night, I'm really a part of me . . .
> I've got me under my skin.
> So why
> don't I take all of me

When I begin the beguine . . .
I get accustomed to my face,
The thought of me makes me stop
before I begin
Yes, I've got me under my skin,
and I get a kick out of me . . .
Day and night, night and day . . .
Shall I compare me to a summer's day? (pp. 28–9)

What Albert does not perceive is that such a detached view of human life necessarily involves a proportional rise in self-importance. It takes an outsider to underline the fact. Fraser, a would-be suicide, climbs the bridge to prepare for his leap and, finding Albert in song, declares sarcastically, 'Very nice, very nice. The egotist school of songwriting.' (p. 29) His arrival, and the irritation it provokes, further emphasises the way in which the bridge has become Albert's private sanctuary:

*Albert:* You came up to go down?
*Fraser:* To jump.
*Albert:* Jump?
*Fraser:* Off.
*Albert:* Jump off? You'd kill yourself. Ah.
*Fraser:* Yes.
*Albert:* I see. All right then.   (p. 31)

By this stage we can see how Stoppard is furthering the theme introduced with Brown and Gladys, as he gently scrutinises not only the desirability but also the morality of such a detached stance. Albert's wife and child are a distraction from the more essential life of the bridge, and he abandons them. An intruder climbs up to violate his private sanctuary, and he hastens him down again, indifferent to the means. Unfortunately (for Albert) Fraser decides to *climb* down, only to return at regular intervals to reassure himself that, from such a height, life can be coped with. 'I'm a victim of perspective!' (p. 35) he shouts as he is forcibly chased down at one point. Both Gladys and Albert are victims of perspective too. Albert is seduced by the remoteness and untouchability of life viewed from the bridge just as Gladys is imprisoned in the impersonal horror of a view into the heart of infinity. Malquist, too, is such a victim in his lordly declaration, 'Nothing is the history of the world viewed from a suitable distance.' (p. 8) There is a majesty about these views, but they are not of a human perspective, and where Gladys revolts against such an extremity of isolation, Albert (like Malquist) becomes increasingly inhuman in response.

The imaginative leap forward in *If You're Glad*, in terms of dramatic form, is meanwhile consolidated, with Albert acting as even more of a centrifugal force within the play, since Kate (unlike Frank) becomes little more than peripheral, a scarcely developed cipher for the ordinary life which Albert deserts. At no point do we become emotionally involved with her plight and since our view of her is largely gleaned through Albert's eyes, she is not required to be psychologically convincing as Persephone is in *Enter a Free Man*. Her relationship with Albert thereby avoids the kind of square-on emotional contact which Stoppard rarely brings off with total success. When Kate sobs

> I've begun talking to myself, over the sink and stove . . . I talk to myself because nobody else listens, and you won't talk to me, so I talk to the sink and the stove and the baby, and maybe one day one of them will answer me   (p. 28)

Albert is not even listening. Their non-communication, as with several Stoppard couples in later plays, is used to dramatic advantage as the search for naturalistic 'truth' is abandoned.

Like the G.P.O. officials in *If You're Glad*, *Albert's Bridge* also contains a comic collection of bureaucrats presented in broadly satirical terms. This is the Bridge Sub-Committee, a shambling body which includes a yes-man called Dave whose sole contribution to meetings is his perpetual 'hear hear's, and Fitch, who is the 'genius' with the figures:

> *Fitch:* This cycle is not a fortuitous one. It is contrived by relating the area of the surfaces to be painted – call it A – to the rate of the painting – B – and the durability of the paint – C. The resultant equation determines the variable factor X – i.e. the number of painters required to paint surfaces A at speed B within time C. For example –
> *Chairman:* E.g.
> *Fitch:* Quite. Er, e.g. with X plus one painters the work could proceed at a higher rate – i.e. B, plus, e.g. Q.   (p. 12)

It is not hard to deduce how a gigantic error comes to be made. After two years, the Committee's realisation that Albert has only painted one-quarter of the bridge with the new eight-year paint leaves only one solution open, namely to employ 1800 painters to paint the rest of the bridge in a single day. This has an unexpected side-effect: as the army of painters marches onto it without breaking step, the bridge collapses, taking the army, Fraser and Albert down with it.

\*     \*     \*     \*

The four plays we have been discussing form a group of sorts and make clear a number of significant developments in Stoppard's art. Where *Rosencrantz and Guildenstern are Dead* deals with figures stranded on the edge of their environment (the play *Hamlet*), these plays present distinctive individuals who, in various ways, consciously set themselves apart from their environments, the ordinary currents of modern society. George Riley moulds for himself a world of eccentric inventions, John Brown seeks out a gentle and protective refuge and Gladys and Albert contemplate the lives of their fellow-men from otherworldly distances of time and space. Each 'hero' is not merely seeking some kind of escape, but also some kind of certainty, however restricted, amidst the flux and chaos of life. It is a search for refuge, but also a search for order.

The plays are not merely structured around those sensibilities; they are, to a steadily increasing extent, attempts to *create* those sensibilities in dramatic terms. To this end Stoppard progressively eschews realistic criteria in establishing characters and settings – a fact which goes some way towards explaining why the two pieces for radio are the most successful of these early plays; with their freedom from the dogmas of naturalistic stage conventions, they enable Stoppard to use images of language and sound with something approaching a sculptor's freedom at times. In *Albert's Bridge*, for example, Kate has only to mention the Eiffel Tower and we are instantly transported there: to the accompaniment of clichéd French accordion music, we hear her yelling at Albert to come down (p. 26). By using this kind of fluidity to the full, Stoppard starts to govern his dramatic structures by the pursuance of an idea, an association or a piece of wordplay, emphasising his authorial rôle as manipulator and puppetteer. As the naturalistic arrangement of his characters is progressively slackened, so too is the nuptial bond, from *Enter a Free Man*, where Riley is constrained by it, to *If You're Glad*, where a relationship of tenderness is created between Gladys and Frank precisely because they cannot meet, to *Albert's Bridge*, where Albert deserts his family. The central characters are thus developed in increasing isolation as Stoppard's sense of individual style evolves and it is highly significant that the only characters who function in groups in the two radio plays – the G.P.O. hierarchy and the Bridge Sub-Committee – are formulated in wholly satiric terms.

One of the few critics to comment at any length on these early plays is Jill Levenson, in an article written in 1971 entitled 'Views from a Revolving Door: Tom Stoppard's Canon to date'.[22] In it she pursues a similar tack to many critics of *Rosencrantz* by pressing Stoppard's affinities with the Theatre of the Absurd, and specifically with the work of Samuel Beckett, rather too far. For instance, she asserts that Riley, Gladys and Albert – 'objectify human needs and frustrations without convincing us that they are men'.[23] With Gladys and Albert alienation and dehumanisation are, as I have shown, explicit themes. But in the more naturalistic play *Enter a Free Man*, Stoppard is concerned precisely to convince us that Riley is a real, ordinary man at heart: while his hopes are *not* real, his pain and his human status *are*. The pathos, the feeling of shared sympathies generated by the play, suggests the ordinary human vulnerability and bewilderment which endows Riley with a three-dimensional, living stature. This is a realistic technique, and it is not the same as the limited pity and sympathy which it is possible to have for one of Beckett's grotesques. It is a distortion of Riley's character, and thereby of Stoppard's intention, to represent it, out of context, by the line:

> *nothing*, absolutely nothing. I give nothing, I gain nothing, it is nothing – (p. 34)

and suggest that this represents Riley's diagnosis of his existence. He is addressing Florence in the pub here, who has asked him 'Don't you like your home?' and to which he produces, to order, a 'sob story':

> My wife and I and Linda, we get up in the morning and the water is cold . . . fried bread and sausage and tea. . . . (p. 34)

What is really depressing Riley, as Stoppard makes clear, is the failure of his inspiration. When Miss Levenson quotes Riley further:

A man must resist. A man must stand apart, make a clean break on his own two feet! Faith is the key – faith in oneself  (p. 16)

she is much closer to the heart of the real George Riley with what she calls his 'ideology of individuality and resistance'. [24]

This description is equally true, in broad terms, of Gladys and Albert (and John Brown, whom Miss Levenson does not consider). They choose their eccentric, individual paths; they make conscious decisions about the direction of their future. George Riley tries to do the same, but his failures continually lead him back to the domestic hearth. The concept of determinism, the philosophical linchpin of the Theatre of the Absurd's attempt to illustrate 'the human condition', is found only in *Rosencrantz and Guildenstern are Dead*, where, as we have seen, the influence of Beckett becomes tangible. But Miss Levenson exaggerates the debt in all the other plays which she considers, for while these illuminate in various ways a development whose first real laurel is *Rosencrantz and Guildenstern are Dead*, they themselves are more concerned with the implications of human eccentricity than with imaginative planes of being. To dramatise escape-routes from the routine, humdrum processes of ordinary life is not necessarily to joust with determinism. The systemised eccentricity of the Absurd, even in such a diluted form as the work of N. F. Simpson, diverges sharply from Stoppard's individualised eccentricity. In *A Resounding Tinkle*, for instance, Simpson maintains the illusion of normality through progressively outrageous stages:

*Nora (loudly):* Aha! Whose is the wastepaper basket! It looks rather interesting.

*Mrs Paradock:* That's Mr. Malden's. We lent him a couple of lampshades Myrtle has grown out of for his little boy; he said we were welcome to his wastepaper basket if we could make anything of it.

*Mr Paradock:* It might be all right for Myrtle when she's older. It looks to me like one he had when he was at school. [25]

Here the supposed ridiculousness of suburbia is exposed – rather too obviously – by using familiar objects in nonsensical contexts. As in the work of other Absurd dramatists, Simpson constantly mechanises identities in his plays to suggest the conditioned drudgery and predictability of modern life, and his characters are markedly less than human. In *If You're Glad*, on the other hand, Stoppard utilises the idea of the speaking clock girl not to mechanise her identity, as Simpson might have done, but, on the contrary, to illustrate her revolt against the mechanised order of her little realm. As a result the human status is not crushed but amplified; the residual humanity of Stoppard's relatively undeveloped characters asserts itself under pressure, emphasising the sympathetic, individual sensibility at the heart of each play.

# 6 Nuts and Bolts

After the grand success of *Rosencrantz*, first in London, secondly on Broadway and then in a multiplying number of other countries and languages, Stoppard's attention switched increasingly towards writing for the stage. He wrote nothing for television between *Neutral Ground*, written in 1965,[1] and *The Boundary*, co-written with Clive Exton in 1975, and accepted only one radio commission, to create a play for the BBC's Schools Service, *Where Are They Now?* (considered later in this chapter). In part, this may have been a simple question of opportunity, but it is surely also bound up with the intrinsic theatricality of his talents. As he once confessed to Jon Bradshaw:

> I'd rather write for the stage than television . . . because in a theatre one has the full attention of one's audience, whereas while watching television one tends to glance at the newspaper, to talk or to answer the telephone. I'm not terribly keen on having my plays performed in that sort of situation.[2]

After his adventurous experiments in dramatic form on radio with *If You're Glad I'll Be Frank* and *Albert's Bridge*, it is not therefore surprising that for the next few years Stoppard should have chosen to direct his almost exclusive attentions to the live theatre.

Apart from the belated West End opening of *Enter a Free Man*, the next stage play after *Rosencrantz* was *The Real Inspector Hound*, first performed in June 1968 at the Criterion Theatre, London (with a curtain-raiser called *The Audition* by Sean Patrick Vincent) in a production by Robert Chetwyn, starring Richard Briers and Ronnie Barker. Two years later, in April 1970, came the first performance of *After Magritte* in a West Indian restaurant (the Green Banana) for Ed Berman's Ambiance Lunch-hour Theatre Club, the first of several Stoppard plays written for Berman's Inter-Action organisation.[3] The cast included Stephen Moore and

Prunella Scales and the director was Geoffrey Reeves. Both are short, one-act plays and they offer several points of comparison. Stoppard once defined them as

> an attempt to bring off a sort of comic coup in purely mechanistic terms[4]

and, in the same interview, described *After Magritte* as 'not an intellectual play; it's a nuts-and-bolts comedy'.[5] This should not be taken as an indication that these plays are wholly lightweight, farcical exercises, though both are full of lively, ebullient comedy. Reasons of length alone prevent the development in them of intellectual ideas comparable to the exploration of rôle-playing found in *Rosencrantz and Guildenstern are Dead*, but they are ingeniously and seriously constructed with quite different characteristics from those shorter-length plays examined in the previous chapter. In each play, a puzzle of some kind is set up, and the discovery of its solution involves characters and audience alike.[6] These puzzles hinge on the manner in which differences of perspective can cause nightmarish confusion in the lives of those involved in the task of trying to separate appearances from reality. They are 'nuts-and-bolts' plays in the sense that the puzzle at the heart of each is, in essence, that of relating the right nuts to the right bolts. But, as one learns to expect with any play of Stoppard's, the process is a good deal more complicated than it first seems.

Like *Rosencrantz and Guildenstern are Dead*, *The Real Inspector Hound* is concerned with the nature of theatre. The earlier play extracts characters from the confines of *Hamlet* and re-houses them in a different context which nevertheless requires them to continue their performance. In a comparable way, *The Real Inspector Hound* utilises the idea of the 'play within a play'. As two critics watch a particularly poor (and, unintentionally, extremely funny) thriller, correspondences gradually emerge between themselves and the characters in the play, until finally Stoppard breaks down the barriers between the two and the critics themselves start to take part in the thriller.

The two critics, Birdboot and Moon, are watching a 'whodunnit' of the kind perfected by the late Agatha Christie, but this one is a travesty of the genre, set in the inevitable country house drawing-room with its equally inevitable quota of mysterious house-guests. Thrown into the reckoning are cottages on clifftops, suddenly descending fogs and, of course, an unexplained corpse, hidden for much of the play beneath a large, high sofa. The chief characters are Lady Cynthia Muldoon, the owner of the house, her young friend Felicity Cunningham, her husband's half-brother Magnus, the cleaner Mrs Drudge and an uninvited house guest, Simon Gascoyne. This last character, in particular, highlights the way in which the thriller corresponds in several of its details to Agatha Christie's play *The Unexpected Guest*; both plays' ingredients include a man reported dead who figures in the *dénouement*, a remote Canadian connection and a man in a wheelchair.[7] These, and a wild array of other details, are pieced together with an uncanny instinct for parody which incorporates the stage business, the furniture, the props, the choice of characters, the kind of language they use and the thriller's tendency to convey pieces of necessary information directly to the audience without pretence of subtlety. For instance, after Mrs Drudge has turned on the radio at just the right moment to catch a pertinent police message, she busies herself preparing for the next piece of information:

> *The phone rings. Mrs. Drudge seems to have been waiting for it to do so and for the last few seconds has been dusting it with an intense concentration. She snatches it up.*[8]

Her conversation with the caller then provides, with ridiculous, hilarious obviousness, further information:

> Hello, the drawing-room of Lady Muldoon's country residence one morning in early spring? . . . H*ello*! – the draw – Who? Who did you wish to speak to? I'm afraid there is no one of that name here, this is all very mysterious and I'm sure it's leading up to something. I hope nothing is amiss for we, that is Lady Muldoon and her house-guests, are here cut off from the world, including Magnus, the wheelchair-ridden half-brother of her ladyship's husband Lord Albert Muldoon who ten years ago went out for a walk on the cliffs and was never seen again – and all alone, for they had no children.   (p. 15)

The production is evidently badly stage-managed – Mrs Drudge's intensive dusting is clearly covering up for a late cue – and, even by the standard of thrillers, badly written. The breathless rush of information she offers in response to a wrong number is entirely unjustified, and her alarm that 'I'm sure it's leading up to something' is a wholly artificial attempt to create tension. Yet at the same time as he produces this multi-layered parody of the genre, Stoppard is deftly conveying the information his audience needs. The parody provides effective humour of a fairly obvious kind, but Stoppard extends and complicates the comedy by interspersing parody of the critical jargon of reviewers. Moon is a pseudo-literary hack whose utterances are riddled with pretence and contradiction:

> There are moments, and I would not begrudge it this, when the play, if we can call it that, and I think on balance we can, aligns itself uncompromisingly on the side of life. *Je suis*, it seems to be saying, *ergo sum*. But is that enough? I think we are entitled to ask. For what in fact is this play concerned with? It is my belief that here we are concerned with what I have referred to elsewhere as the nature of identity. I think we are entitled to ask – and here one is irresistibly reminded of Voltaire's cry, *'Voilà!'* – I think we are entitled to ask – *'Where is God?'* (p. 28)

The posturing and the pomposity are self-evident in the wandering syntax, the name-dropping and the generally contrived tone of this cant. Nothing that Moon says here is in any way related to the trivial piece that he is actually watching; he is merely exercising his own ego and attempting to get one-up on his senior, Higgs, the paper's first-string critic. Moon toys wistfully with the idea of Higgs's death, the only path that seems to betoken fame and success; like his namesake in Stoppard's novel, he feels removed from the centre of action, but whereas that Moon carries a bomb, this Moon carries only his secret yearnings. At one point, contemplating the third-string critic beneath him, it occurs to Moon that he may be part of a chain of such yearning:

> I wonder if it's the same for Puckeridge? . . .
> Does he wait for Higgs and I to write each other's obituary – does he dream – ? (pp. 17–18)

The significance of this passing thought is made painfully clear to him before the thriller has run its course. The parody of Birdboot, in comparison, rests on his shamelessly dishonest rôle of star-maker. With his eye on one of the actresses, he declares:

all this would be for nothing were it not for a performance which I consider to be one of the summits in the range of contemporary theatre. In what is possibly the finest Cynthia since the war. (p. 35)

The elevated tone is still present, but here its objective is simply sexual. Birdoot is a merchant of reputations, and expects the due rewards for his praise:

*Birdboot:*   – the radiance, the inner sadness –
*Moon:*   Does she actually come across with it?
*Birdboot:*   The part as written is a mere cypher but she manages to make Cynthia a real person –
*Moon:*   *Cynthia?*
*Birdboot:*   And should she, as a result, care to meet me over a drink, simply by way of er – thanking me, as it were –
*Moon:*   Well, you fickle old bastard!   (p. 27)

As his fancy directs, Birdboot is also fully prepared to forsake one debutante actress for another, for, as we gather from Moon, he spent the previous evening in the company of the actress playing Felicity! Yet, rebuffing Moon's gentle insinuations with hypocritical outrage, Birdboot insists on his utter devotion to his wife, Myrtle.

It is important to draw a clear distinction between Stoppard's parody of the critics and his parody of the thriller because the relationship between the two becomes increasingly complicated as the thriller progresses. Both kinds of parody have made the audience very aware of the nature of theatre: they have been kept at a critical distance from the action not simply in the normal comic manner but also by being continually reminded of how convention operates in the theatre. However, in establishing these two levels of parody, Stoppard is only preparing the ground for a far more disturbing assault on theatrical convention by ingeniously confusing the two levels and leaving the audience to contemplate which level of statement (if either) can claim to relate to 'truth' or 'reality.' This further extension of the complex system of parody centres on the private dreams and motivations of the two critics, which bear a remarkable proximity to situations within the thriller. It is these 'parallels' which lead them to be enmeshed in its plot. For in the unfolding design of the 'whodunnit' it happens that Simon, having had an affair with Felicity, switches *his* affections to Cynthia, thereby paralleling Birdboot's involvement with the two actresses playing these rôles. It also transpires that, according to the traditional conventions of the thriller, not all of the characters are what they seem, Magnus and Inspector Hound in particular. Magnus purports to be the disabled half-brother of Albert Muldoon, Cynthia's long-lost husband, but he is in fact a policeman, Inspector Hound, in disguise. In this way he tricks the real killer, who has returned to the scene of the crime disguised as Hound and shot a second victim, Simon, when he realises that Simon has recognised the original corpse as a man against whom he (the bogus Hound) has borne 'a deep-seated grudge' (p. 47). Finally unmasked by Magnus, the murderer is shot dead trying to escape.

Unfortunately, neither Moon nor Birdboot knows that the original corpse is, in fact, Higgs, Moon's senior critic, and that the actor playing Magnus is Puckeridge, his junior. The third-stringer has killed Higgs and sets an ambush for Moon, conniving to involve both him and Birdboot in the play. Birdboot is drawn into the action in the rôle of Simon and Moon as Inspector Hound – and Puckeridge, having cast himself as the eventual hero, Magnus, therefore kills them both. When the play is over, both critics (and Higgs) lie dead, killed, to all appearances, according to the workings to the plot. But in the meantime Puckeridge, acting where Moon only dreams, leapfrogs to the position of top critic.

What Stoppard does in *The Real Inspector Hound* is to establish the action according to a particular set of theatrical conventions, and then shift all the terms of reference. Two separate planes of theatrical reality are established, as with *Rosencrantz and Guildenstern are Dead*. The courtiers exist both within *Hamlet* (their 'on-stage' reality) and outside it, in the world which Stoppard creates for them (their 'off-stage' reality). Yet, however thinly drawn their characters and experiences may be, their identities at least remain broadly consistent. For Moon and Birdboot the experience is both more abrupt and more alarming. Stoppard precipitates them from a plane in which they are not even participants, but only spectators and critics, into rôles as actors on a quite different plane – one which promptly enmeshes them in its cogs. As the two plays unexpectedly coalesce, they are taken from the security of one set of conventions and transplanted into a far more dangerous world. The audience is, of course, equally confounded when the shift occurs, but before considering the implications that this carries for them, it is important to examine closely how Stoppard executes it.

It is the on-stage telephone which makes the initial breach between the two sets of conventions, when, in the interval following the second act, it turns from a 'prop' into a real telephone. For the caller is Myrtle, Birdboot's wife, apparently (and not without cause!) checking up on her husband. Birdboot, having gone onto the stage to answer her call, becomes inextricably trapped when the action abruptly recommences. Thus, suddenly, the scope of the play is enlarged; it snowballs menacingly outwards to engulf first Birdboot, who finds himself in the 'parallel' rôle of Simon, and later Moon. But contrary to expectations (ours included), it is not the third act which follows the first two at this point, but a re-run of the first. Felicity delivers to Birdboot lines identical to those she addressed to Simon in the original encounter, but now with a double import. Without departing from the text, she can break out of her rôle and address Birdboot personally. Thus:

*Felicity (stiffly):*   What are you trying to say?
*Simon:*   I love another.
*Felicity:*   I see.
*Simon:*   I didn't make any promises – I merely –
*Felicity:*   You don't have to say any more –
*Simon:*   Oh, I didn't want to hurt you –
*Felicity:*   Of all the nerve!   (p. 20)

becomes

*Felicity (stiffly):*   What are you trying to say?
*Birdboot:*   I want to call it off.
*Felicity:*   I see.
*Birdboot:*   I didn't promise anything – and the fact is I do have my reputation – people do talk –
*Felicity:*   You don't have to say any more –
*Birdboot:*   And my wife too – I don't know how she got to hear of it, but –
*Felicity:*   Of all the nerve!   (p. 37)

Cynthia's arrival then gives Birdboot the opportunity to pursue his newly-conceived fancy for her, just as Simon does in the 'authentic' text. In the process:

*Cynthia:*   We can't go on meeting like this!

*Simon:*  We have nothing to be ashamed of!
*Cynthia:* But darling, this is madness! (p. 22)

re-emerges as:

*Cynthia:* We can't go on meeting like this!
*Birdboot:* I am not ashamed to proclaim nightly my love for
    you! – but fortunately that will not be necessary – I
    know of a very good hotel, discreet – run by a man of
    the world —
*Cynthia:* But darling, this is madness! (p. 38)

The fidelity to the original text is, however, soon submerged in the
mounting chaos, and the act ends, as the second act originally did,
with someone shooting Simon from off-stage. Just before the shot,
Simon had found and recognised the original corpse. Birdboot now
does the same:

*Birdboot (dead-voiced):* It's Higgs.
*Moon:* What?
*Birdboot:* It's Higgs.
*Moon:* Don't be silly.
*Birdboot:* I tell you it's Higgs! I don't understand . . . He's dead.
*Moon:* Dead?
*Birdboot:* Who would want to . . . ?
*Moon:* He must have been lying there all the time . . .
*Birdboot:* . . . kill Higgs?
*Moon:* But what's he doing here? I was standing in
    tonight . . .
*Birdboot (turning):* Moon? . . .
*Moon (in wonder, quietly):* So it's me and Puckeridge now.
*Birdboot:* Moon . . . ?
*Moon (faltering):* But I swear I . . .
*Birdboot:* I've got it –
*Moon:* But I didn't –
*Birdboot (quietly):* My God . . . so that was it . . . Moon – now
    I see –
*Moon:* – I swear I didn't –
*Birdboot:* Now – finally – I see it all –
 *(There is a shot and Birdboot falls dead.)* (pp. 43–4)

This time the bullet is real and Moon, rushing onto the stage to his colleague's side, finds himself similarly trapped in the action, in his case in the rôle of Hound. Despite his obvious reluctance, he feels obliged to keep the action going, and therefore starts to bluff his way towards the third act *dénouement*. As he does so, he slowly realises that this hinges on his own rôle, and specifically on Magnus unmasking him as an imposter:

| | |
|---|---|
| *Magnus:* | I put it to you! – are you the real Inspector Hound?! |
| *Moon:* | You know damn well I'm not! What's it all about? |
| *Magnus:* | I thought as much. |
| *Moon:* | I only dreamed . . . sometimes I dreamed – |
| *Cynthia:* | So it was you! |
| *Mrs Drudge:* | The madman! |
| *Felicity:* | The killer!   (p. 47) |

Magnus then throws off his disguise and Moon realises, much too late, how everything falls into place. Magnus is the 'real' Inspector Hound – and he is Puckeridge too, shooting Moon down before he can reach the door. Stoppard then treats himself to a final, delicious piece of parody. Magnus is not merely a policeman in disguise: he is also Cynthia's long-lost husband, Albert!

This necessarily lengthy exposition of the play's complicated plot shows, I hope, that it is as ingenious as it is complex. But if Stoppard's breach of the conventions he initially establishes is to be seen as more than a calculated piece of virtuosity, it is necessary to consider carefully the rôle of the audience. At the start of the play we are part of an audience which includes Birdboot and Moon; we are watching the thriller, as they are, and also their response to it. A certain ambiguity is, however, suggested, by the initial stage direction:

> *The first thing is that the audience appear to be confronted by their own reflection in a huge mirror. Impossible. However, back there in the gloom – not at the footlights – a bank of plush seats and pale smudges of faces.*   (p. 9)

The 'mirror' audience is then whittled down to the two critics in its front row, but this effect creates at once an unexpected element of alienation and detachment from the play which progressively increases as Stoppard develops the twin parodies of the critics and the thriller, and finally curdles as our fellow-spectators become actors and the scenes begin to fall out of chronological order. Finally the disturbing symmetry is completed as Simon and Hound occupy the critics' seats and deliver their own critical judgements on the play. The audience is thus required to play two distinct rôles: one watching the thriller and one watching the critics. When these rôles are merged in the deliberate confusion Stoppard creates, there is a deep sense of disorientation. The mental adjustment is simple to make in itself, but its implications are genuinely disturbing, for Stoppard is not merely juggling with conventions and characters; he is jolting us from one kind of assumed 'reality' into another with quite different terms of reference.

In short, the audience is led to question *its* 'reality.' As the critics' 'reality' is absorbed in the expanding playworld, so the 'authentic' thriller characters become increasingly remote. The 'reality' is no longer contained in the world of the conventional thriller with its Magnuses and its Cynthias; the 'reality' becomes Puckeridge pointing a gun at Moon. We are made strongly aware of the actors and actresses who are playing all the rôles; of Felicity, for instance, as a character wooed and then dropped by Simon and at the same time an actress wooed and then dropped by Birdboot. Which is more real? Birdboot seems more real than Simon only because he believes himself to be outside the world of illusion in which Simon is contained, but the interplay between fact and fiction (or at least between fiction and fiction-within-fiction) shatters his illusion. Stoppard demonstrates with frightening ease that planes of reality are neither exclusive nor even consistent and he underlines this relativity in the quintessential irony of his *dénouement*, when Magnus asks Moon, 'I put it to you! – are you the real Inspector Hound?!' (p. 47) Moon's negative reply is true on three planes: he is neither Hound nor even the actor who is meant to be playing Hound, nor is the character of Hound 'real', for it is Magnus, in the workings of the thriller, who is really Hound. This is beautifully handled and shows most clearly that the jolt from one system of 'reality' to another need not stop where it does – with Puckeridge's triumph; as it spirals outwards, the play demonstrates the unreality of *all* acting, and invites the audience to consider whether, in terms of another focus beyond their perception, they too are no more than actors in a play. By showing, through the shape of his play, how one man's fate is another man's fiction Stoppard leaves us begging the inevitable, logical question: whose illusion is our reality?

\*     \*     \*

Stoppard's next play, *After Magritte*, also makes fundamental use of the conflict between appearances and reality, but whereas *Hound* explores this in terms of theatrical 'layers', *After Magritte* rests on a single controlling idea familiar from Stoppard's novel – that there can be logical explanations for even the most bizarre appearances. The conflicting evidence of four independent pairs of eyes must be resolved in order to discover the true nature of a strange person observed in Ponsonby Place one morning and variously described as a black-and-white minstrel with a broken crutch, a blind one-legged man in pyjamas carrying a tortoise, a West Bromwich Albion footballer with shaving-cream on his face and an escaped prisoner with a handbag and cricket bat playing hopscotch. These bizarre and divergent descriptions emanate, respectively, from an elderly lady who observed the spectacle and from Reginald Harris and his wife and mother, who were driving their car away when the figure appeared.[9] The unravelling of this puzzle provides the linchpin of the action, with Stoppard supplying a number of secondary puzzles, some related, others not, to complete a play whose chief characteristic is its capacity to generate confusion.

As the curtain goes up the first puzzle is presented at once: making sense of the weird scene in the Harrises' living room. Why (to mention only some of the perplexing details) is the furniture stacked up against the front door; why is a police constable looking through the window; why is Mother lying prostrate on the ironing board wearing a black bathing cap; why is Thelma Harris sniffing around on the floor on her hands and knees, and why is her husband, naked to the waist, wearing waders over his evening dress trousers and blowing into the lampshade? The answers emerge slowly, indirectly and deviously. A casual remark of Mother's, for instance, serves to explain the presence of Harris's waders and his attempt to cool the light bulb in the living-room:

> *Mother:* The bulb in the bathroom's gone again. *(She leaves by the other door. Harris gets up and goes to the cupboard, extracting his waders. Mother returns, hopping, carrying a large felt bag.)* I let the water out.[10]

That there exists a logical explanation of this kind for each manifestation of seemingly erratic behaviour is the axiom of the play. Yet before the audience is in possession of all the facts which explain the first scene, it is plunged into the complication of a second, concerning the mysterious figure in Ponsonby Place. While the family is arguing about him, Police Inspector Foot bursts in, demanding 'What is the meaning of this bizarre spectacle?' (p. 24) He has received a report that extraordinary scenes are taking place from the constable who was at the window at the start of the play. By this time, however, the bizarre spectacle is no more: all the furniture has been moved to its ordinary position, the ironing board and bathing cap have disappeared, Mother is seated in a chair, Thelma is relaxing, smoking and holding a drink, and Harris is fully dressed.

Basing his accusations on the constable's eye-witness account, the Inspector nevertheless proceeds:

*Foot:*     I have reason to believe that within the last hour in this room you performed without anaesthetic an illegal operation on a bald nigger minstrel about five-foot-two or Pakistani and that is only the beginning!
*Harris:* I deny it!
*Foot:*     Furthermore, that this is a disorderly house! . . .

    tarted-up harpies staggering about drunk to the wide, naked men in rubber garments hanging from the lampshade – Have you got a music licence?
*Harris:* There is obviously a perfectly logical reason for everything. (pp. 31–2)

This, as Stoppard leisurely proceeds to demonstrate, is precisely the case. The Inspector, however, will not let matters rest so easily and proceeds to his main investigation, triggered by the report from the old lady in Ponsonby Place. Working with remorseless logic from her description, he builds up a full picture:

The facts appear to be that shortly after two o'clock this afternoon, the talented though handicapped doyen of the Victoria Palace Happy Minstrel Troupe emerged from his dressing-room in blackface, and entered the sanctum of the box-office staff; whereupon, having broken his crutch over the heads of these good ladies, the intrepid uniped made off with the advance takings stuffed into the crocodile boot which, it goes without saying, he had surplus to his conventional requirements. (pp. 33–4)

The connection with the Harris family then emerges: Foot has traced them from the parking ticket which their car received while illegally parked in Ponsonby Place at the exact time that the minstrel was sighted and, suspecting that they could be accomplices, has sent Constable Holmes round to investigate, with unexpected results. He now explains to Mother, who is sharp enough to spot an apparent incongruity in the story so far, how he came to check for parking tickets:

> *Foot:*	My dear lady, you have put your finger on one of the ironies of this extraordinary case. I myself live at number four Ponsonby Place, and it was I, glancing out of an upstairs window, who saw your car pulling away from the kerb.
> *Mother:* And yet, you never saw the minstrel?
> *Foot:*	No, the first I knew about it was when I got to the station late this afternoon and read the eye-witness report sent in by the old lady. I must have missed him by seconds, which led me to suspect that he had driven off in your car. I remembered seeing a yellow parking ticket stuck in your windscreen, and the rest was child's play.	(p. 41)

At this point the seams of Stoppard's plot, even on its own far-fetched premises, are stretched close to breaking point. But he is only setting the stage for the final irony, which caps all that has preceded: the very man supposedly investigating these mysterious reports has himself been their cause. It was Foot who, with his face half-covered in shaving foam and with both legs inside one pyjama leg, hopped out onto the street with his wife's handbag and parasol (it was raining) to put a coin in the parking meter outside his house before the wardens came round. With the kind of symmetry that Stoppard never misses an opportunity to capitalise upon, the play then closes with a scene every bit as bizarre as the opening tableau: Mother is standing on one foot (having burnt the other), with a woollen sock on one hand (she has just changed a hot bulb), playing the tuba; Foot is standing with one bare foot (Mother has the sock), wearing sunglasses (for his migraine) and eating a banana (from the basket of fruit suspended from the ceiling throughout the play as a counterweight for the height-adjustable ceiling light); Harris, gowned and blindfolded, is standing on one leg and counting (testing Foot's thesis that a blind man cannot stand on one leg, advanced in order to contradict Harris's claim that the figure in Ponsonby Place was a blind, one-legged musician), and Thelma is crawling on the floor (searching for a dropped needle) dressed in her underwear (she is trying to mend her evening dress).

Behind this parade of puzzling scenes and descriptions lies a comic method that rests, perhaps rather obviously, on the relationship between appearances and reality. Because this is such a singular concern, characterisation serves even more functional ends than in Stoppard's previous work, without the slightest attempt at any kind of psychological depth or verisimilitude. John Russell Taylor likens this approach to character with N. F. Simpson's:

> Foot works with ruthless logic from a basically idiotic premise, just as many of Simpson's characters do, and the somewhat strenuous exchanges of absurdities which result from his appearance in the Harrises' dining-room just as they preparing to compete in an evening's ballroom dancing have a decidedly Simpsonish flavour.[11]

The resemblance, however, is only superficial. In Simpson's puzzles there are only square holes for round pegs; the nuts and bolts are impossible to marry. Though the logic is indeed ruthlessly watertight, it is used to develop situations of ever-increasing lunacy and absurdity and his whole point is that logic alone is *not* enough. In *After Magritte*, however, logic works in the opposite direction, eventually explaining all the curiosities that the play has thrown at us. Stoppard's fundamental premise is that appearances finally do make sense and it is his shameless, self-conscious manoeuvring of essentially normal characters into their prescribed places in his puzzles that creates the eccentricity. There is no detail about any of the characters that is not in some way related to these puzzles. Inspector Foot's name, for instance, is given him purely to give Harris the opportunity for a wise-crack:

*Harris:* Not Foot of the Y –
*Foot:*  *Silence!*  (p. 26)

and when the Inspector reveals that his constable is called Holmes, the moment is obviously ripe for Thelma's attempt at a sequel:

*Thelma:* Not –
*Foot (screams):*  *Be quiet!*  (p. 27)

Similarly, all that we need to know about Mother is that she plays, and is a devotee of, the tuba. It does not even matter whose mother she is – as Harris and Thelma demonstrate at one point when they argue over it!   (pp. 22–3)

Mother's passion for the tuba has one particularly important consequence. It is because of this fixation that the Harrises have taken her to the Tate Gallery to see an exhibition of Magritte's paintings in which, reputedly, tubas proliferate. (This actually took place, in 1969.) As a result they park in Ponsonby Place and initiate the chain of events above, but their journey also sets up the pun in the title which is a valuable pointer to the playwright's intentions. The play deals with what happened 'after Magritte' in two senses. Firstly, it takes place after the family's visit to the Magritte exhibition, and secondly it is clearly meant to be seen as constructed in the style of Magritte, whose own examination of appearance and reality is typified by his picture of a pipe labelled 'This is not a pipe' or his painting of a man with a bowler hat, his face obliterated by a dove – conceptual works designed to disturb and disorientate the viewer. In the first example, a tension is created between two opposing kinds of visual 'reality' – a physical image and a written instruction. In the second, a violent juxtaposition grafts the 'reality' of the bird over the 'reality' of the man's face; because they originate from such different planes of being, their forceful fusion makes the work both sinister and disturbing to our notions of a consistent, harmonious 'reality'. Magritte's work suggests it is only by doing violence to our expectations that the artist can demonstrate that 'reality' is no more than the sum of consistent appearances and customary expectations.

Following Magritte's theory, Stoppard creates a pair of three-dimensional, quasi-surrealistic canvases in which there is a minimum of movement – only the counterweighted basket of fruit and ceiling light move – and the visual arrangement of the settings takes absolute primacy.[12] The descriptions of the controversial figure in Ponsonby Place have a certain surreal quality too, though since the figure is never seen, these lack the same kind of pictorial power. In each case, like most surrealistic canvasses and montages, these 'images' do not create a rational, comprehensible whole – they remain an assemblage of erratic parts. This is, of course, the intention of surrealism: to create works of art which evade rational analysis, making their appeal instead to the imagination or the subconscious which, according to the movement's claims, is the original source of inspiration for their composition. Yet in *After Magritte*, while the juxtaposition of details is certainly comic, it is questionable whether the correspondence between surrealistic art and drama can be sustained. When Stoppard explores layers of theatrical reality in *Rosencrantz and Guildenstern are Dead* and *The Real Inspector Hound*, he pursues his subject wholly within the terms of his chosen medium, achieving, as a result, a persuasive unity of form and content. Here, however, Stoppard's two planes never fuse, and two distinct levels of operation are always discernible: an 'artistic' reality in which bizarre composite images are presented to the audience and a 'theatrical' reality in which these images are unravelled and explained with comic glee.[13] Stoppard is, I think, fully aware of the impossibility of any true reconciliation between an essentially static and an essentially dynamic medium and what he creates can perhaps best be regarded as a theatrical commentary upon his artistic subject. In this light *After Magritte* is a playful, parodic attempt to show that rational sense can sometimes be made of the unlikeliest nonsense, rather than an attempt to analyse, criticise or even present surrealism theatrically. The comic tone also reflects Stoppard's professed admiration for Magritte's work,[14] and while one hesitates to see the play simply as a tribute, Mother's humorous verdict on the exhibition:

Tubas on fire, tubas stuck to lions and naked women, tubas hanging in the sky – there was one woman with a tuba with a sack over her head as far as I could make out. I doubt he'd ever tried to play one; in fact if you ask me, the man must have been some kind of lunatic  (p. 37)

confirms the level on which the play operates. Stoppard's customary mischievousness is again in evidence as he teases his audience's expectations by presenting apparently surrealistic scenes that turn out to be perfectly explainable. It is not the workings of the subconscious which are being called into play, but those of an ingenious, at times almost cheeky, dramatic inventiveness.

\*        \*        \*

*Where Are They Now?* is the title of a short one-act radio play which Stoppard was commissioned to write for Schools Radio. It was first broadcast in January 1970 in a production by Dickon Reed with Carleton Hobbs, John Bentley and David Brierley among the cast, and though it stands largely by itself, a wistful piece with an equivocal balancing of humour and serious thought, it does offer certain points of resemblance to the other plays under examination, with the audience required to unravel a number of 'clues'. Its main setting is a public school Old Boys' Dinner in a smart hotel at which three former pupils, who used to be known as the 'Marx Brothers', exchange reminiscences with each other and with their erstwhile Latin master Dobson, an elderly man still teaching at the school. Much of the conversation revolves around the late French master, the tyrannical Mr Jenkins, and in a rather obvious and lightweight 'sub-plot' a quite different Jenkins takes his place at the table. His reminiscences do not seem to correspond with anyone else's and it eventually transpires that he is at the wrong dinner altogether. The important story-line derives from the evident differences which have grown up between the three former cronies; while two of them have followed careers and developed attitudes broadly in keeping with their privileged education, the other – the 'crusading journalist' Gale – has not.

Again, there is a puzzle at the core. Unlike *Hound* or *Magritte*, however, there is neither a satire on the tradition of detective fiction involved, nor a parodic structure such as the thriller genre or Magritte-inspired tableaux offer. In this play the audience of listeners is quite alone in their sleuth-like rôle, trying to establish which of the three men corresponds to which Marx Brother (and, to a lesser extent, what the wrong Mr Jenkins is doing at their reunion) from the flashback sequences Stoppard periodically employs to switch the action to a school dinner some twenty-four years earlier, in 1945, when the boys were thirteen. As Stoppard makes clear in a note to the published text:

> The idea is to move between the two without using any of the familiar grammar or fading down and fading up; the action is continuous.[15]

This advance is important, for although he uses contrasting scene switches with great applomb in *If You're Glad* and *Rosencrantz*, all his earlier plays utilise a broadly linear time-scale. *Where Are They Now?* is the first in which Stoppard consciously explores the dramatic possibilities of manipulating this fourth dimension, using the abrupt replacement of adult murmur by high childish voices, and vice-versa, to make each transition. It is soon established that the boys' own characteristics are very roughly like those of the 'heroes' from whom their nicknames are derived: that Groucho demonstrates a lively, independent and somewhat mischievous spirit, that Chico is his cheerfully obedient sidekick and that Harpo has earned his nickname not from bring dumb so much as dumbstruck:

> *Dobson:* Why haven't you been eating? Do you hear me, boy? . . . What did he say?
> *Chico:* He says he's not feeling well.
> *Dobson:* Not feeling well? Why should anyone expect to feel *well*? Has he got a mog chit? . . .
> do stop crying, and take your plate away. You really shouldn't get into such a state over Mr. Jenkins. (p. 68)

The third member of the trio thus emerges as a cowering youngster petrified in particular by the tyrannical French master.

At the reunion dinner, it is Marks and Brindley who emerge as the talkative old chums, full of breezy conviviality, enthusiastically comparing the quality of the wine and smoked salmon in previous years. Gale, on the other hand, says nothing at all at this stage, ignoring the attempts at polite conversation which his colleagues address to him (as if deaf) and hogging the Chablis. Since we know from the first flashback that Brindley is Chico, it is obvious to assume that his chum Marks must be Groucho and that the silent Gale is Harpo. Once Gale starts talking, however, it transpires that the truth is the other way round. It is, therefore, with the utmost irony that Marks, who seems to have suffered most as a child (Harpo), should assert of his schooldays that he'd 'love to have them again' (p. 72) and that he has done the next best thing by sending his son to the school. He even declares of Jenkins, 'I don't think I was actually afraid of him' (p. 66) and provides the loudest, heartiest 'hear, hear' when the headmaster, paying tribute to his late colleague, remarks of Jenkins that 'many of you will remember him with affection and respect' (p. 74). And it is Marks who glorifies and romanticises the viciousness of the old regime with the greatest enthusiam:

> Do you remember Runcible? And Grant-Menzies? They were kings! Grant-Menzies used a cane with a silver knob and kept a pre-war Lagonda garaged in town. They could reduce the lockers to trembling silence with one look. (p. 68)

With ruthless neatness Stoppard then proceeds to hoist Marks with his own petard by means of a further flashback to the much more recent past in which his own son is given a sound, undeserved beating.

The solution to the puzzle turns, then, on the enigmatic character of Gale and it is on him that Stoppard's use of the flashback as a tool of ironic hindsight really rests. For although he was apparently the happiest schoolboy of the trio (Groucho), he has only come to the dinner for the purpose of seeking out Jenkins and perhaps, thereby, exorcising this powerful shadow that hangs larger-than-life over all their childhood memories:

> We walked into French like condemned men. We were too afraid to *learn*. All our energy went into ingratiating ourselves and deflecting his sadism onto our friends. We brought him lumps of French to propitiate him until the bell went. . . .
>
> What a *stupid* man. I think we would have liked French. It is not, after all, a complex language.   (p. 75)

Gale has been cruelly thwarted by discovering that Jenkins has died just a few days earlier, yet despite this, Jenkins emerges as the play's most vital character, a catalyst who reveals the prejudices, preoccupations and self-deceptions of his former pupils, and the way in which time can colour the truth either favourably or adversely, nurturing forgetfulness as well as grievances. The most pertinent question in the play thus lies not in its title 'Where are they now?', but in Gale's fierce reversal of it, 'Where were they *then*?' (p. 76) and it remains unanswered, since none of the characters is in touch with his 'true' past – neither Marks, Brindley, Gale, nor for that matter the enigmatic Mr Jenkins who is, so to speak, in the wrong play altogether.

It is instructive to compare Stoppard's flashback technique with the more conventional use of time-patterns in an almost contemporary stage play, Peter Nichols's *Forget-me-not Lane*,[16] in which the middle-aged central character, Frank, confronts both his wartime adolescent self and his authoritarian father of three decades earlier, as his memories are dramatised like ghosts. The boy is by turns rebellious towards, angry with and embarrassed at his father, whom he nicknames 'Hitler'. Time, however, alters the perspective and the mature Frank now sees his father in a very different light:

'Poor man. Thirty years too late I can see what he must have been suffering . . . .'[17] Like *Where Are They Now*?, the theme is the way in which time alters memories and relationships, but whereas Nichols traces its shifts within the confines of Frank's memories, Stoppard's flashbacks do not take place within the memory of any of his characters, but are self-consciously organised by Stoppard himself, both to establish the comic puzzle and to contradict the characters' beliefs about their own childhoods. In other words, while the audience joins Frank as he muses on his past in Nichols's play,[18] it is *only* the audience who are in a position to muse on the Marx Brothers' pasts in Stoppard's; as in *Rosencrantz*, *Hound* and *Magritte*, our rôle is not to share the action with the characters but to collaborate with the author at the characters' expense. Here, however, the complete assurance of tone that characterises these earlier works is missing and the conspiracy with the author feels only half-achieved. The scene with Marks Junior delivers a neat come-uppance to his father's glibness, but the implied critique of the force-fed educational system that they endured as children is never crystallised.

Instead, the play's energies are dissipated by the increasing emphasis upon the turbulent character of Gale. His rôle as the detached outsider who, unlike his colleagues, has *not* forgotten past injustices becomes progressively overshadowed by his obsessive need to reconcile himself with his own past. A mood of un-mistakably Proustian or Wordsworthian origin is struck:

> childhood is Last Chance Gulch for happiness. After that, you know too much. I remember once – I was seven, my first term at prep school – I remember walking down one of the corridors, trailing my finger along a raised edge along the wall and I was suddenly happy, not elated or particularly pleased, or anything like that – I mean I experienced happiness as a state of being: everywhere I looked, in my mind, *nothing was wrong*. You never get that back when you grow up; it's a condition of maturity that almost *everything* is wrong, *all the time*, and happiness is a borrowed word for something else – a passing change of emphasis. . . .
>
> Maturity is a high price to pay for growing up.    (p. 77)

It is as if Gale holds Jenkins to blame for starting up the process of his maturity, robbing him of the childhood happiness that was his natural birthright. (This recalls John Brown's desire to escape into a

mollycoddled hospital world in *A Separate Peace*.) With desperate,
almost pathetic intensity, he launches into a lament for a vanished
innocence in which both the tone and the pastiche style of Eliot's
poem 'A Cooking Egg' can be discerned:

> Oh, where the Fat Owl of the Remove, where the incorruptible
> Steerforth? Where the Harrow match and your best friend's
> beribboned sister? Whither Mr. Chips? Oh no, it's farewell to the
> radiators and the punishable whisper, cheerio to the un-
> comprehending trudge through *Macbeth* and sunbeams defined
> by chalkdust.    (p. 76)

In striving for poignancy in this instance, Stoppard merely succeeds
in making the character of Gale all the less comprehensible, denying
him any coherent rôle as a corrective force to Marks's unthinking
conformism and furnishing us instead with another distinctive echo
of Moon's obsessive intensity from *Lord Malquist and Mr Moon*.
Gale's vendetta against Jenkins then reaches its climax as the
headmaster requests that a minute's silence be observed in his
memory, at which Gale remains obstinately in his seat, muttering a
counter-tribute with conspiratorial determination.

Though Gale dominates the closing stages of the play, his
relatively late entry as a speaking character makes it impossible for
him to provide the same kind of concentrated focal point as Gladys
or Albert offer in the earlier radio plays. What Stoppard seems to
have aimed for instead (but seems almost to jettison before the end)
is the kind of structural unity achieved in *The Real Inspector Hound*
and *After Magritte*: intricate explorations into our notions of 'reality'
pivoting on a massive reversal of audience expectations. Like
O'Hara, the racist coachman in Stoppard's novel who turns out,
when Moon finally sees his face, to be not only an Irish Catholic but
also a Negro,[19] we build up to the expected revelation that the silent
Gale is Harpo, who was always so petrified of Jenkins, only to
discover that he was Groucho all along and is nursing a fiercesome
grudge. Stoppard's exploration of the nature and partiality of
memory is, however, disappointingly slight and within his canon
the importance of the play lies less in its content than in its
impressively supple form, where the adroit balancing of different
perspectives provides a highly significant preparation for the
masterly formal execution of his next radio play, *Artist Descending a
Staircase*, and subsequently for *Travesties*.

\*          \*          \*

Stoppard's earlier plays demonstrate his progression towards a dramatic form which, while relying heavily on comic, parodic and at times farcical effects, has a definite structure of thought or ideas, organised through and around the sensibility of the central characters. This process is most fully realised in *Rosencrantz and Guildenstern are Dead*, where the courtiers' lives are caught up within an inescapable dramatic pattern. What subsequently emerges in *The Real Inspector Hound, After Magritte* and *Where Are They Now?* is an even greater emphasis on the patterning and dramatic shape of the play and, in proportion, a further reduction in the importance of developed characterisation. While Gladys, Albert, Rosencrantz and Guildenstern are all victims of the strange perspectives in which they find or place themselves, the later plays increasingly embody unworldly perspectives in their actual dramatic form. In both *Hound* and *Magritte* the concept of 'reality' is conceived in anarchy, twisting and altering like a zoom lens out of control. Moon and Birdboot think they are watching a play, but it swallows them alive. The footballer-felon-minstrel turns out to be the police inspector investigating the case of the footballer-felon-minstrel. And in *Where Are They Now?* the perspectives which memory provides are belied by the 'true' past which the flashback sequences reveal.

Stoppard has sometimes been accused of being a rather bloodless, cerebral playwright and these three plays, in which rounded characterisation is eschewed still further, might at first sight seem to fuel such views. Philip Roberts, for instance, complains that they 'reel away from seriousness as from a contagious disease.'[20] Behind this aggressive comment is, of course, a glimmer of truth. Stoppard's plays might be described as reeling away from stark, direct engagement with the 'seriousness' of specific causes or issues (at least at this stage of his writing career), but this is not the kind of seriousness that comic playwrights are generally expected to espouse. What seems remarkable, on the other hand, is how often serious implications are threaded through these lightweight one-acters, inextricably mingled with the comedy; while their frameworks are shamelessly, ingeniously comic, the implications of the theatrical puzzles which Stoppard sets up within them are often far-reaching. As Jim Hunter suggests, 'Stoppard's playing is about thinking; but his claim on our attention is not as a thinker but as a player. His equations and solutions are theatrical.'[21] *Hound*, in particular, is a brilliantly executed set-piece in which, as in *Rosencrantz*, Stoppard utilises the theatrical process itself to develop a humorous and disturbing analogy between the play's structure and the patterning of people's lives. The other two, on balance, are rather less successful. The design of *Where Are They Now?* careers awkwardly off in pursuit of Gale's private vendetta with his past, while *After Magritte* relies rather too singularly on the execution of its main confusion-engendering principle. In both plays, there is rather more ingenuity than humour, especially when the 'explanations' are known and the dextrous mechanics alone impress, while in comparison *The Real Inspector Hound*, with its alarming shifts of convention, continues to baffle and disturb.

# 7 Ethics on the Wane

It was not until 1972, nearly five years after *Rosencrantz and Guildenstern are Dead* first opened in London, that Stoppard's next full-length work, *Jumpers*, reached the stage. And that stage was again at the National Theatre, whose directors' faith in their original discovery was further rewarded by the astonishing success of this new play. *Jumpers* ran for two seasons in 1972 and 1973, with the *Evening Standard* readers who had voted Stoppard the Most Promising Playwright of 1967 now voting *Jumpers* the Best Play of 1972,[1] and it resurfaced in the 1976/77 repertoire, following the National Theatre's move to its new South Bank complex. The original production, which opened at the Old Vic Theatre on 2 February 1972, starred Michael Hordern as George, Diana Rigg as Dotty and Graham Crowden as Archie, and was directed by Peter Wood. For the revival of his production at the Lyttleton Theatre, Michael Hordern recreated his marvellous playing of the central rôle, with Julie Covington as Dotty and Julian Glover as Archie.

In establishing a playwright's reputation, the successor to his first triumph is often regarded as the crucial test. Stoppard's one-act plays after *Rosencrantz*, though accomplished pieces of work, left some questions in the air which only a work of equal weight could dispel, and this distinction is one which Stoppard himself stressed during an interview conducted for *Theatre Quarterly* in 1974:

> I find it confusing to talk about 'my plays' as though *Hound* and *Jumpers* were the same sort of thing. . . . *Jumpers* is a serious play dealt with in the farcical terms which in *Hound* actually constitute the play.[2]

At the same time he outlined his specific objective in the longer plays:

What I try to do is to end up by contriving the perfect marriage between the play of ideas and farce or perhaps even high comedy.[3]

This comment provides a particularly useful gloss in the light of the play's critical reception. B. A. Young of the *Financial Times* echoed the opinion of almost all of his fellow-reviewers when he wrote:

I can't hope to do justice to the richness and sparkle of the evening's proceedings, as gay and original a farce as we have seen for years, but a farce for people who relish truly civilised wit.[4]

The play is indeed highly 'original' (though Stoppard derives some of the strands of its plot from his earlier television play *Another Moon Called Earth*[5]) and Peter Wood's production certainly showed just how 'gay' and 'sparkling' it could be in performance. But Stoppard's insistence that *Jumpers* is more than a witty farce – a 'play of ideas', in fact, in the mould of *Rosencrantz and Guildenstern are Dead* – has not been altogether conceded by the reviewers. Alan Brien in *The Listener*, for instance, considered that 'the fencing matches between the two branches of philosophy are often more showy than significant'.[6] John Weightman took a more studied view of the play, only to conclude that 'According to my antennae, quite a few bits of this play have not been brought fully into intellectual or aesthetic focus'[7] while Jonathan Bennett, writing about *Jumpers* and *Rosencrantz* in *Philosophy*, called the play 'a mildly surrealistic farce . . . which lacks structure and lacks seriousness'.[8] Michael Billington's short *Guardian* review seemed almost alone in recognising that 'Under the guise of a madcap farce, Mr Stoppard has written a deeply moral play.'[9] This takes us to the heart of the critical dichotomy about Stoppard outlined in the Introduction. *Pace* Billington, the distinct impression gleaned is that the philosophical subject-matter of the play is not entirely at ease in the comedy which surrounds it – a criticism not made of *Rosencrantz*, even by its detractors. *Jumpers* seems an altogether more naturalistic play, but since Stoppard is evidently attempting a similar 'marriage', the question that must be confronted is whether in utilising many of the mechanics of farce, Stoppard has blurred or even buried his serious intentions.

What, in fact, is the precise nature of these intentions? In the course of the *Theatre Quarterly* interview, Stoppard said:

*Jumpers* obviously isn't a political act, nor is it a play about politics, nor is it a play about ideology. . . . On the other hand, the play reflects my belief that all political acts have a moral basis to them and are meaningless without it.

*Is that disputable?*

Absolutely. For a start it goes against Marxist-Leninism in particular, and against all materialist philosophy . . . *Jumpers* was the first play in which I specifically set out to ask a question and try to answer it, or at any rate put the counter-question.[10]

His thinking clearly pivots upon ways of exploring the morality or immorality of philosophical and political creeds, an idea carried through to *Travesties* (which he had just completed at the time this interview was conducted) and, more obviously, to *Professional Foul*. What is particularly striking here is the way in which the questioner blandly asks 'Is that disputable?' seemingly taking Stoppard's earnest point for granted. It is quite possible – and, I think, quite likely – that the critical response to *Jumpers* has tended to make a similar assumption, thereby failing to recognise the way in which this concern is carried through the comedy into the dialetic between 'question' and 'counter-question' that is such an integral part of Stoppard's conception.

*Jumpers* tells the story of a work-obsessed philosophy professor named George Moore (but unconnected with the famous philosopher of the same name) and his nervy wife, Dotty, a former cabaret star, whose lives are complicated by the shooting of one of a troupe of University gymnasts performing in their Mayfair flat. This occurs while the man is forming part of a human pyramid at a party Dotty is throwing to celebrate an election victory that has brought the Radical-Liberal party to power, and he is subsequently identified as the late Professor McFee, also of the Philosophy Department. In the wake of the murder, elements of the 'whodunnit', familiar from *The Real Inspector Hound* and *After Magritte*, are introduced as Dotty, who seems to have shot the 'jumper' herself, tries to dispose of the corpse in her lavishly appointed bedroom. In this task she is aided by the University's Vice-Chancellor, Archie, who is in the habit of visiting her regularly and at all hours, and hindered by the arrival of Inspector Bones. During all this, her husband remains quite impervious to the goings-on and, with the disorganisation and impracticality traditionally the preserve of University professors, he continues to prepare a paper for an imminent symposium on the subject 'Man: good, bad or indifferent?', making use of an unlikely collection of study-aids that includes a bow and arrow, a pet hare (named Thumper) and a tortoise (Pat). Eventually Dotty is rescued from the clutches of the law by the resourceful Archie, who gets rid of both the body and the inspector, and then proceeds to oppose George at the symposium as a late replacement for McFee. With their debate, presented in a distorted, dream-like form, the play ends.

It is only at this point, in the 'coda' symposium, that Stoppard's 'question' and 'counter-question' confront each other directly, although they do so without dialectical clarity, as if projected out of a private nightmare of George's. Nevertheless the nature of the rival philosophical systems is made clear and is effectively under debate throughout the play as George prepares his case against the prevailing attitudes represented by Archie and McFee, which insist upon a materialistic, pragmatic view of man and the universe. To this end he sets out to defend a God in whom he can't altogether bring himself to believe in order to support his determined belief in the moral and aesthetic standards which he holds to be a necessary basis for civilised human activity. Stoppard sets up George and Archie as the protagonists in a 'play of ideas' by providing a constant interplay for and against the philosophy of Logical Positivism. McFee and Archie are the zealous proponents of the philosophy, George the muddled but vehement opponent. (Even his servant, Crouch, is an enthusiastic amateur.) The debate spans the whole of *Jumpers*, neatly assimilating all the various strands of its plot into a subtle structural unity. For Stoppard is concerned not merely to conduct a theoretical debate, but to illuminate the Logical Positivist philosophy in action, with all its attendant consequences.[11] He does this through a futuristic situation in which it has become so philosophically orthodox that Radical-Liberalism, its political arm, has just won a general election. The seemingly diverse elements of *Jumpers* represent the tragi-comic consequences of a world that is running mad as a result. In spite of this, Jonathan Bennett, a philosopher, treats the philosophical content of *Jumpers* as not altogether integral to Stoppard's conception, and concludes his dismissive comments with the assertion that 'there is nothing here that deserves the attention of philosophers'.[12] To demonstrate how integral I take the play's philosophy to be, it will first be expedient to sketch, in necessarily broad terms, the main tenets of Logical Positivism.

*　　　　*　　　　*

Logical Positivism originated in Vienna in the early 1920s where the Professor of Philosophy at the University, Moritz Schlick, and a group of like-minded colleagues who included leading mathematicians and scientists established the 'Vienna Circle'. Its members' fundamental stance is neatly summarised by Neurath's profession:

> All the representatives of the Circle are in agreement that 'philosophy' does not exist as a discipline, alongside of science, with propositions of its own; the body of scientific propositions exhausts the sum of all meaningful statements.[13]

The intention was thus to deprive philosophy of its traditional position of privileged independence, which the Circle considered obsolete, and to rationalise it along strictly scientific lines. At the heart of this attempt at demystification was the verification principle, an insistence that observability, either actual or possible, was a predicate of all knowledge that could be regarded as genuine. Strictly factual statements whose validity could be tested in practice were to be regarded as the only meaningful, only truly philosophical order of assertions.

This zealous dismissal of traditional areas of metaphysical, ethical or aesthetic enquiry, recognised for centuries as the legitimate preserve of the philosopher, attracted often rabid hostility to Logical Positivism, especially after the Second World War when, largely under the influence of A. J. Ayer (who had studied under Schlick in Vienna), it more or less became the new orthodoxy in British academic circles. Opponents insisted that this extreme empiricism was not only misguided but actually dangerous. A particularly influential critic in this country was C. E. M. Joad, whose book *A Critique of Logical Positivism*, published in 1950 when the influence and academic respectability of Logical Positivism was at its height, seeks to point out the implications of practical living on the basis of Logical Positivist assumptions. His particular target was A. J. Ayer's book *Language, Truth and Logic*, a handbook of Logical Positivist orthodoxy. For example, he describes Ayer's intractable position on God as being

neither atheist nor agnostic; it cuts deeper than either by asserting
that all talk about God, whether pro or anti, is twaddle[14]

on the basis of Ayer's clinical and carefully worded assertion that, to
the Logical Positivist, 'all utterances about the nature of God are
nonsensical.'[15] Ayer's statement insists that *logical* talk about God is
impossible because, if he exists, his existence is evidently of a
metaphysical nature. Joad's concern is with the implication: that
one should not therefore bother oneself with whether God exists or
not.

With ethics, too, the Logical Positivist concludes that since we
cannot 'know' goodness in the sense in which we can 'know' that
grass is green, we cannot really know it at all. Ayer declares that
sentences

> which express moral judgements do not say anything. They are
> pure expressions of feeling and as such do not come under the
> category of truth and falsehood.[16]

But if ethics are to be excluded from the field of truth, is the field
worth having? The total relativity that results is liable to render
them almost insignificant and the caveat which Ayer enters:

> To say that moral judgements are not fact-stating is not to say
> that they are unimportant, or even that there cannot be
> arguments in their favour. But these arguments do not work in the
> way that logical or scientific arguments do[17]

sounds almost patronising, since the *primacy* of 'logical or scientific
arguments' is not conceded. Instead, he gives the distinct impression
of trying to have it both ways. As Joad, defending the inscrutable,
says:

> The claim is that clarity of thought is so effectively promoted that
> when exhibited in the light of the logical positivist method of
> analysis and translation many, perhaps most, of the problems of
> philosophy disappear. And so, no doubt, they do. But they
> disappear not because they have been solved but because they are
> dismissed.[18]

What is fundamentally at issue, then, is whether its reduction of
all philosophy to logical premises which can be accepted or rejected

effectively means that Logical Positivism put into practice would authorise the most solipsistic and pragmatic forms of conduct. This is the question which Joad's book and Stoppard's play both pose, and the two writers clearly share a belief that academic debate about philosophy does not take place in an irrelevant vacuum, and that trends in academic thought percolate into the social and cultural climates to affect the way that we all live and think. Thus Stoppard's aim is broadly that of Joad, who states at the outset of his *Critique*:

> I am concerned to enquire what effects are liable to be produced by Logical Positivism upon the minds of those who are brought into contact with it and to consider whether these are such as are desirable.[19]

Such an enquiry provides the implicit and unifying structure of *Jumpers*: it presents domestic, academic and even extra-terrestial situations where human values seem to be corroding and explores them as the direct and adverse consequences of materialistic habits of thought.

\*　　　\*　　　\*

The central representative of Logical Positivist orthodoxy in *Jumpers* is the University's Vice-Chancellor, Sir Archibald Jumper, a dandy of multitudinous talents in the fields of philosophy, law, medical therapy, politics and, not least, gymnastics, which provides a pun on his own name (his students are 'Jumpers' in two senses) as well as suggesting a continuation of the ancient Greeks' mixture of recreational and intellectual pursuits. As one of the stalwarts of the Radical-Liberals, he seems to be running the victory celebrations at Dotty's flat with which the play opens. The party's success at the polls initiates a regime committed to wholesale rationalisation of the nation and its institutions, and we have several hints as to how they intend to pursue their radicalism; among their earliest actions, for instance, is the appointment of Sam Clegthorpe, the atheist Radical-Liberal spokesman for agriculture, as Archbishop of Canterbury. His importance as the party's only leader mentioned by name in *Jumpers* (apart from Archie) is reinforced when he figures in the nightmarish 'coda' sequence. Before this, however, George spots him from the window of his flat:

Good God! I can actually *see* Clegthorpe! – marching along, attended by two chaplains in belted raincoats.[20]

This 'rationalisation' of the church (like the railways!) thus establishes an episcopal hierarchy more reminiscent of the mafia than the clergy, while the military implications of the election success are suggested when Archie declares that 'the Police Force will be thinned out to a ceremonial front for the peace-keeping activities of the Army' (p. 65) and when George and Dotty hear jets flying low overhead:

> *George:* Oh yes, the Radical-Liberals. . . . It seems in dubious taste. . . . Soldiers . . . fighter-planes. . . . After all, it was a general election, not a *coup d'état*.
> *Dotty:* It's funny you should say that.
> *George:* Why
> *Dotty:* Archie says it was a *coup d'état*, not a general election. (p. 34)

'Archie says' is a recurrent phrase of Dotty's which serves to indicate both the influence he has over her and the influence he has gained through insinuating himself into as many disciplines as he can. This is not dilettantism, but a power complex, and it is largely realised when the Radical-Liberals win the election after a campaign centred on the philosophy – 'No problem is insoluble given a big enough plastic bag' (p. 40) – a motto which emphasises the narrow scope of 'problems' that Logical Positivists are prepared to recognise. When Dotty is trying to dispose of the corpse she shows her susceptibility to the philosophy by asking George, 'You don't happen to have a large plastic bag, do you?' (p. 41) which seems absurdly comic, but the joke rebounds when this turns out to be precisely the manner in which Archie and his gymnasts do dispose of the problem! *Jumpers* shows us the disturbing extent to which the Vice-Chancellor practises precisely what he preaches, and his behaviour throughout the play illustrates the moral limbo that opponents insist is a consequence of Logical Positivism's narrowing emphasis upon the practical aspects of rational behaviour.

A further example is demonstrated in the English moon expedition which Dotty watches on her bedroom television. There, with an ironic reversal of Oates's chivalry and self-sacrifice on the famous British Antarctic expedition of 1912, we see the astronaut in command, Captain Scott, fight with his subordinate officer Oates for a place in the capsule, after it has been damaged on landing. Scott originally figured in the coda in person, but Stoppard has deleted this from the published edition, leaving him as a symbol of Logical Positivism stretching the horizons of its deadening rationality right out into the universe. For what could be more rational than wanting to save your own neck when the reward for practising abnegation is a slow and airless martyrdom on the surface of the moon? In such a situation the Logical Positivist can console himself in the knowledge that generosity and selflessness are merely emotional whims.

This darkening sense of established values being overtaken is central to *Jumpers*, although it is established only indirectly, by such means as television newsreel, people in the street below and Dotty's snippets of Archie's opinions. The play itself, in fact, never moves outside the setting of George and Dotty's flat – which, besides being dramatically convenient, also suggests someting of man's alienation from political actuality. The action alternates between study and bedroom to focus in turn upon George's losing battle against his materialist academic colleagues, Dotty's losing battle against her own nerves and, obliquely hinted at, their losing battle to keep their marriage afloat (though this is offered as a subject for humour rather than trauma). In several respects, the play thereby recalls its most naturalistic predecessor, *Enter a Free Man*. Both Georges are obsessed with their work, escaping from their more-or-less estranged wives' realms (Persephone's sitting-room, Dotty's bedroom) into their own domain (Riley to his pub, Moore to his study). There, however, the resemblances end. *Jumpers* is an incomparably more sophisticated and original work and Moore's role, though handled comically, is essentially serious. Although his attempts to refute the rationality of the Logical Positivist cause constantly flounder, his ultimate intention (which ensures our sympathy) is to prove that there is a source of meaning and values in the universe. His position is not that of the convinced Christian but of the determined humanist:

If God exists, he certainly existed before religion. He is a philosopher's God, logically inferred from self-evident premises. That he should have been taken up by a glorified supporters' club is only a matter of psychological interest. (pp. 39–40)

Nevertheless, George needs a Godhead to support his beliefs that values are not arbitrary and that science cannot exhaust truth. He tries to convince Dotty that reason alone cannot provide a sufficient touchstone:

> The National Gallery is a monument to irrationality! Every concert hall is a monument to irrationality! and so is a nicely kept garden, or a lover's favour, or a home for stray dogs! You stupid woman, if rationality were the criterion for things being allowed to exist, the world would be one gigantic field of soya beans! . . .
>
> The irrational, the emotional, the whimsical . . . these are the stamp of humanity which makes reason a civilising force! (p. 40)

Rationality is, however, the criterion of the uncivil Radical-Liberals in all things, and as George widens the argument to include aesthetics and art and love, the shortcomings of their criterion are magnified. But George, nevertheless, remains unable to translate his objections to Logical Positivism into the coherent alternative philosophy for which he is constantly searching.

His wife's fragile state has apparently sprung largely from the violent blow dealt to her sensibility when men first landed on the moon and quashed all her treasured romantic associations:

> They thought it was overwork or alcohol, but it was just those little grey men in goldfish bowls, clumping about in their lead boots on the television news; it was very interesting, but it certainly spoiled that Juney old moon; and much else besides. (p. 39)

Now Scott's behaviour takes the process a stage further, coinciding with the Radical-Liberals' victory to suggest the decline of human values within the ever-onward march of materialism. Dotty's singing career came to an abrupt end with the rape of her 'spoony, Juney moon' and she remains highly strung throughout the play. Her resultant vulnerability estranges her from the intellectual George and leads her to an emotional dependence upon Archie, but she is not wholly won over to Logical Positivism, and we can see the idealistic and irrational within her rebelling against the philosophy to which, under Archie's influence, she pays lip service:

There's no question of things getting better. Things are one way or they are another way; 'better' is how we see them, Archie says . . .

Things and actions, you understand, can have any number of real and verifiable properties. But good and bad, better and worse, these are not real properties of things, they are just expressions of our feelings about them.   (p. 41)

It is precisely this tension between her nominal acceptance of the rational and her inward clinging to the irrational which produces her mental disorder, and from which her appeal as a character largely springs. The rupture of her fond and dreamy associations of the moon, derived from the songs whose clichés she can no longer manage to sing, becomes symbolic of the shattering demands constantly being made on us by the march of scientific progress. Yet Dotty's position, although unenviable, is in a sense a privileged one, showing the resilience of human sensibility to the implacable demands of reason and materialism. It is therefore appropriate that her neurosis should culminate in a vision of apocalyptic proportions:

Well, it's all over now. Not only are we no longer the still centre of God's universe, we're not even uniquely graced by his footprint in man's image . . .

and all our absolutes, the thou-shalts and thou-shalt-nots that seemed to be the very condition of our existence, how did *they* look to two moonmen with a single neck to save between them? Like the local customs of another place. When that thought drips through to the bottom, people won't just carry on. There is going to be such . . . breakage, such gnashing of unclean meats, such coveting of neighbours' oxen and knowing of neighbours' wives, such dishonourings of mothers and fathers, and bowing and scraping to images graven and incarnate, such killing of goldfish and maybe more –
(*Looks up, tear-stained*)
Because the truths that have been taken on trust, they've never had edges before, there was no vantage point to stand on and see where they stopped.   (p. 75)[21]

Dotty's 'vision' here is intuitive and heartfelt, a revolt from 'logical' progression of science and philosophy that reduces man from God's beloved, unique creation to just another scientific specimen in a global jar, and the implied question 'Where's it all going to stop?' again recalls the sad figure of Moon in Stoppard's novel, the little man who feels overwhelmed by the multiplying technology and population of his world, and who stands in central relationship to almost all of Stoppard's sympathetic and humane characters. Archie's clipped question in response to this passionate torrent – 'When did you first become aware of these feelings?' (p. 75) – is all the more ironic when one considers that to the Logical Positivist all value-statements *are* simply illogical 'expressions of feeling'.

Dotty's response provides her character with what is broadly required to create the pun on her name; she simply fails to cope with the pressures of the brave new reality and passes most of the play drifting about her bedroom in a confused state. Her reaction to the new rationalism is matched by the Christians who storm Lambeth Palace in rebellion against the government's anti-religious dictates – 'my chaplains had to use tear-gas to disperse them' admits the frantic Clegthorpe (p. 84) – and also, as Crouch tells George, by Dotty's apparent victim, McFee. The Professor of Logic himself stumbled from the pinnacle of Logical Positivist orthodoxy shortly before his death:

It was the astronauts fighting on the Moon that finally turned him, sir. Henry, he said to me, Henry, I am giving philosophical respectability to a new pragmatism in public life, of which there have been many disturbing examples both here and on the moon. Duncan, I said, Duncan, don't let it get you down, have another can of beer. But he kept harking back to the first Captain Oates, out there in the Antarctic wastes, sacrificing his life to give his companions a slim chance of survival . . . Henry, he said, what made him do it? – out of the tent and into the jaws of the blizzard. If altruism is a possibility, he said, my argument is up a gum-tree . . . Duncan, I said, Duncan, don't you worry your head about all that. That astronaut yobbo is good for twenty years hard. Yes, he said, yes, *maybe*, but when he comes out, he's going to find he was only twenty years ahead of his time. I have seen the future, Henry, he said, and it's yellow. (pp. 79–80)

This revelation is crucial to the whole balance of *Jumpers* and

McFee's apprehensive notion of 'giving philosophical respectability to a new pragmatism' is the linchpin of Stoppard's 'play of ideas'. It serves to put Dotty's apocalyptic vision into a more rational and accurate perspective – one that is correspondingly more disturbing. By contrasting Scott on the moon with Oates at the Antarctic it also stresses how the gulf between bravery and unselfishness and cowardice and self-interest is left without any kind of demarcation by the Logical Positivists' reduction of all value-judgements to the interplay of relative emotions. As the Radical-Liberals with their yellow flags and the Jumpers with their yellow tracksuits attire themselves in the colour traditionally associated with cowardly behaviour, Stoppard draws out the obvious moral implications, emphasising them finally in McFee's horrified vision of a yellow future.

Within the play, McFee's retraction also isolates Archie as the sole dedicated adherent of Logical Positivism, and it is inevitably he who coolly steps in to oppose George in the 'coda' symposium. *Jumpers* seems to reveal only one breach in his clinical poise, only one pointer to any humane content in his life: his fondness for Dotty as he helps her out of the murder scrape, and administers skin therapy to alleviate her neurosis. But close examination casts doubt even on this. Perhaps his dermatological experiments are merely an extension of his scientific personality, a wry reminder that, as Joad says, 'For logical positivists the world consists only of sensual facts.'[22] The pun seems appropriate in view of the constant ambiguity that Stoppard suggests in Archie's bedroom activities with Dotty, which is never resolved either way, with the audience left as much in the dark as George. Alongside Archie's professed 'medical' interest in Dotty is his defence of her after Bones has found the corpse. Bones is prepared to be as lenient as he can, and his own values are not wholly unprejudiced – 'Show business is my main interest, closely followed by crime detection' (p. 46) – but this is not sufficient for Archie:

*Bones:* My advice to you is, number one, get her lawyer over here –
*Archie:* That will not be necessary. I am Miss Moore's legal adviser.
*Bones:* Number two, completely off the record, get her off on expert evidence – nervous strain, appalling pressure, and one day – snap! – blackout, can't remember a thing. Put

her in the box and you're half-way there. The other half
is, get something on Mad Jock McFee, and if you don't
get a Scottish judge it'll be three years probation and the
sympathy of the court.

*Archie:* That is most civil of you, Inspector, but a court
appearance would be most embarrassing to my client
and patient; and three years' probation is not an
insignificant curtailment of a person's liberty.

*Bones:* For God's sake, man, we're talking about a murder
charge.

*Archie:* You are. What I had in mind is that McFee, suffering
from nervous strain brought on by the appalling pressure
of overwork – for which I blame myself entirely – left
here last night in a mood of deep depression, and
wandered into the park, where he crawled into a large
plastic bag and shot himself . . . (*Pause. Bones opens his
mouth to speak*) . . . leaving this note . . . (*Archie produces
it from his pocket*) . . . which was found in the bag
together with his body by some gymnasts on an early
morning keep-fit run. (*Pause. Bones opens his mouth to
speak.*) Here is the coroner's certificate. (*Archie produces
another note, which Bones takes from him. Bones reads it*)

*Bones:* Is this genuine?

*Archie:* Of course it's genuine. I'm a coroner, not a forger.
(pp. 64–5)

Once again, Archie has wheedled his way into all the necessary
spheres of influence, but where Bones's desire to aid Dotty clearly
springs from his admiration and affection for her, Archie's seems to
be based on the principle that corruption is all right provided that it
works – which, a detractor might add, is a fairly Logical Positivist
stance. Indeed, after offers of bribery and patronage fail, Archie is
forced to resort to blackmail, marshalling Dotty to fabricate a bogus
cry of rape against the Inspector in order to get rid of him. The very
considerable wit with which Stoppard manages this scene does not
in the least diminish the wholly amoral and unprincipled conduct
which it exhibits.

For a murder has been committed; McFee is dead, and the
'whodunnit' elements in *Jumpers* are wholly integral to the interplay
of ideas for and against Logical Positivism. The fact that it *looks* as if
Dotty shot him leads all concerned, including the audience, to

assume that she has, but this is hardly proof, as we recall from Archie's indignation when George casts doubt on his activities in Dotty's bedroom:

> Well, what would it have *looked* like if it had *looked* as if I was making a dermatographical examination? (p. 78)

And indeed it *looks* as if Bones has tried to rape Dotty only because she has contrived, at Archie's initiation, to make it look like that. Perhaps, similarly, it has been *made* to look as if Dotty is guilty of the murder for, as Archie says,

> The truth to us philosophers, Mr. Crouch, is always an interim judgement. We will never know for certain who did shoot McFee. (p. 81)

Such a conclusion falls considerably short of satisfying both the inspector (who mistrusts philosophy anyway) and the 'whodunnit' enthusiasts in Stoppard's audiences, however consistent it may seem with the stringent demands of the Vice-Chancellor's logical principles. However, the fact that this follows hard upon the revelation of McFee's despairing retraction and his intention of entering a monastery, circumscribes these closing words of Archie's with a sinister implication which could put a rather different interpretation upon his motives for trying to get Dotty off the hook. For in an earlier encounter with Bones the following dialogue occurred:

*Archie:* With the possible exception of McFee's fellow gymnasts, anybody could have fired the shot, and anybody could have had a reason for doing so, including, incidentally, myself.
*Bones:* And what might *your* motive be, sir?
*Archie:* Who knows? Perhaps McFee, my faithful protégé, had secretly turned against me, gone off the rails and decided that he was St. Paul to Moore's Messiah . . .

> McFee was the guardian and figurehead of philosophical orthodoxy, and if he threatened to start calling on his masters to return to the true path, then I'm afraid it would certainly have been an ice-pick in the back of the skull. (pp. 63–4)

At that stage of the play the idea sounded ludicrous; it is, however, as we subsequently learn from Crouch, precisely what *did* happen to McFee. The inspector has no way of knowing of this, but, shortly afterwards, Archie tests out George's knowledge of the previous night's events:

> *Archie:* Oh he could be very violent, you know . . . In fact we had a furious row last night – perhaps the Inspector had asked you about that . . . ?
> *George:* No . . .
> *Archie:* It was a purely trivial matter. He took offence at my description of Edinburgh as the Reykjavik of the South. (pp. 68–9)

Together these quotations comprise a strong case for believing that a violent disagreement actually did take place between McFee and Archie when the Vice-Chancellor discovered the nature of his protégé's recent apprehensions, and that Archie responded in almost as murderous a manner as the one he incautiously describes to Bones.

These suspicions are further justified by the fact that when George learns of the murder, Dotty says, casually, 'I thought Archie did it' (p. 78) (throughout the play no-one has actually *asked* her if she did it!) and by the manner of Clegthorpe's death in the coda as Archie controls the symposium in neo-fascist style. (Interestingly, this is one of Joad's stated concerns: that the moral vacuum created by the attempted debasement of ethics is susceptible to fascist infiltration.) In the coda the moral current moves inexorably towards solipsistic self-interest, and even Clegthorpe, having been besieged by the Christian rebels, draws back from the abyss:

> *Clegthorpe:* In my opinion the Government is going too fast.
> *Archie:* Surely that is a matter best left to the Government?
> *Clegthorpe:* They were shouting 'Give us the blood of the lamb. Give us the bread of the body of Christ' –
> *Archie:* That's hardly a rational demand.
> *Clegthorpe:* They won't go away! . . . Surely belief in man could find room for man's beliefs . . . ? (p. 84)

But the Radical-Liberals' 'belief in man' is a humanism steered rigidly along Logical Positivist lines, and Clegthorpe is promptly executed, shot out of a pyramid of Jumpers, just as McFee was. Archie rids himself of his 'turbulent priest' by transforming the symposium into a trial, but this hardly offers a solution to the problems posed by the irrational basis of Christian belief. Once again, the problems are not being solved but dismissed.

This is Archie's method in all things, and it strongly suggests that the status of the coda is not entirely subjective – a bizarre experience of George's – but is designed to put beyond doubt our suspicions of Archie that have accumulated at the end of the play proper. The audience alone is in a position to make the logical deduction: that the help Archie gives Dotty is designed to defray suspicion from himself.

George might, of course, have won the symposium with his 'opponent' taking his side. But Archie preserves the Logical Positivist case by disposing of the renegade McFee and stepping into the gap, seemingly with impunity. His first speech is an incoherent, Joycean babble, that is extremely funny and earns him shattering applause (and scores of '9.7', '9.9' and '9.8' from the ushers) but hardly advances the Logical Positivist cause. After George's speech, however, he has the chance to defend himself, the only point in the play when the two philosophical positions come truly face to face. George's case rests on the value and importance of the non-scientific, non-verifiable content of life, but having struggled unsuccessfully throughout the play to express this convincingly he chooses in the Coda to outline instead the double standards he regards as necessarily implicit in Logical Positivism:

A remarkable number of apparently intelligent people are baffled by the fact that a different group of apparently intelligent people profess to a knowledge of God when common sense tells *them* – the first group of apparently intelligent people – that knowledge is only a possibility in matters than can be demonstrated to be true or false, such as that the Bristol train leaves from Paddington. And yet these same apparently intelligent people, who in extreme cases will not even admit that the Bristol train left from Paddington yesterday . . .

will, nevertheless, and without any sense of inconsistency, claim to *know* that life is better than death, that love is better than hate, and that the light shining through the east window of their bloody gymnasium is more beautiful than a rotting corpse! (pp. 86–7)

However much this fails to 'prove' non-logical positives, it at least presents another cogent illustration of the limitations of merely logical ones and, with some dexterity, suggests that the Logical Positivist is in practice forced to maintain fundamentally contradictory attitudes towards ethical and aesthetic standards.

In response, Archie puts forward a pragmatically optimistic but evasive and discreditable defence:

> Do not despair – many are happy much of the time; more eat than starve, more are healthy than sick, more curable than dying; not so many dying as dead; and one of the thieves was saved. Hell's bells and all's well – half the world is at peace with itself, and so is the other half; vast areas are unpolluted; millions of children grow up without suffering deprivation, and millions, while deprived, grow up without suffering cruelties, and millions, while deprived and cruelly treated, none the less grow up. (p. 87)

The shortcomings of this comically glib account are as evident as the Beckettian influence on Stoppard's style here. But where Beckett hovers mercilessly on the edge of the holocaust, Stoppard steers us safely clear of the brink with this tongue-in-cheek illumination of the immorality that *could* be logically acceptable to an order perpetrating such rigid rationality: lack of respect for life, the pursuit of hate, equanimity in the face of deprivation and suffering, a chaos of values, all potentially stemming from the Logical Positivist's indifference to those 'facts' which cannot stand by logical tests alone. In this manner, albeit within a comic framework, Stoppard powerfully demonstrates the perversity of holding evaluation to be a matter of merely emotional significance, and suggests some of the deplorable values that might be shielded behind the philosophy's facade of rose-tinted logic.

*      *      *

It should now be clear that the play's 'question' and 'counterquestion' are of rather more than theoretical interest to its author. In broad terms, George is the play's hero and Stoppard's own mouthpiece. Archie, on the other hand, the representative of Logical Positivism, is indicted as the villain of the piece in two senses as the 'whodunnit' puzzle and the 'play of ideas' slowly converge. The manner of Dotty's emotional recoil from the implications of Logical Positivism and its spheres of influence also provides a counterpart to her husband's intellectual repulsion. And even in the heart of some of the funniest sequences between the characters he creates in *Jumpers*, Stoppard rarely steps very far away from the relentless illumination of the ultimate consequences of an all-pervasive logicality. Here George is trying to explain McFee's position to Inspector Bones:

*George:* The point is it allows him to conclude that telling lies is not *sinful* but simply anti-social.
*Bones:* And murder?
*George:* And murder, too, yes.
*Bones:* He thinks there's nothing *wrong* with killing people?
*George:* Well, put like that of course . . . but *philosophically* he doesn't think it's actually, inherently wrong in itself, no.
*Bones (amazed):* What sort of philosophy is that?
*George:* Maintream, I'd call it. Orthodox mainstream.
(pp. 48–9)

This, of course, is exactly what we see happen in the course of the play and it also demonstrates the way in which George's role within the ranks of Academe, ironically, is that of the sceptic. Archie's patronising regard for George is demonstrated when he refers to him as

our tame believer, pointed out to visitors in much the same spirit as we point out the magnificent stained glass in what is now the gymnasium. (p. 63)

Throughout, George is clearly regarded as the local eccentric. John Weightman has evidently not perceived the irony when he describes him as 'an eccentric who is trying to set back moral philosophy forty years,'[23] for this is, of course, to endorse Archie's position. What Stoppard wants us to see in George is the norm distorted by his environment into the apparent eccentric. His efforts may seem as futile as Canute's, because within the world of ebbing values that Stoppard depicts, esteem for George's whole area of concern has been so far undermined that

Only the Chair of Divinity lies further beyond the salt, and *that's* been vacant for six months since the last occupant accepted a position as curate in a West Midland diocese. (p. 51)

Yet the consequences of such a debasement of ethics are the running theme of the entire comedy.

In making a final assessment of *Jumpers*, the pertinent question must be whether the dramatic form that Stoppard employs with such zest and originality makes the serious elements of his concept sufficiently discernible. Is the skill and intricacy of his design such that more than a single viewing or reading may be necessary to appreciate its full range? Here we need to recognise that, however passionate Stoppard's concern with his philosophical argument, he is not writing a treatise but a play which has to work as a comedy on the stage. As he told Penelope Mortimer, with slightly too much modesty:

> It's a very primitive work indeed if you judge it intellectually. It's about the sort of basics that a first year philosophy student could understand. But if you want to write about moral philosophy on an entirely different level, more discursively, then my kind of theatre is not appropriate.[24]

Equally, though, to take the play merely as a clever farce is to see the farcical mechanics – the sexual ambiguity, the body swinging away from view each time Dotty's bedroom door opens, George's bizarre appearance on the Inspector's arrival, foamed for a shave and carrying a tortoise, bow and arrow – in isolation, without recognising the intellectual pattern by which Stoppard schematises them. And this pattern, of all the brilliant patterns we encounter in his plays, is probably the most accomplished. Perhaps Stoppard's objective is in some ways 'a Shavian mix', as Katharine Worth suggests,[25] though one which differs sharply from what Shaw achieved in practice. As Hunter puts it:

> Shaw works as a barrister presenting a case, always towards an end, a last word, a judgement . . . . Theatre, though enjoyable enough, is merely the rhetoric he uses to win the jury.[26]

Shaw shares with Stoppard the idea that a play can be a vehicle for debating views on life, rather than a method of presenting slices of it, but his rhetorical instinct often seems stronger than his theatrical instinct. In *Heartbreak House*, for instance, the comic elements of the play are practically swamped by his earnestness. With *Jumpers*, this equation can almost be reversed: the serious argument runs the danger of being swamped by the relentless comic energy – until the final and decisive synthesis of his largely abstract argument with his 'whodunnit' mystery secures the 'marriage' knot.[27] And where the play succeeds is not only in the remarkable shrewdness of its total design, but often in its very smallest units, where the two 'marriage' partners truly converge in wit of the very highest standard, simultaneously provoking ironic laughter and thoughtfulness:

*George:*   Poor Duncan . . . I like to think he'll be there in spirit.
*Archie:*   If only to make sure the materialistic argument is properly presented.  (p. 69)

# 8 The Importance of Being Carr

In 1973 the Royal Shakespeare Company commissioned a new full length play from Stoppard, no doubt influenced both by the fact that they had let *Rosencrantz* slip out of their hands in 1966[1] and by the enormous success that the National Theatre was enjoying with *Jumpers*. The result was *Travesties*, given its first performance at the Aldwych Theatre, London, on 10 June 1974 with John Wood in the leading rôle of Henry Carr and with Peter Wood, director of the National Theatre's *Jumpers*. again directing. The play won the *Evening Standard*'s Best Play Award of 1974 and by the following year, when its success in both critical and commercial terms had rivalled its illustrious predecessor, it was reintroduced into the RSC's Aldwych repertoire for a second season, just as *Jumpers* had been at the Old Vic. The play then moved to Broadway in 1975 ( *Jumpers* had been produced there the previous year) with spectacular success, capturing three of the annual 'Tony' awards: to Stoppard (Best Writer), to John Wood (Best Actor) and to *Travesties* itself (Best Play). A number of productions in British regional theatres have since followed.

The play breaks with Stoppard's previous custom by treating historical figures in an historical setting. Set in Zurich, it contrives to bring together a number of distinguished exiles who were in the city in the later years of the Great War: Lenin, on the verge of revolutionary success in Russia; James Joyce, engaged in creating the revolutionary prose edifice of *Ulysses*; and the artist Tristan Tzara, who, with his fellow Dadaists, revolted against practically all established notions of art and culture. These three revolutionary figures – two in the arts, one in the fiercer world of politics – provide the play with its main themes and its central characters. But in general Stoppard does not treat them historically and their individual lives and achievements serve chiefly as the pretext for a playfully disrespectful comedy which, as its title suggests, makes 'travesties' of the characters which it presents.

For at the hub of the drama is a fourth 'real' character, Henry Carr, who also chanced to be in Zurich in 1917, based at the British Consulate in Zurich while recovering from a serious wound sustained in action in France. There is no evidence to suggest that Carr ever met Tzara or Lenin, but it is by dramatising his humorous, bigoted and largely fictitious recollections of the great men living alongside him in the city that the travesties are perpetrated. And since Carr provides the frame for the entire action, it appears to be he, rather than Stoppard, who is their source. His one genuine connection is with Joyce and this is well-documented. They met when Carr was enlisted to play the rôle of Algernon Moncrieff in a production of *The Importance of Being Earnest* given in the city with Joyce as business manager (and an English actor named Claude Sykes as producer) and their relationship, never amicable, blew up into a storm after the production when they commenced legal proceedings against each other – Carr seeking reimbursement for clothes he had bought specifically for his performance and Joyce, by way of riposte, demanding money for the tickets that Carr had sold. As a result Carr assumes sufficient importance to figure in Richard Ellmann's biography of Joyce,[2] and Stoppard liberally expands upon the minimal information offered therein:

> From these meagre facts about Henry Carr – and being able to discover no others – I conjured up an elderly gentleman still living in Zurich, married to a girl he met in the Library during the Lenin years, and recollecting, perhaps not with entire accuracy, his encounters with Joyce and the Dadaist Tzara.[3]

The character thereby created is, of course, just as much of a travesty as those which Carr himself perpetrates – a fact obscured by the real Carr's relative unimportance in historical terms, but wryly under-lined when Mrs Noel Carr, his widow, wrote to Stoppard after the play's reviews had appeared!

Carr's rôle, then, is roughly that of the pseudo-biographer and Stoppard employs a series of devices to warn us of the unreliability of his hazy recollections. He presents the character in two distinct guises: in the present time, as a rambling old man fancifully recalling his past, and as his imagined younger self, reliving that

past in 1917. Both Carrs are played by the same actor, moving from
the theatre fore-stage of Old Carr's drawing room – where the play
begins and ends and to which, intermittently, it briefly returns – to
the scene, behind it, of his imaginary former glories, the elegant
drawing room of the British Consulate in Zurich (though this is
swiftly transformed for a number of scenes into the city's Public
Library). Here, as Old Carr invests himself with an importance very
much greater than that which history actually afforded him,[4] we
meet Young Carr the British Consul, intimately mingling with the
great artists and revolutionaries exiled in the city. Stoppard thus
brings to life a Zurich landscape that exists only inside Carr's head,
where fact, fiction and jumbled reminiscence whirl around in
glorious abandon. The time-scale, for instance, is obviously im-
plausible; the characters were never all in Zurich at *exactly* the same
time and by the opening of *The Importance of Being Earnest* in April
1918, Lenin had been back in Russia for almost a year. Old Carr
himself eventually concedes at the end of the first act that he may
not have got all the details quite right as his memory travels back
over sixty years, mixing wile with forgetfulness:

> Incidentally, you may or may not have noticed that I got my
> wires crossed a bit here and there, you know how it is when the old
> think box gets stuck in a groove and before you know where you
> are you've jumped the points.   (p. 64)

Right from the start, though, Stoppard demonstrates his concern to
emphasise that his character's hit-or-miss recollections are based
much less on first-hand memory than on what he has subsequently
read or heard about the great men in question by deflating the
pompous literary tone of Old Carr's first explanatory soliloquy. An
enormously long monologue, crowded with contradictions, puns,
inaccurate quotations and humorous wordplay, it provides a
mischievously telling parody of the august tone adopted by so many
biographers and autobiographers, while at the same time enabling
Stoppard to lay much of the groundwork for what follows, not only
in respect of the suspect basis of Carr's memoirs but by sketching the
characters whom we subsequently encounter in scenes which,
because they reflect the confusion in Carr's thinking, can be equally
confusing for the audience.

These main 'dramatised' sections of the play are often rapid,
chaotic and contradictory, but one strand provides a constant point

of reference: the rôle of Algy which Carr played in *The Importance of Being Earnest* and which is his sole authentic link with his subjects. As his 'wires' cross and re-cross, he frequently attributes to those around him lines and structures borrowed from the play in which he performed (apparently with considerable distinction) in Zurich and although these are often employed in fairly unlikely contexts, they produce a quite remarkable effect. For Stoppard so engineers the quotations and borrowings from *The Importance of Being Earnest* that Tzara, Joyce and Carr's younger self consistently act 'in character', enabling him to create an elaborate parallel structure between his play and Wilde's. In addition to these three parallel characters (Lenin is omitted for reasons examined below), he subordinates with cheeky appropriateness the real British consul at the time, Bennett, to the rôle of Carr's manservant and invents a sister for Carr named Gwendolen and a librarian called Cecily to complete the essential cast as follows:

| | |
|---|---|
| Algernon Moncrieff: | Henry Carr |
| John Worthing: | Tristan Tzara |
| Lane: | Bennett |
| Aunt Augusta (Lady Bracknell): | James Joyce |
| Gwendolen Fairfax: | Gwendolen Carr |
| Cecily Cardew: | Cecily Carruthers |

In this way the only true correspondence – that Carr recalls playing Algy – becomes the starting point from which Stoppard organises practically the entire course of his play along the lines of Wilde's, with Carr in romantic pursuit of Cecily and Tzara of Gwendolen. In defence of this improbable schema, two remarkable further coincidences may be cited: that Joyce was in reality mis-registered at birth as 'James Augusta' (in error for Augustine) and that the actor playing Worthing in the English Players' production was indeed named Tristan. Carr's mistakes are therefore almost plausible, enabling Stoppard to use *The Importance of Being Earnest* – with considerable ingenuity and dexterity – to furnish the audience with familiar and coherent bearings. The concept of setting characters within borrowed cultural patterns plainly owes much to Joyce, since *Ulysses* – in the use it makes of *The Odyssey* – provides the archetype for this kind of structure. Stoppard himself had earlier attempted a similar experiment in the use to which he puts *Hamlet* in

*Rosencrantz*. Here, however, the whole point of the 'play-within-a-play' concept is the absence of any real mutual dependence of the one on the other. Wilde's play is thus used to provide a steadily identifiable but essentially bogus focus, unifying the otherwise disparate strands of Stoppard's complicated subject and creating a narrative thrust that Carr alone cannot offer. Charles Marowitz has therefore described *Travesties*, with some justice, as 'a play-within-a-monologue',[5] neatly highlighting the patent discrepancy between Carr's real existence in Zurich in 1917 and his fantastic representation of it, which – as if to 'seal in' these discrepancies – is everywhere permeated by the characters, structure and even *tone* of Wilde's play. Even where there is no direct mimicry, one senses the way in which Carr's account is shot through with a joyous sense of play-acting:

> It is this complete absence of bellicosity, coupled with an ostentatious punctuality of public clocks, that gives the place its reassuring air of permanence. Switzerland, one instinctively feels, will not go away.   (p. 26)

The epithets, if not Wilde's own, bear the unmistable stamp of his delight in artifice and style as Stoppard cultivates for Young Carr a tone of extravagant loquaciousness that carries as far as possible the image of a cultivated Victorian–Edwardian world of gentlemanly leisure – a world which Carr capriciously desires to believe in but which, in its turn, travesties the *real* mood of 1917.

Carr's fantasy does not therefore exist merely for the pleasure its playful variations on *The Importance of Being Earnest* undoubtedly provide. As the central characters might suggest, both political activity and philosophical theory – especially as reflected in artistic theory – are major preoccupations in this play, as in *Jumpers*. *Travesties* represents a further advance in Stoppard's attempt to marry the 'play of ideas' with 'farce or high comedy';[6] indeed, the presence of the 'ideas' is rather more ostentatious here, especially in respect of the character of Lenin. Stoppard is primarily concerned with the concepts of art and revolution and the possible relationship between them. Inside the frame established by Carr runs a broad-based discussion of these two subjects in which each character has a clear-cut contribution to make. Lenin is presented as a man of absolute commitment to action, burning with fervent determination to implement the theories he has spent his life formulating.

Joyce demonstrates a scarcely lesser commitment to his art, and pursues it with a passion and conviction that verge upon religious dedication. Tzara exemplifies the artist's zealous commitment to the destruction of the false and outmoded gods of established culture. In addition, Lenin holds important views on art, Tzara on revolution. Between them the three provide a wealth of possibilities and opportunities, but without any self-evident focal point. It is Young Carr's role as prompter and catalyst which provides this, as his trenchant and reactionary views fuel – not to say inflame – the various stages of the debate. Unlike *Jumpers*, the rôle of the central character therefore exists both outside the action – as Old Carr, presenting his fabricated portrait of Zurich – and within it, as Young Carr, an active combatant in a similar sense to George in his pitched battle against the legions of Logical Positivism.

*      *      *

Carr himself is fractionally more sympathetic to Joyce's views than those of the others, but the portrait is quite predictably coloured by his strong personal bias. Having crossed swords with his subject in the Zurich courts, he makes from the start no secret of his difficulty in maintaining the biographer's traditional objectivity:

> To be in his presence was to be aware of . . .

> a complex personality, an enigma, a contradictory spokesman for the truth, an obsessive litigant and yet an essentially private man who wished his total indifference to public notice to be universally recognised – in short, a liar and a hypocrite, a tight-fisted, sponging, fornicating drunk not worth the paper, that's that bit done. (pp. 22–3)

The stage manifestation of Joyce we subsequently encounter reflects the tenor of this initial sketch, a crude caricature shaped by Carr's long-nursed grudge who serves as a continual reminder that *all* our impressions are being gleaned from a far-from-neutral source. Many of the details of this 'portrait' are lifted from Ellmann's biography and are used to belittle or ridicule the artist. Thus Joyce's fondness for creating limericks gives rise to an hilarious scene in which Tzara, Joyce, Carr and Gwendolen converse entirely in limericks:

| | |
|---|---|
| *Carr:* | If it's money you want, I'm afraid . . . |
| *Gwendolen:* | Oh Henry! – he's mounting a play, |
| | and Mr Joyce thought |
| | your official support . . . |
| *Carr:* | Ah . . . ! |
| *Joyce:* | And a couple of pounds till I'm paid. |
| *Carr:* | I don't see why not. For my part, |
| | H.M.G. is considered pro-Art. |
| *Tzara:* | Consider me anti. |
| *Gwendolen:* | Consider your auntie? |
| *Joyce:* | A pound would do for a start.   (p. 34) |

But behind this comedy is a stinging reminder of Joyce's reputation for frequently trying to borrow or save money,[7] later reinforced by his declaration:

I am an Irishman. The proudest boast of an Irishman is – I paid back my way.   (p. 50)

Similarly, Joyce's appearance in the two acts of *Travesties* wearing the opposite halves of two suits has its origin in a casual remark of Ellmann's that when Joyce began some private teaching:

Ordinarily he came to his lessons neatly, if not elegantly, dressed. He never wore a complete suit, always the jacket of one and trousers of another.[8]

For this almost slapstick touch, Stoppard's character offers the excuse that

My wardrobe got out of step in Trieste, and its reciprocal members pass each other endlessly in the night.   (p. 96)

This obscures the real origin of the device, but further bolsters Carr's impression of Joyce as a muddle-headed clodpoll.

The historical background to his legal confrontation with Joyce provides a valuable insight into Carr's personal animus as portrayed in *Travesties*. Joyce enjoyed less than friendly relations with British officials for many years, following an early bruise in Trieste in 1904 when he was suddenly arrested:

He urgently demanded to see the British consul, who came reluctant to interfere. Had not Joyce jumped ship? he asked.

Joyce angrily protested that he was a Bachelor of Arts at the Royal University of Ireland and had come to teach in the Berlitz school. The consul was not taken in by this unlikely story. Had Joyce not committed some crime in England? At last he effected Joyce's release, but in the worst grace. His coldness helped to intrench Joyce's loathing and contempt for English officialdom which he corroborated afterwards by many instances.[9]

Thirteen years later, the consul in Zurich was A. Percy Bennett, whom Joyce visited to seek official support for the English Players' planned production. According to Ellmann, the consul

treated him in an offhand and superior way until Joyce needled him with some remark, after which he lapsed into silence and pretended to be looking for something thrown by mistake into his waste-paper basket.[10]

Joyce duly produced a limerick to commemorate this unlikely encounter:

There's an anthropoid consul called Bennett
With the jowl of a jackass or jennet,
   He must muzzle or mask it
   In the waste-paper basket,
When he rises to bray in the senate.[11]

Ellmann suggests that Carr, who had 'a small job'[12] under Bennett, was happy to accept Joyce's invitation (made on the basis of a recommendation) to play the rôle of Algy, though he nevertheless 'evidently accepted the official view that Joyce's conduct in Zurich was not quite cricket'.[13] After the performance Carr excused himself from the cast dinner and on the next day remonstrated with the producer, Claude Sykes, about Joyce's constant high-handedness with him, further demanding 150 francs for the trousers, hat and gloves that he had bought specially for his performance. At the consulate, Joyce subsequently retorted by demanding twenty-five francs that he claimed Carr owed him for tickets that he had been given to sell. Knowing that Sykes and Joyce had made a profit from the show and that he had received a mere ten francs (although this was the sum agreed in advance), the enraged Carr allegedly shouted at Joyce

You're a cad. You've cheated me and pocketed the proceeds. You're a swindler. If you don't get down, I'll throw you downstairs. Next time I catch you outside I'll wring your neck.[14]

Legal action duly proceeded on the basis of Carr's demand for 150 francs against Joyce's for 25, and in addition Joyce sued for slander on the strength of the words 'cad' and 'swindler' – expressions which Stoppard duly incorporates into the text of *Travesties* (p. 96). Meanwhile, the English Players took their production on a short tour with a new Algernon, and Joyce continued to press for the injustice to be righted, despatching letters to Bennett and, when the consul supported Carr and withdrew official backing from the Players, to Sir Horace Rumbold, British Minister to Berne.[15]

The eventual outcome of the first action was the court's decision against Carr, based on the fact that 'his clothes were not stage costumes but ordinary wearing apparel capable of further use'.[16] The second action for slander was lost by default as Carr had by this time left Zurich and witnesses of the conversation from the consular office were understandably unhelpful. After the first decision, Joyce composed a celebratory song to the tune of Tipperary which included the stanza:

When the play was over Carr with rage began to dance,
Saying I want twenty quid for them there dandy pants,
So fork us out the tin or Comrade Bennett here and me,
We're going to wring your bloody necks, we're out for liberty.[17]

But a worse fate awaited Carr in *Ulysses*, where Joyce extracted his full vengeance in the 'Circe' episode of the novel, set in the brothel zone of Nighttown. Here Private Carr and Private Compton are two drunken and insulting British soldiers who accost Stephen, and the former assaults him to the accompaniment of such choice epithets as

I'll wring the neck of any fucking bastard says a word against my bleeding fucking King.[18]

Carr also shows total disrespect towards his superior officer, who, although he does not appear in the novel, is naturally called Bennett:

God fuck old Bennett! He's a whitearsed bugger. I don't give a shit for him.[19]

Bennett receives scarcely better shrift from Carr in *Travesties*, cast in the rôle of his valet, but Joyce, naturally, is his main target. Having been so rudely travestied himself in *Ulysses*, Carr duly seeks his revenge (with Stoppard's aid) in *Travesties*.

On this level, if on no other, he succeeds, for Joyce's rôle in the play consists largely of composing limericks, hectoring Tzara, scrounging money and chaperoning Carr's sister, Gwendolen. But it certainly cannot be said of this figure, as he winds his way in and out of the 'dramatised' scenes of the play, that he adds up to a character. According to John Weightman:

> The character of Joyce is a failure, a sort of blank, because it is easier to show how non-art is silly and political dogmatism limited than it is to explain how good art comes to be good.[20]

This criticism is open to the objection that since the characters are pieced together from the unreliable fragments of Carr's memory, they ought not to be judged as independent creations in this way. With Joyce, there is also the added complication of Carr's personal grudge to contend with. It nevertheless seems legitimate to expect Stoppard to present a stage version of Joyce capable, in some way, of transcending these self-induced obstacles. In the event, this is only achieved by Old Carr's inability to sustain his attack on Joyce's character:

> I dreamed about him, dreamed I had him in the witness box, a masterly cross-examination, case practically won, admitted it all, the whole thing, the trousers, everything, and I *flung* at him – 'And what did you do in the Great War?' 'I wrote *Ulysses*,' he said. 'What did you do?' Bloody nerve.   (p. 65)

Carr's grudging admission of the partiality of his own viewpoint goes some small way towards countering the thinness and paucity of the stage travesty. But beyond this one brief reference, the quality and importance of Joyce's work is never brought into focus; when, for instance, we first encounter Joyce in the Zurich library in the opening scene of the play, he is dictating to Gwendolen a section of

*Ulysses* ('Oxen of the Sun') that shows the book at its most intractable and inaccessible:

> Send us bright one, light one, Horhorn, quickening and wombfruit.  (p. 18)

This, which, as Ellmann has pointed out, is 'itself a travesty of English prose styles',[21] is deliberately bracketed with Tzara's nonsensical re-arrangement of the individual words of poems:

> Eel ate enormous appletzara
> key dairy chef's hat he'll learn oomparah!
> Ill raced alas whispers kill later nut east,
> noon avuncular ill day Clara![22]   (p. 18)

The crucial distinction between Tzara's international nonsense and Joyce's difficult sense is entirely absent, which would not matter if all the characters were presented in the same jokey vein. It is, however, comparatively easy to demonstrate Stoppard's concern to outline the philosophies, beliefs and influence of both Lenin and Tzara in far more depth.

There is only one scene in which the character of Joyce sustains any kind of theatrical energy and even here Stoppard's concern is much less with Joyce's art than with Tzara's, as the Irishman cross-examines and castigates the Dadaist. Their lengthy exchange provides one of the strongest parallels with a scene from *The Importance of Being Earnest*, namely that in which Aunt Augusta examines the pedigree of her daughter's suitor, John Worthing. In Stoppard's play, Joyce instead appraises the personalities, credentials and artistic manifesto of the Dadaists; here, for example, Tzara's colleague Arp is the subject of discussion:

| | |
|---|---|
| *Joyce:* | By what familiarity, indicating possession and amicability in equal parts, do you habitually refer to him? |
| *Tzara:* | My friend Arp. |
| *Joyce:* | Alternating with what colloquialism redolent of virtue and longevity? |
| *Tzara:* | Good old Arp. |
| *Joyce:* | Grasping any opportunity for paradox as might occur, in what way is the first name of your friend Arp singular? |

*Tzara:* In that it is duplicate.

*Joyce:* Namely?

*Tzara:* Hans Arp. Jean Arp.

*Joyce:* How can this contradiction of two distinct and equal first names be accounted for?

*Tzara:* Linguistically, each being a translation of the other, from German into French and conversely.

*Joyce:* Given a superficial knowledge of your friend's birth and parentage on the one hand, and of the political history of nineteenth-century Europe on the other, how would his bi-lingual nomination strike one?

*Tzara:* As understandable.

*Joyce:* Why?

*Tzara:* He is a native of Alsace, of French background, and a German citizen by virtue of the conquest of 1870. (pp. 56–7)

The combination of alert humour with polite formality catches passing echoes of the tone of Wilde's original scene which reinforce our sense of Joyce's rôle as Lady Bracknell.[23] But even stronger echoes are also at work, reminding us irresistibly of 'Ithaca', the lengthy question-and-answer section that forms Chapter XVII of *Ulysses.* The layers of reference thus multiply to perform at least three functions: a verbal tribute to Joyce's art, a cementing of Joyce's rôle within the *Earnest* structure and an opportunity to fill out the audience's understanding of the history and beliefs of Dadaism. The length of the scene reflects a common tendency of Stoppard's to provide his audience with so much information that he runs the risk of becoming repetitive. In this case, however, the risk is more than usually justified, since Tzara is undoubtedly the least familiar of the main characters and because the scene offers one of a regrettably small number of instances in which the character of Joyce is developed.

This increasingly irate conversation propels us into an important branch of Stoppard's dialogue on art and revolution, a confrontation of opposing artistic spirits which helps to define their sharply differing responses to the crisis of twentieth-century existence. As the temperature of the discussion rises, Joyce, coolly provocative, begins to produce, conjuror-style, from his top hat a string of streamers and flags and finally a rabbit, all the time calmly continuing his dialogue with Tzara. This saucy piece of magic underlines Joyce's conception of the artist as a man magically transmuting the unexceptional into art and emphasises the diametrical opposition of this view to Tzara's, especially since it is the same hat into which Tzara has just defiantly shredded a Shakespearean sonnet! The mood quickly switches to outright mutual attack:

> *Tzara:*     Your art has failed. You've turned literature into a religion and it's as dead as all the rest, it's an over-ripe corpse and you're cutting fancy figures at the wake. It's too late for geniuses! Now we need vandals and desecrators, simple-minded demolition men . . . !
>
> *Joyce:*     You are an over-excitable little man, with a need for self-expression far beyond the scope of your natural gifts. This is not discreditable. Neither does it make you an artist. An artist is the magician put among men to gratify – capriciously – their urge for immortality. (p. 62)

There is some substance in each of these criticisms and even if Joyce does underestimate the importance of the Dada rebellion (an important and acute response to the horrific carnage of the First World War), his put-down is beautifully measured. As for Tzara's complaint, it is frequently observed of Joyce's reverence for art that it is in some respects a substitute for a lost religious sense, a comparison he himself made on at least one occasion, writing to his brother Stanislaus:

> Don't you think there is a certain resemblance between the mystery of the Mass and what I am trying to do? I mean that I am trying . . . to give people some kind of intellectual pleasure or spiritual enjoyment by converting the bread of everyday life into something that has a permanent artistic life of its own . . . for their mental, moral and spiritual uplift.[24]

There is, however, a quality of Joyce's own character that irradiates even this brief quotation and which is entirely absent from *Travesties*: a sense of integrity and innermost searching which inspired his life and work. Largely because of the restrictions imposed on him by the ill-matched parallel with Aunt Augusta and the distortions of Carr's bias, Stoppard's Joyce never begins to suggest this level of seriousness or commitment, and it is an important failure.[25] Nonetheless, within the scheme of Stoppard's debate he has a useful contribution to make and beneath his obvious hostility towards Tzara – a hostility of temperament as much as philosophy – there is one sense in which their positions coincide, as both men adopt the romantic view of the artist as a man of special vision and insight (in Tzara's case, largely the insight to demolish). Though each artist denies the other's right to consider himself thus special, the point is of considerable significance, for such a conception presupposes a certain level of freedom for the artist which at least one of the other characters is not at all disposed to accept.

*       *       *

Tzara is the joker in the *Travesties* pack, the clown revolutionary brimful of energy and passion who chants 'dada' thirty-four times in rhythmic succession (p. 37) and creates several new poems from the random re-assortment of old ones. As a result, his character is strongly established, entertaining and naturally theatrical, especially in comparison with the relatively colourless figure of Joyce.[26] The stylish and romantic Worthing offers Stoppard a far more promising parallel and since Tzara lacks any authentic link with Carr, his Wildean rôle assumes correspondingly greater importance. The pretext that Old Carr cannot separate him in his jumbled recollections from Tristan Rawson, the actor who played Worthing for the English Players, is splendidly plausible too. Hence Tzara 'parrots' Worthing's opening lines from *The Importance of Being Earnest*:

> Oh pleasure, pleasure! What else should bring anyone anywhere?[27]

in three successive scenes as the cogs of Carr's memory whirr around, propelling him on each occasion into an improbable variation of Wilde's true opening scene. In the first he appears in the guise of what Stoppard calls 'a Rumanian nonsense', speaking with a joke German accent:

> Vhat is all the teapots etcetera? Somebody comink?
> It is Gwendolen I hopp!   (p. 32)

until Joyce follows hard on his heels and the scene turns into a bout of limericks. On the second and third occasions, Carr's account is fractionally more intelligible, but only because he now has the characters of Tzara and Worthing inextricably confused:

> *Tzara:*  Hello–why the extra cup?–why cucumber sandwiches? Who's coming to tea?
>
> *Carr:*  It is merely set for Gwendolen–she usually returns at about this hour.
>
> *Tzara:*  How perfectly delightful, and to be honest not unexpected. I am in love with Gwendolen and have come expressly to propose to her.
>
> *Carr:*  Well, that is a surprise.
>
> *Tzara:*  Surely not, Henry; I have made my feelings for Gwendolen quite plain.
>
> *Carr:*  Of course you have, my dear fellow. The way you pass her the cucumber sandwiches puts me in mind of nothing so much as a curate assisting at his first Holy Communion.[28]   (p. 43)

Besides once more illustrating how well Stoppard catches the measure of Wilde's idiom – and the last speech demonstrates how his wit can at times rival Wilde's own – this passage emphasises the advantage of portraying Carr and Tzara as close, long-standing friends and this is further strengthened in the second half when Carr impersonates his friend in the Zurich Public Library in order to meet the beautiful unknown Cecily (just as Algy impersonates Worthing in Wilde's play in order to meet his young ward of the same name). Here, and throughout the play, there is a sense of witty congruity about the Dadaist's rôle as Worthing; the danger, as with Joyce, is that we lose sight of the serious artist beneath.

Tzara and his fellow Dadaists possessed a sense of lively and urgent theatricality precisely because they were so comprehensively destructive in their judgements. Growing up in Zurich with the First World War ravaging all of Europe around them, these young artists, Tzara, Arp, Ball, Janco, Huelsenbeck and a score of lesser figures, created what was, in origin, a protest movement. They believed that the established and traditional means of artistic expression were rendered futile by the unprecedented scale of the war and that only the 'art' of anarchy was appropriate to the new situation. As Arnold Hauser says:

> Dadaism . . . pleaded, out of despair at the inadequacy of

cultural forces, for the destruction of art and for a return to chaos.[29]

Thus Tzara demanded the right to urinate in different colours and created 'simultanist verse' from re-arranged poems, while Arp invented a game called the Eggboard in which all the participants emerged covered in egg-yolk. More tangible Dada creations were meanwhile exhibited at a Zurich gallery in the Bahnhofstrasse where cabaret-type performances, equally trenchant in their expression of disgust, were also staged. Negative revolt of this kind can, of course, give rise to creative achievements of the highest kind, but the Dadaists are more properly regarded as propagandists for, and to a lesser extent agents of, destruction than as creative artists in their own right. Their importance lay less in what they achieved than in what they subsequently made possible; as Sir Herbert Read has said:

> The foundation of the Dada Group in 1916 (in Zurich) was the first conscious negation of the aesthetic principle in art[30]

and it was the direct inspiration of Dada which gave rise to Surrealism in Paris after the war, guided by André Breton but aided and abetted by several members of the original Dada group. Yet through both movements runs an essential contradiction:

> Dadaism demands the complete destruction of the current and exhausted means of expression. It demands entirely spontaneous expression, and thereby bases its theory of art on a contradiction. For how is one to make oneself understood – which at any rate surrealism intends to do – and at the same time deny and destroy all means of communication?[31]

In either direction, there is inevitably some form of servitude: either to the established, often *passé* conventions of the day or to the arbitrary dictates of chance or the subconscious, and within *Travesties* the role of *agent provocateur* in raising the debate between these positions is quite naturally Tzara himself.

Tzara's reputed personality and Wilde's vivid character of John Worthing combine to suggest the kind of flamboyant creation that Stoppard invents with particular success in several earlier works – the Player in *Rosencrantz and Guildenstern are Dead*, for instance, or

George Riley or Lord Malquist (whose linguistic style is even similar). A distinct advantage, especially over Joyce, is the simplicity of demonstrating Tzara's passions and beliefs – as when he asserts the comprehensive principle that 'everything is chance, including design' (p. 37). In one of several scenes with Carr that begin with exchanges from *The Importance of Being Earnest* and become increasingly frenzied, he declares that

> Nowadays, an artist is someone who makes art mean the things he does. A man may be an artist by exhibiting his hindquarters. He may be a poet by drawing words out of a hat.  (p. 38)

Carr, as a traditionalist and a reactionary, naturally refuses to accept this and steadfastly advances the contrary position:

> An artist is someone who is gifted in some way that enables him to do something more or less well which can only be done badly or not at all by someone who is not thus gifted . . .
>
> you are simply asking me to accept that the word Art means whatever you wish it to mean; but I do not accept it.  (pp. 38–9)

At once Tzara replies:

> Why not? You do exactly the same thing with words like *patriotism, duty, love, freedom*, king and country, brave little Belgium, saucy little Serbia –  (p. 39)

This exchange introduces the first of the connections between art and politics which develop in importance as the play progresses. It rests on the associations, especially the more emotive ones, that words acquire within a living system of language. Tzara cannot, of course, make arbitrary sense of words, for they live only through meaning and association. All he can do is *contest* established meanings and associations – unless he is to treat language as merely a system of sounds. Carr's insistence that the word 'art' has limited and known applications is entirely proper, yet when it comes to politics, his uncritical acceptance of the meaning of words points an equal, opposite danger:

> I went to war because it was my *duty*, because my country needed me, and that's *patriotism*. I went to war because I believed that

those boring little Belgians and incompetent Frogs had the right to be defended from German militarism, and that's *love of freedom*. (p. 40)

The issue is finally one of linguistic philosophy: what right has an individual to determine the meaning and interpretation of words? Stoppard's tendency here, and throughout the first half of *Travesties*, is to leave such questions hanging temptingly in mid-air, with the play's diversity and eclecticism constantly steering the audience's attention into a new frame. No sooner have the outlines of an argument been sketched – in this case that Tzara's conception of the 'new' artist is self-contradictory and that Carr's conception of the war is naïvely uncritical – than the investigation ceases and the action sweeps forward once again.

In his vigorous exchanges with Tzara, Carr provides more cogent opposition to Dadaism than Joyce, thereby further weakening the latter's position within the crucial clashes of opinion and philosophy within the play. Carr also sets his sights on much more basic principles:

> What is an artist? For every thousand people there's nine hundred doing the work, ninety doing well, nine going good and one lucky bastard who's the artist. (p. 46)

As his argument develops, he pits himself against a philosophy to which both Tzara and Joyce, despite their differences, adhere:

> Artists are members of a privileged class. Art is absurdly overrated by artists, which is understandable, but what is strange is that it is absurdly overrated by everyone else . . .
>
> the idea of the artist as a special human being is art's greatest achievement, and it's a fake! (pp. 46–7)

On this issue, one of the play's crucial concerns, the span of opinion across the four protagonists is most visible. For it later emerges that Lenin – an improbable ally for the philistine Englishman – is in broad agreement with Carr. He is determined that such a romantic notion of the artist shall be exorcised under Communism, and that the artist will become the custodian of socialist values. These contrasting viewpoints emphasise, as Stoppard intends, that the frontiers of revolution in art and in politics run in quite separate directions. Tzara, for one, is prepared to concede the irony of this:

> I am the natural enemy of bourgeois art and the natural ally of the political left, but the odd thing about revolution is that the further left you go politically, the more bourgeois they like their art. (p. 45)

With this neat barb, Tzara, the character most effectively woven into the Wildean parallels, thereby spikes Lenin, the character whom Stoppard deliberately leaves in the cold – only for the Russian to demonstrate, by way of riposte, just how much stronger than the artist the politician can be.

*　　　*　　　*

As the character of Lenin does not participate in the parallel structure linked to *The Importance of Being Earnest*, he does not figure in any of the scenes set in Algy's drawing room – though this is scarcely surprising since it is supposedly the drawing room of the British Consulate! The only setting in which Lenin is encountered is in the Public Library, where at the start of the play he receives from his equally startled and excited wife Nadya the news that revolution has broken out in Russia. In this scene only, they converse in Russian, which provides a further ironic counterpoint to the apparent nonsense Joyce is dictating and the actual nonsense Tzara is proclaiming aloud. While the artists play, however, the politicians act: the Lenins leave the library at once and disappear completely until the second act when the action returns to the library and picks up their preparations for departure from Switzerland. This re-introduction is achieved with some awkwardness by means of a potted history of the background to the Russian Revolution presented in the form of a lecture by the librarian Cecily, an admirer of Lenin's work. This lecture continues intermittently throughout the act and is taken up by Lenin and Nadya themselves when Cecily is detached from the narrative to participate with Carr and Tzara in more parallel scenes from *The Importance of Being Earnest*. The main trouble is that the lecture format is open to the very evident objection that it removes (or certainly *appears* to remove) the action from the supposed context of Old Carr's confused memories. Stoppard himself seems somewhat equivocal about its importance too, directing that

*The performance of the whole of this lecture is not a requirement, but is an option. After 'To resume' it could pick up at any point, e.g. 'Lenin was convinced . . .' or 'Karl Marx had taken it as an axiom . . .' but no later than that.* (p. 66)

Yet whatever its length, the lecture is not assimilated into the dramatic structure in the same way as the comparable passage in which Joyce 'interrogates' Tzara. The function of these two scenes is broadly the same, to convey to the audience important background information on the central characters, but the comparison magnifies the lecture's intractibility and lack of humour or conversational relief. This difference serves to emphasise Stoppard's very special concern to map out for his audience the precise contours of Lenin's importance, both before and after his years in Zurich.

Exiled since the abortive revolution of 1905, Lenin and his wife had in fact lived in Zurich for about a year when the 1917 revolution broke out and, according to Adam B. Ulam:

When they moved from Berne to Zurich in 1916 (there was a better library in Zurich) they lived first in a shabby boarding house, among whose inmates were a prostitute and a criminal.[32]

Thus it was the city's library which drew the Russians to Zurich. In Carr's recollections Lenin is working there on one of his major works, *Imperialism, the Highest Stage of Capitalism* – a treatise actually completed in 1916. (Once again, Carr's memory is snowballing together the Zurich years.) More salubrious accommodation was found shortly afterwards when he and Nadya moved to a shoemaker's house at 14, Spiegelgasse, though Edmund Wilson draws attention to the sausage factory opposite, from which 'the stench was so overwhelming that they . . . spent most of their time in the library'.[33] The stench was obviously found less objectionable by the Dadaists, who frequented the Meierei Bar at 1, Spiegelgasse, a coincidence that prompts Carr to the excited remark:

now here's a thing: two revolutions formed *in the same street.* Face to face in Spiegelgasse! *Street of Revolution! A sketch.* (p. 24)

In the event this comparison, as with so much else in Carr's train of thought, is not pursued. Throughout the play, though, Lenin is treated in sharp contrast to the other characters, with fu!l seriousness, as a figure embarking on a mission that radically changed the history of the world, a mission in which the nature of his own character has been recognised as decisive. As Ulam writes:

> Lenin imported to Bolshevism and communism not only ideology and tactics, but also many of his personal characteristics. The cult of Lenin has always united communists of the most divergent views.[34]

He was not a warm man or one who laughed easily, taking himself and others with the utmost seriousness. Edmund Wilson quotes Pyotr Struve's observation of 'something lifeless and repulsively cold' about his manner.[35] Gorky, in *Days With Lenin*, quotes the occasion (omitted from the official Russian version) on which Lenin fiercely demanded to know, 'Is regard for humanity possible in such an unheard-of ferocious struggle?'[36] and elsewhere, in a memorable phrase, describes Lenin's speeches as giving the impression of 'the cold glitter of steel shavings'.[37]

Cecily's lecture charts Lenin's career with a simple and (for *Travesties*) untypical regard for historical authenticity, and one senses at once that Stoppard has ceased trying to entertain:

> Lenin was convinced, like Marx, that history worked dialectically, that it advanced through the clash of opposing forces and not through the pragmatic negotiation of stiles and stepping-stones. He was a hard-liner. The class war was war, and to direct it effectively the Party had to be a compact group of professional revolutionaries who gave the orders.   (p. 68)

When Lenin and Nadya take over the narrative, its factual basis continues, with frequent extracts from Lenin's own letters and writings advancing the story to their departure from Russia in the famous 'sealed train'. Meanwhile, in an entirely different vein, the *Earnest* pastiche resumes alongside the Lenins' account, with a passage paralleling Wilde's frivolous impersonation scene. Having learnt that Tzara is passing himself off as his own (fictitious) brother Jack to avoid being hectored in the library as one of the unpopular Dadaists, Carr slips into the loophole, passing himself off as Tristan in order to meet the librarian Cecily. These two strands advance together in uneasy relationship:

*Lenin:* My dear Vyacheslav Alexeyevich. I am considering carefully and from every point of view what will be the best way of travelling to Russia . . .

You must disappear from Geneva for at least two or three weeks, until you receive a telegram from me in Scandinavia . . .

*Cecily:* Jack!

*Tzara (turning one way):* Cecily!

*Cecily:* I have such a surprise for you. Your brother is here.

*Tzara:* What nonsense! I haven't got a brother.   (pp. 79–80)

While Lenin plots, Carr is preoccupied with self-disguise and romantic conquests, although in his own account he has supposedly been telegraphed by the British Government to watch Lenin and ascertain his intentions, following the new developments in Russia. This 'spying' connection is no more satisfactory than the lecture as a means of linking Lenin to the main action of *Travesties*, but it enables Carr to embark on one of his milder pieces of self-aggrandisement:

I'd got pretty close to him, had a stroke of luck with a certain little lady, and I'd got a pretty good idea of his plans, in fact I might have stopped the whole Bolshevik thing in its tracks, but – here's the point. *I was uncertain.* What was the right thing? And then there were my feelings for Cecily. And don't forget, *he wasn't Lenin then! I mean who was he?* as it were. So there I was, the lives of millions of people hanging on which way I'd move, or whether I'd move at all, another man might have cracked –   (p. 81)

Carr, of course, has no *real* case to answer, yet his bloated defence begs the question: did the governments of either Britain or Germany realise the possible consequences of Lenin's return? This, juxtaposed with Lenin's actual departure and the subsequent extracts from some of his most noteworthy speeches, serves as a chilling reminder to the audience that 'the lives of millions of people' *did* hang on Lenin's fate, and from this perspective, Carr, Cecily, *The Importance of Being Earnest* all fade into trivial insignificance, belittled by the menacing shadow of the. 'lecture'.

Yet the characterisation of Lenin has less to do with the clumsy comedy of Carr than with the deep convictions of his creator. Unwilling to make Lenin's political dogmatism comic, Stoppard

consciously strives to make it frightening. Like *Jumpers* and several
of the following plays, *Travesties* should be viewed in the light of the
author's insistence that

> all political acts must be judged in moral terms, in terms of their
> consequences. . . . The repression which for better or worse
> turned out to be Leninism in action after 1917 was very much
> worse than anything which had gone on in Tsarist Russia. I
> mean, in purely mundane boring statistical terms, which some-
> times can contain the essence of a situation, it is simply true that
> in the ten years after 1917 fifty times more people were done to
> death than in the *fifty years* before 1917.[38]

In consequence, Lenin is not only not incorporated into the Wilde
pastiche, he is scarcely travestied at all. There is barely a joke
directed at him in the whole play and, whereas Carr can call Joyce

> a liar and a hypocrite, a tight-fisted, sponging, fornicating drunk
> (p. 23)

and Tzara

> you little Rumanian wog – you bloody dago – you jumped-up
> phrase-making smart-alecy arty-intellectual Balkan turd!!!
> (p. 40)

the nearest approach to a joke at the expense of Vladimir Ilyich
Ulyanov is in Tzara's fairly impersonal comment that

> at the Zum Adler Lenin was raging away against the chauvinist
> moderates who didn't necessarily want to bayonet every man
> over the rank of N.C.O.   (p. 45)

and the same character's description, on reading some of Lenin's
ideas from *Imperialism, the Highest Stage of Capitalism*, that the
experience was 'like sharing a cell with a fanatic in search of a
mania'.   (p. 96)

For much of the second half of the play, the solemn, towering
figure of Lenin unquestionably restricts the comic momentum,
weakening in particular the overall effect of the *Earnest* pastiche. Yet
we can now see this as a risk which Stoppard deliberately takes, for
one of his major concerns is precisely to suggest how art can be

overshadowed and even controlled by the currents of political activity – even when his own brilliance may be jeopardised in the process. In this way the rôle of Lenin completes the intermittent debate on art and revolution; even though he never converses with the other characters, his is the most important single contribution. Like Carr, he regards the notion of the artist-magician heralded by Joyce as anathema, but for quite different reasons:

> Down with literary supermen! Literature must become a part of the common cause of the proletariat . . .
>
> The freedom of the bourgeois writer, artist or actor is simply disguised dependence on the money-bag, on corruption, on prostitution. Socialist literature and art will be free because the idea of socialism and sympathy with the working people will bring ever new forces to its ranks.  (p. 85)

Here, and throughout the act, Stoppard's approach is to use Lenin's own recorded statements whenever possible so that he may stand condemned, literally, by his own words. Behind his insistence that the artist's true freedom can emerge only through decisive political change is, of course, his obsessive and singular concern with that political change. Unlike the other main characters of *Travesties*, he has no first-hand knowledge of the processes that make individuals produce art and its ambiguous importance to him personally is further shown in Stoppard's final quotation, which Lenin delivers to the background swell of Beethoven's *Appassionata*:

> I don't know of anything greater than the Appassionata. Amazing, superhuman music. It always makes me feel, perhaps naïvely, it makes me feel proud of the miracles that human beings can perform. But I can't listen to music often. It affects my nerves, makes me want to say nice stupid things and pat the heads of those people who while living in this vile hell can create such beauty. Nowadays we can't pat heads or we'll get our hands bitten off. We've got to *hit* heads, hit them without mercy, though ideally we're against doing violence to people . . . Hm, one's duty is infernally hard.  (p. 89)

This is the decisive verdict Stoppard has sought from his character. There must be no miracles and no beauty; in the final analysis, art is seen as a potential counter-revolutionary force, uniting or at least emasculating those who should consider themselves enemies. As such, whether it is the art of Joyce or of Tzara, it must be resisted until something new can take its place.

Stoppard has suggested that 'ideological differences are often temperamental differences in ideological disguise'[39] and the stifling dominance of 'Socialist Realism' in post-revolutionary Russia can certainly be traced to Lenin's own views on art. One man's idiosyncratic beliefs can thus be transformed into an orthodoxy laying claim to an absolute moral righteousness and *Travesties* uses Lenin to show how political dictatorship – in whatever guise – must include artistic dictatorship. No doctrine in fact cuts deeper into the notions of artistic freedom and, as Carr declares early in the play,

> The easiest way of knowing whether good has triumphed over evil is to examine the freedom of the artist.   (p. 39)

This, surely, amounts to Stoppard's own view and his concern, underlying the whole of *Travesties*, is whether artists of any persuasion can survive in a climate dominated by a man such Lenin. In a special sense, therefore, the play does not merely circumnavigate the beliefs of the three main characters: it arranges them in such a fashion as to spotlight the various directions open to twentieth-century art. Joyce, though his own art is done scant justice, provides the yardstick by which the more traditional art is continually re-shaped; Tzara, though his own 'art' is contradictory and destructive, provides the yardstick by which it is subjected to constant challenge; Lenin, as an absolute dogmatist, provides a yardstick by which art is throttled in the grip of political intolerance, and it is towards his direct challenge to the artist that Stoppard relentlessly draws our attention in the second half of the play. Lenin is, of course, free to love the *Appassionata* and hate Dadaism, just as Tzara is free to do the opposite, but Tzara did not force his views onto a nation of several hundred million people. Stoppard's concern is over the vulnerability of the artist's freedom.

> Aren't you ashamed for printing 5 000 copies of Mayakovsky's new book? It is nonsense, stupidity, double-dyed stupidity and affectation. I believe such things should be published one in ten, and not more than 1 500 copies, for libraries and cranks. As for Lunacharsky, he should be flogged for his futurism.   (p. 87)

These words – Lenin's own in a memo to the Commissar for Education in 1919 – point towards repression, not change, and the sixty succeeding years have demonstrated their importance.

As a remarkable feat of dramatic engineering, *Travesties* provides the clearest example yet of Stoppard's rich inventive powers, exceeding even the verve of *Jumpers*. The fertile use of Carr both as eccentric narrator and participant in his own mêlée and the structural dovetailing of the various transmogrified scenes from *The Importance of Being Earnest* combine to create a carnival atmosphere of stylish and joyous comedy. As a tract – and this certainly is a no less important aspect of the play – it can finally be seen as a plea for tolerance of the individual artist in pursuing his chosen path. Carr's muddle-headed last words provide a comic attempt to try and tie together the threads of the whole debate he has set in motion:

> Firstly, you're either a revolutionary or you're not, and if you're not you might as well be an artist as anything else. Secondly, if you can't be an artist, you might as well be a revolutionary. (pp. 98–9)

This 'conclusion' does not crystallise the play's moral concerns into a single nucleus, as in *Jumpers*, where the indictment of Archie as McFee's murderer completes the indictment of his dangerous Logical Positivist views. The more open-ended structure of *Travesties* (it has been described by Tynan, not altogether fairly, as a 'triple-decker bus that isn't going anywhere'[40]) militates against such a neat *coup de grâce*. Sir Herbert Read's lucid statement of the different natures of artistic and political revolution offers a more promising position:

> There are two senses in which one can be a revolutionary. One can set out with a definite aim – to replace a monarchy by a republic, for example – and if one achieves that aim, the revolution is complete, finished. One is no longer a revolutionary. But that is not the kind of revolutionary that Picasso was, or Klee, or Joyce. . . . These painters and writers had no new constitution in their pockets: they did not know where they were going or what they might discover. They were quite sure about the sterility and rottenness of the academic standards which then prevailed everywhere, but they had no preconceived ideas about new standards. They were explorers, but they had no compass bearings.[41]

Read provides here a cogent summary of the central premise that Stoppard defends in *Travesties*. Lenin's political aim is definite, defined, but he summons art to follow, as it cannot. Joyce and Tzara are not revolutionaries in this sense, and cannot be. Stoppard lauds the rights of the artist and opposes the cruelty and immorality of imposing dogmatism upon them, and though the character of Lenin who personifies this dogmatism is without precedent in any of his previous plays, his shadow is firmly cast over several of those that follow.

# 9 More Puzzles

The two shorter plays to be discussed in this chapter, *Artist Descending a Staircase*, written for radio and broadcast in 1972, and *The Boundary*, a collaboration with Clive Exton in the BBC television series *Eleventh Hour*, screened in 1975, are divided by the major achievement of *Travesties*. It is appropriate to consider them together because of certain important resemblances, and each, to some extent, can also be seen as an extension of the 'nuts and bolts' plays discussed in Chapter 6, since Stoppard again creates a puzzle at the core of each play. As in *The Real Inspector Hound*, a dead or apparently dead body provides the heart of the mystery and each 'whodunnit' is solved – and each dramatic pattern simultaneously rounded off – by an abrupt twist of perspective at the end, confounding the expectations which have previously been established. The earlier piece, *Artist Descending a Staircase*, also reveals important similarities both of theme and style to *Travesties*. At earlier stages in his writing career, Stoppard frequently remodelled ideas and even specific lines from one play into another,[1] and certain sections of *Travesties* are similarly a clear development of ideas first explored in *Artist Descending a Staircase*. The latter, however, is very much more than a 'work-out' for *Travesties*; it is by some margin Stoppard's most accomplished play for radio, both in the richly inventive use it makes of the medium and in the quality of its humour and thought.

*Artist Descending a Staircase* was commissioned by the BBC to mark British entry into the E.E.C. as the first in an exchange scheme of European radio plays and was first broadcast in November 1972 with a cast including Dinsdale Landen and Carleton Hobbs. Like so many of Stoppard's plays, it is constructed by steadily expanding upon a strong initial image, as with the pyramid of actors in *Jumpers*, the painters on Albert's bridge or the elusive pseudo-surrealistic drawing-room scene in *After Magritte*. In a television interview in 1976, he stressed the way in which his imagination needs to be constantly fuelled by such images:

> I rather enjoy other people's plays when nothing's happening at
> all. You know, there are people coming in and they're washing up
> the breakfast cups or something for twelve minutes and then
> somebody comes in and says the sun's come out, and then she
> dries the breakfast cups for eight minutes, and I can see that the
> thing's working! I'm having a nice time. When *I'm* writing a play
> the first cup is not dry before Batman has smashed through the
> kitchen window, because I'm thinking no, they're going to leave,
> no, wait a minute, I'll have . . . I tell you what I'll do . . . I
> know, there'll be a body on the floor![2]

And, indeed, *Artist Descending a Staircase* starts with a body on the
floor, though in this case the image must be conveyed aurally. We
grasp the situation only slowly, hearing, as the play begins, a
succession of enigmatic noises which are being played and replayed
on a tape recorder. The sequence of sounds, contained on a long
continuous loop of tape, is as follows:

(a) Donner dozing: an irregular droning noise.
(b) Careful footsteps approach. The effect is stealthy. A board
    creaks.
(c) This wakes Donner, i.e. the droning stops in mid-beat.
(d) The footsteps freeze.
(e) Donner's voice, unalarmed: 'Ah! There you are . . .'
(f) Two more quick steps, and then Thump!
(g) Donner cries out.
(h) Wood cracks as he falls through a balustrade.
(i) He falls heavily down the stairs, with a final sickening thump
    when he hits the bottom. Silence.[3]

These vivid aural 'images' remain the hub of the play as the possible
interpretations of the sounds are investigated.

Three aged artists have lived together for years at the top of a
house; now Donner's corpse has been discovered at the bottom of
the stairs by Beauchamp and Martello, each of whom is gravely
suspicious of the other, having construed from the sounds unmistakable evidence of foul play by someone whom Donner must
have known sufficiently well to recognise without alarm. The
absence of any obvious motive on either side sends the pair combing

back through their pasts in a multiplying series of flashbacks. We learn of the three men's close friendship sustained since boyhood, of the artistic endeavours with which they have filled the intervening years and of their close relations in the early 1920s with a blind girl named Sophie, the play's only other character. We wait in vain, however, for the vital clue which will incriminate either Beauchamp or Martello. Instead, the play concludes its flashbacks at the year 1914 and then rolls rapidly forwards again, picking up and concluding each of the previous flashbacks in turn and returning us finally to the present where the 'murder' riddle is abruptly solved. Donner's descent, which provides the play with its title in a parody of Marcel Duchamp's series of paintings, *Nude Descending a Staircase*, was not murder at all. Listening to the replayed sounds a final time, we realise that the 'snoring' noise corresponds exactly to the sound of a fly still buzzing in the room; as Beauchamp then swats it, on the top of the bannister rail, he unconsciously recreates the entire sequence of sounds which led to Donner's fall. It suddenly becomes clear how deceptive the 'evidence' of the tape has been, and that Donner's crash through the rickety bannister has been a genuine accident. But, with beautiful ambiguity, Stoppard leaves us guessing whether or not the artists themselves have made the vital connection.

As it develops, the purpose of the play becomes very much broader than the solving of this given puzzle. In *After Magritte* Stoppard dabbled playfully with the subject of surrealism for almost wholly comic ends. In *Artist Descending a Staircase* his intentions are rather more ambitious as he integrates within a stylish comic framework both a serious discussion of the rôle of the artist in society and a simultaneous satire on trends in modern art over some fifty years. Much of this discussion specifically prefigures the lengthier debate in *Travesties* and the character of Tzara is clearly modelled in part on the three genial bohemians. Like him, they are concerned with the nature of art at a critical point of its development in the early years of the twentieth century. Beauchamp, for instance, holidaying in France on the eve of World War One, declares:

> All my life I have wanted to ride through the French countryside in summer, with my two best friends, and make indefensible statements about art. (p. 42)

The war – of which they are so blissfully ignorant – duly brings this jaunt to an abrupt end, but not before Beauchamp has managed to introduce a crucial question: 'how can the artist justify himself?' (p. 43). He has also answered it:

> The answer is that he cannot, and should stop boring people with his egocentric need to try. The artist is a lucky dog. That is all there is to say about him. In any community of a thousand souls there will be nine hundred doing the work, ninety doing well, nine doing good, and one lucky dog painting or writing about the other nine hundred and ninety-nine. (p. 43)

In *Travesties* this contention is put, in practically the same words, into the mouth of Henry Carr, but where his attitude suggests resentment towards the one-per-cent artist, Beauchamp, Donner and Martello are merely glad to belong to this fortunate minority fraternity. For them, it is a vocation that carries virtually no obligations and which offers the opportunity for constant and carefree pursuit of the *avant-garde*. They are thus discovered, at various stages of the play, experimenting with sculptures made entirely from sugar, creating gramophone records and later tapes which resemble '*a bubbling cauldron of squeaks, gurgles, crackles and other unharmonious noises*' (p. 19)[4] and planning a mixed media carving of a wooden man with a real leg. This terrain, first paced out by the Dadaists, provides them with more than fifty years of creative endeavour.

The artists' confident pursuit of these chosen ends does not, however, pass without question. Carr's role, that of the sceptic, is provided in *Artist Descending a Staircase* by Sophie, who gently opposes their dutiful service to Duchamp's maxim, which Donner quotes:

> There are two ways of becoming an artist. The first way is to do the things by which is meant art. The second way is to make art mean the things you do.[5] (p. 24)

It is the second way that Stoppard's artists live and work, drawing all kinds of simplistic objects and bizarre creations into the realm of 'art'. Sophie's role is to remind them of the presence of the first:

> The more difficult it is to make the painting, the more there is to wonder at. It is not the only thing, but it is one of the things. And

since I do not hope to impress you by tying up my own shoelace, why should you hope to have impressed me by painting a row of black stripes on a white background? (p. 38)

She then counters Martello's riposte with equal effectiveness:

*Martello:* And what, after all, is the point of excellence in naturalistic art –? How does one account for, and justify, the very notion of emulating nature? The greater the success, the more false the result. It is only when the imagination is dragged away from what the eye sees that a picture becomes interesting.

*Sophie:* I think it is chiefly interesting to the artist, and to those who respond to a sense of the history of art rather than to pictures. I don't think I shall much miss what is to come, from what I know, and I am glad that I saw much of the pre-Raphaelites before my sight went completely. (p. 39)

Sophie's critique of modern art anticipates Carr's less tolerant views and provides a commonsensical counterweight to the evident excesses of the artists' more self-indulgent work. She hints at the artist's responsibility to the other nine hundred and ninety-nine members of his community, against that to his fellow artists, and it seems likely that Sophie is voicing Stoppard's own conception of the desirable rôle of the artist: that this man in a thousand should work in a way calculated to be of more than small minority interest. In the event, Sophie's views do not prevail for two reasons: because the artists are blithely set on their chosen paths with romantic self-assurance and because Sophie herself dies in a sudden, tragic accident.

The complicated involvement between the artists and Sophie provides the basis for the play's complex technical structure. Stoppard pursues the use of time-patterns introduced in *Where Are They Now?*, this time deploying no less than six basic settings in the following order: A (here and now), B (a couple of hours ago), C (last week), D (1922), E (1920), F (1914), E, D, C, B and A – with the last five scenes as respective continuations of those previously started. It is the 'D' and 'E' scenes which concern Sophie and they have a crucial importance for the 'A', 'B' and 'C' scenes. Sophie falls in love with Beauchamp and lives with him for the two-year period between scenes 'D' and 'E', but from the day on which she first visits the artists (the 'E' scenes), it is Donner who loves her the most, recognising her, with a start, as a girl he vividly noticed on the occasion of an *avant-garde* exhibition entitled 'The Frontiers of Art' which he, Beauchamp and Martello mounted in the Russell Gallery. Sophie also recalls the encounter, as the only occasion she saw them before going wholly blind. They all looked similar and were dressed alike in army uniforms, but she can offer a clue to the man who particularly caught *her* eye.

| | |
|---|---|
| *Beauchamp:* | Is it that you remember one of our faces particularly, Miss Farthingale? |
| *Sophie:* | Well, yes, Mr. Beauchamp. |
| *Beauchamp:* | Oh. |
| *Sophie:* | I mean, I thought you were all engaging. |
| *Beauchamp:* | But one of us was more engaging than the others. |
| *Martello:* | Ah. Well, we shall never know! |
| *Donner:* | Oh! but it was my eye you caught. |
| *Sophie:* | As a matter of fact, there is a way of . . . satisfying my curiosity. There was a photographer there, for one of the illustrated magazines . . . |
| *Donner:* | The *Tatler*. |
| *Sophie:* | No, there was no photograph in the *Tatler*, I happened to see . . . but this man posed each of you against a picture you had painted. |
| *Martello:* | I see. And you want to know which of us was the one who posed against the painting you have described. |
| *Sophie:* | Well, yes. It would satisfy my curiosity. It was a background of snow, I think. |
| *Donner:* | Yes, there was a snow scene. Only one. |
| *Sophie:* | A field of snow, occupying the whole canvas – |
| *Martello:* | Not the whole canvas – |
| *Sophie:* | No – there was a railing – |
| *Beauchamp:* | Yes, that's it – a border fence in the snow! |
| *Sophie:* | Yes! (*Pause.*) Well, which of you – |
| *Donner:* | It was Beauchamp you had in mind.   (pp. 40–1) |

Thus it comes about that Beauchamp and not the hopeful Donner wins Sophie's love, and although he accepts the 'evidence' of the painting, Donner's unrequited love nevertheless remains steadfast while Beauchamp's falls steadily away. Two years later, when the artists contemplate moving across the Thames to Chelsea (the 'D' scenes), Beauchamp agrees to Donner's proposal that he should stay behind with Sophie while Beauchamp and Martello move away. But when Donner explains this proposition to her, her despairing response is permeated with a tragic irony which we, and Donner, cannot at the time perceive:

> I have lost the capability of falling in love. The last image that I have of love is him larking about in that gallery where you had your first exhibition . . .

> It was quick: one moment the sick apprehension of something irrevocable which I had not chosen, and then he was the secret in the deep centre of my life. (pp. 33–4)

Minutes later, Sophie is dead, crashing through the fifth-floor window in a moment of blind panic after Donner has briefly descended the staircase to bid his friends goodbye.

It is much, much later (in the 'C' scenes) that the whimsical train of Martello's thoughts turns up the crucial, uncomfortable key to this whole tragically miscarrying affair, when he stumbles upon the long forgotten memory of a picture which Donner had exhibited, bearing a striking similarity to Beauchamp's:

*Donner:* What occurred to you, Martello?
*Martello:* Well, your painting of the white fence –
*Donner:* White fence?
*Martello:* Thick white posts, top to bottom across the whole canvas, an inch or two apart, black in the gaps –
*Donner:* Yes, I remember it. Oh God.
*Martello:* Like looking at the dark through gaps in a white fence.
*Donner:* Oh my God.
*Martello:* Well, one might be wrong, but her sight was not good even then.
*Donner:* Oh my God.
*Martello:* When one thinks of the brief happiness she enjoyed . . . well, we thought she was enjoying it with Beauchamp but she was really enjoying it with you. As it were. (p. 52)

This sickening blow, as the unfortunate Donner realises the circumstances which have, so to speak, defrauded him of the happiness he might so easily have enjoyed with Sophie, and she with him, has such a profound effect that it causes him to abandon the principles of a lifetime: he begins to paint a naturalistic portrait of her. This 'conversion' is important for two reasons. First it is designed to imply that nothing less than a naturalistic, lifelike portrait from memory can do justice to the depth of his emotion, certainly not the comparatively playful and bloodless works of his younger days. At the same time the volte-face has, of course, steered Donner towards Sophie's own views. The tribute is thus doubly strong, even if his own untimely death ensures that it is never completed.

Stoppard's satire on modern art is greatly reinforced by the poignant emotional expression given to this whole theme by the Sophie sub-plot. Though the process by which her lover is identified is an improbable, elaborate conceit, the deep ironic sadness Stoppard subsequently generates throws the humorous inconsequentiality of the artists' bohemianism into fierce relief. The implied indictment of abstract art as the bringer of both thwarted love and premature death is made playfully – hard though it is to see how anything else could have caused the particular confusion which Stoppard evokes! But if the *cause* is suggested playfully, the result and the character's pain is not, and there is writing here of an emotional intensity not generally recognised in Stoppard's work. Here Donner is proposing himself to Sophie as Beauchamp's successor:

> *Sophie:*  You're staying?
> *Donner:*  Yes.
> *Sophie:*  Why?
> *Donner:*  Either way it's what I want to do.
> *Sophie:*  Either way?
> *Donner:*  If you're going with them, I don't want to live so close to you any more.
> *Sophie:*  *If* I'm going . . . ?
> *Donner:*  Sophie, you know I love you . . . how long I've loved you . . .
> *Sophie:*  He wants me to stay? With you?
> *Donner (cries out):*  Why do you want to go? *(quietly)* He's stopped caring for you. He only hurts you now, and I can't bear it. When he made you happy I couldn't bear it, and now that he hurts you I . . . just can't bear it –  (p. 32)

This level of emotion is not a gratuitous addition to the comedy; there is a deliberate, rasping antithesis. Sophie's violent death at the end of this scene even raises the possibility that Donner might have taken his own life, years later, in a similar fashion. But almost as soon as Stoppard raises the dark shadow of possible suicide he quells it, as the swift momentum of the play brings the action back to its starting point (scene 'A'), resolves the mystery in a quite different manner and exposes the whole Sophie sub-plot, for all its importance, as an elaborate red herring. Stoppard's playfulness thereby has the last word, as the comedy demands it must, and on swatting the fly, Beauchamp makes a casual reference to *King Lear* full of the keenest irony:

As flies to wanton boys are we to the Gods:
they kill us for their sport.  (p. 54)

Though he scarcely realises it, this 'epitaph' to the fly is doubly true of poor Donner: both in his pursuit of the fly that led to his accidental death, and in his pursuit of Sophie that led to their mutual, 'accidental' unhappiness.

Though its scale is smaller, *Artist Descending a Staircase* stands up to comparison with *Travesties* surprisingly well. Its arguments about art are less protracted and the connection with the fiercer world of politics is not made. The flashbacks into the artists' distant pasts and the transposing of senility and youthful exuberance are not exploited with the versatility of the later play; there is nothing either to compare with the marvellous travesty of *The Importance of Being Earnest*, the fertile limerick sequences or the pseudo-High Victorian thrusts, parries and ripostes between the various characters. Technically, however, it can be considered superior to *Travesties* since it marshalls its formidable range of materials, arguments and scenes into a masterfully complete unity. Whereas the Lenin episodes in *Travesties* extend the play's boundaries at some expense to its furiously paced, intricately layered fabric, Sophie – who provides the comparable serious kernel in *Artist Descending a Staircase* – is perfectly contained within the structure, mingling and living with the artists and meeting a fate inextricably linked to theirs. No less impressive is the way in which the subjective nature of modern art is turned into an outward-spiralling metaphor which exposes the deceptive, subjective nature of reality. This crucial theme is kept in steady focus behind the action throughout.

Beauchamp's painting of a black railing in the snow is Donner's
painting of a white fence in the dark. Donner's ripe snoring is the
buzzing of an unwelcome fly. As Sophie enters the artists' drawing
room for the first time she hears what she takes to be a ping-pong
game in progress, only to learn that it is an example of Beauchamp's
disembodied gramophone art – in this case a ping-pong game
between Lloyd George and Clara Bow. Her blind innocence
exposes the hollow sophistication of his 'art', but it also emphasises
the capacity for error latent in all human perception – which recoils
with particular vengeance in her case.

*          *          *          *

Stoppard's collaboration with Clive Exton in the BBC series *Eleventh
Hour* produced a play, *The Boundary*, which offers several bases of
comparison with *Artist Descending a Staircase*. As its title indicates,
the idea on which the series was built was to pair two playwrights
and give them a tight deadline for producing together a thirty-minute
television script – scarcely ideal working conditions. *The Boundary*
proved the most fruitful collaboration in so far as it is the only one
which the BBC chose to repeat, but since it has never been
published, the ensuing discussion will be fairly restricted. The play
was first broadcast on 19 July 1975 and was screened again just two
months later. Leading roles were played by Michael Aldridge,
Frank Thornton and Elvi Hale.

*The Boundary*, a story of two middle-aged lexicographers,
Bunyans and Johnson, and the disasters that befall them, has
sufficient of Stoppard's hallmarks for one to suspect, unfairly, that
there are rather less of Exton's. In fact, the work 'was very much a
fifty-fifty collaboration', according to Exton.

> I suggested the lexicographers because I knew it would appeal to
> him and, with reservations, it did. The reservations were that it
> was too Stoppardian.
>
> We quickly found that it was more fruitful for us to work
> separately and we hit upon the method of precise one-hour stints
> at the typewriter – rather like a game of consequences. The result
> could have been a patchwork but I pride myself that the seams
> are invisible.[6]

And so, indeed, they are. At the start of the play, Johnson enters his
study to find it strewn to a depth of several inches with papers, each

one an individual dictionary entry. Their life's work, in other words, is lying in unfiled, chaotic disarray all over the floor – for no apparent reason. Through the French windows (which have one pane unaccountably broken) a cricket match is visible in the distance and a transistor radio, switched on in the room, is delivering the measured strides of a BBC Test Match commentary by John Arlott and Trevor Bailey. Bunyans's arrival initiates a long conversation between the two dismayed men which pivots on two subjects: the problems posed by this mammoth disruption to their work and the whereabouts of Brenda, Johnson's wife, who is the men's assistant and secretary (and who may or may not have had an affair with Bunyans some thirty years before – another subject on which there is some heated debate). When Johnson alights on a foot beneath the papers they then discover what appears to be Brenda's dead body, at which point the conversation switches to a discussion of her faults, growing increasingly harsh as they realise that the dictionary entries which she has classified for them are riddled with errors. They are abruptly cut short, however, by Brenda herself, rising from beneath the mountain of paper to defend herself angrily against these accusations. With equal suddenness she is then felled again, by a cricket ball flying through the window, breaking a second, adjacent pane and abruptly solving the mystery of her initial unconsciousness. This ball, however, is more conclusive than the first, and the arrival of a cricketer, surreptitiously entering through the French windows to retrieve it and thereby sending the papers flying into a second swirling maelstrom, completes the pattern of explanations with delightful neatness.

The characters in *The Boundary* are not developed with any authentic individuality; the bare facts that they are lexicographers and that one is married to Brenda and the other attracted to her define them in all important essentials. It is rather the irrepressibly humorous verbal patterns woven between the characters that have occupied the authors, especially between the men, whose conversation is characterised by a sparkling, practically incessant use of words with double meanings, a plethora of swapped definitions and constant talking at cross-purposes. As a result, it barely advances at all, being continually caught up in ponderous and pedantic word-spinning of one kind or another. Johnson, for instance, declares that they have had a burglary. Bunyans insists not, though 'it could have been a housebreaking if it took place in the hours of daylight'.[7] Even simple questions are misinterpreted in the light of the prevailing orthodoxy:

| *Bunyans:* | Where's Brenda? |
| *Johnson:* | Breeze to Brethren |

and, with Brenda apparently deceased, Bunyans's attempt to turn his hand to typing is disaster-bound from the start:

| *Johnson:* | Dear Christ, is this the pace at which we shall proceed? |
| *Bunyans:* | I am unfamiliar with the organisation of the keyboard. It's . . . eccentrically arranged. |
| *Johnson:* | It has the letters of the alphabet, I presume. |
| *Bunyans:* | But not in order. QWERTYUIOP. |
| *Johnson:* | Oh, dear God in Heaven – a faulty machine! |

The play abounds with such jocular parodies, and puns are equally prominent; the quintessential example follows Johnson's discovery of the suspiciously familiar foot beneath the papers: 'Did Brenda have bunions?' This felicitous, unconscious pun is beautifully worked on two levels – a bemused enquiry in the light of the extraordinary find and a keen *double entendre* on his colleague's name, following in the wake of a barrage of accusations about an incident at Brize Norton on V.E. night, thirty years earlier. At the same time, Bunyans's name is itself a punning reference to the famous lexicographer C. T. Onions, editor of the Shorter Oxford English Dictionary, the Oxford Dictionary of English Etymology and other publications. A single line thus offers a wealth of meanings and illustrates the kind of cerebral artefact from which the play is very largely created.

This is even more evident when Brenda, having recovered consciousness, is finally roused to action. Already, as her aghast husband and colleague check some of her work it has become evident that she suffers from a form of malapropism which has led her to attribute 'correct' definitions to the wrong words, and unwittingly sabotage the entire collective effort:

| *Bunyans:* | This is one of hers. 'Tampon – iron plate with spikes for walking on ice.' I blame you for this, Johnson. |
| *Johnson:* | Well, I couldn't be looking over her shoulder all the time. |

*Bunyans:*    'Crampon – thin griddled cake made of flour, beaten egg and milk.' We're ruined. We'll have to go over everything.[8]

But Brenda's malady does not end there. Following the stunningly theatrical moment of her spectre-like resurrection is a second, no less brilliant effect. For she actually *speaks* in the same vein, her sentences littered with a hilarious misuse of everyday words:

*Brenda:*    Stop! Enough of this virago!
*Bunyans:*    Brenda, you're alive!
*Johnson:*    My sugar dumpling!
*Brenda:*    Don't you sweetshop me, you sea-lion old taxicographer! I returned from a state of inconsequence several minutes ago. Eavesdropping on your conversation as I drifted back from the barn from which no traveller returns, back from the valley of the château of death, I brought myself into the consequence of what I felt that I could hear from you. I heard every syllabub of your farinaceous attack upon my parson.
*Johnson:*    You were dreaming –
*Brenda:*    Liar! Lying hypnotist![9]

This hilarious outburst and the whole character of Brenda is based, quite literally, on a single linguistic principle. As with so many aspects of this play, what distinguishes it is the ingenuity of the execution – the cunning and elaborate verbal skills with which these simple tools are employed.

Throughout, Stoppard's and Exton's ingenuity is meticulously contained within the ruthlessly neat dramatic structure. This pivots on two main questions which are constantly circumnavigated without being answered: how the room came to be in such a chaotic state and, when she is subsequently uncovered, the cause of Brenda's presence beneath all the paper. Neither question – nor the unexpected connection between them – is answered until the very end of the play. When Brenda recovers, for instance, the two men are too concerned with covering up their abusive remarks to enquire how she came to be unconscious in the first place. Similarly, when Johnson first enters, the authors mischievously provide him with a series of visual and verbal clues that might explain the chaos. Finding all the entries beginning with the letter

'T' uppermost in the mêlée of paper, he alights first upon the entry for 'telephone' and, with characteristic vagueness, realises that this may help his predicament. The problem is that, apparently debilitated by the demands of his unusual profession, he has considerable difficulty in recalling which object in his room corresponds with the definition and makes unsuccessful moves to the television and the telescope before alighting on the correct piece of apparatus. (Ironically, the telescope through which he peers at this point is trained on the wicket, while the cricket commentary on the transistor – another 'T' – provides a further pointer.) Naturally enough, Johnson fails to make these obscure connections; unnaturally enough, however, he proceeds to dial Directory Enquiries and ask for the police station, with an example of 'crossed wires' thinking that recalls both the professorial absent-mindedness of George Moore and the erratic memory of Henry Carr. This sequence, which precedes Bunyans's entry, demonstrates with fairly obvious comic strokes the impracticality and muddled wits of the dictionary compiler. But it also serves to introduce all the important strands in the action: the cricket match in the distance, the strange nature of Johnson's work, the predominant comic register derived from it and the fate of his decades of hard work. With the subsequent development, during his first conversation with Bunyans, of the subject of Brenda and her relationship – past, present and alleged – with both men, the controlling themes are all running smoothly along their intricately engineered courses towards Brenda's resurrection, her second demise and a resolution as inventive and dramatic as any of Stoppard's to date. The play then concludes with one more beautiful comic stroke as John Arlott and Trevor Bailey, such bastions of English speech, start to get their lines just as crossed as the other characters:

> *John Arlott:* Well, with any luck and if the weather holds, we should have five superb days' crumpet.
> *Trevor Bailey:* In short, he'll make a good curtain.
> *John Arlott:* Indeed yes, a very good curtain indeed. Six foot seven and a half high, padded out, a fine medium seam.

The dictionary gremlins have finally proved all-pervasive.

*      *      *

While *The Boundary*, as a two-man collaboration, cannot properly be regarded as a constituent part of Stoppard's canon, it nevertheless provides an interesting comparison with several of his other works. Its ferociously neat structure is, like the other pieces we have categorised as 'nuts and bolts' plays, woven around a 'whodunnit' mystery at its core. There is an especial resemblance to *Artist Descending a Staircase* in that suspicions of murder are raised, only to be dispelled at the end of the play by a sudden, wickedly contrived volte-face. *The Boundary*, however, has no controlling idea of any real magnitude; its playfully symmetrical construction is primarily an end in itself, with the abrupt arrival of a second cricket ball completing the action with smooth finality. Comparison with *Artist Descending a Staircase* and *The Real Inspector Hound* also shows the variation in levels of characterisation: unlike these two plays, *The Boundary* is not at all concerned to involve us in the lives of its characters. Stoppard's own comment on this aspect of his work is of great interest:

> I'm no good at character; it doesn't really interest me very much. What, however, mostly saves me is that the *actor* is interested in character, and *is* a character, and even in a play which is as scrupulously inhuman as *The Real Inspector Hound* . . . I wrote the critics, *mea culpa*, without love, and it was an inhuman joke really. The thing is that the first time this play was done Richard Briers played this critic and I was saved or scuppered or whatever by Richard Briers. When he died, people cared about him.[10]

Though this helps to remind us of the slightness of practically all Stoppard's characters, it risks blurring the quite discernible difference between those found in *The Real Inspector Hound* or *Artist Descending a Staircase* on the one hand and *The Boundary* or *After Magritte* on the other, where our emotions are not brought into play at all. For instance. Sophie provides a core of seriousness and irony in *Artist Descending a Staircase* which highlights and defines the careless frivolities of the artists, both young and old, and offers a sharp contrast between passion and humour. Brenda, in comparison, is a wholly comic creation who functions as the hub of the play's puzzle and as the most comically inept choice for a lexicographical assistant. The affair she may or may not have had with Bunyans in Brize Norton gives rise to nothing more than comic speculation and she completes a triangle of characters, like the

Harris family in *After Magritte*, who exist only to fulfil the obligations of the ingenious pattern. This certainly cannot be said of Sophie, or even the critics in *Hound*, and the plays in which they appear have, as a result, a thread of humane concern that mirrors, albeit in miniature, the concerns of the major plays.

As examples of dramatic pieces written, respectively, for radio and television, comparison between *Artist Descending a Staircase* and *The Boundary* is also instructive. *The Boundary*, with its single, rather static location and its heavy reliance on verbal game-playing, is rather static for a television piece, but since its main subject is lexicography, the play's verbal orientation seems both inevitable and appropriate. It also boasts a number of superb visual effects – the foot discovered beneath the mountains of paper, Brenda's sudden resurrection and the silent cricketer's discreet entry to retrieve his ball, with the draught from the French windows fanning all the paper into still further disarray. Yet in some ways the startling theatricality of these moments is lessened by the confines of the small screen and there remains a lingering sense of unease that a dramatic artefact with such highly stylised dialogue and such nominal characterisation should be housed in such a normalising medium.

In contrast, *Artist Descending a Staircase* is an absolute *tour de force* as a play for radio, a medium in which Stoppard had already demonstrated almost unrivalled inventiveness. From the strange, almost eerie opening as the spools of tape play out the evidence of Donner's fate, to Beauchamp's deceptive aural art; from the joke accordionist in the downstairs flat to the powerful evocation of Sophie's blind presence, it is brilliantly in command of all its verbal and aural effects. Stoppard creates in this play an imaginative equivalent of his audaciously theatrical talent, playing with his audience's expectations with consummate pleasure and composure, while at the same time manipulating a series of thoughtful and poignant ideas. It is a cause for regret that he has, in his maturity, written so few plays for this neglected dramatic medium.

# 10 Eyes East

Stoppard's next play, in 1976, was the hilarious Parliamentary farce, *Dirty Linen*, which I have chosen to examine in Chapter 12 with the two later works to which it most relates, *Dogg's Hamlet, Cahoot's Macbeth* (1980) and *On the Razzle* (1981). In the following year, though, two new works appeared which indicated a marked, though not entirely unexpected shift of emphasis within his work. They were *Every Good Boy Deserves Favour*, a work for actors and orchestra jointly composed with André Previn and set in a psychiatric prison in Soviet Russia, and *Professional Foul*, a television play dealing with the harassment of a dissident student by the Czechoslovakian State authorities and dedicated to the imprisoned Czech playwright, Vaclav Havel, whom Stoppard met in June 1977 on his first return visit to the country of his birth. *Every Good Boy* was given its first, single performance on 14 July 1977 by the Royal Shakespeare Company and the London Symphony Orchestra at the Festival Hall as part of the John Player Festival. The orchestra was conducted by Previn, then its Principal Conductor, and the cast, led by Ian McKellen and John Wood, was directed by Trevor Nunn. This version was then issued by R.C.A. records and recorded for television. A scaled-down version for a chamber orchestra of 32 musicians then ran for a season at the Mermaid Theatre from June 1978, with leading rôles played by John Woodvine, Ian McDiarmid and Frank Windsor and with Michael Lankester conducting. *Professional Foul* was first broadcast on BBC 2 in September 1977, starring Peter Barkworth and John Shrapnel and directed by Michael Lindsay-Hogg. It subsequently received a rare accolade, being repeated twice within a year of its first screening, and received the British Television Critics' award as Best Play of the Year, with Peter Barkworth as Television Actor of the Year.

The subjects of the two plays are closely related and seem to have their genesis in the political exploration first provoked by the character of Lenin in *Travesties*. Each appeared during Amnesty

179

International's 'Prisoner of Conscience' Year and indicate a concern for the breaching of human rights that Stoppard first made public in an article written for *The Sunday Times* in 1977, in which he described a visit he had made to Russian dissidents in Moscow.[1] According to his introduction to the published edition of the two plays, that journey 'unlocked' for him the television play which became *Professional Foul*.[2] By this time, however, the earlier play, *Every Good Boy Deserves Favour*, had already been completed. What 'unlocked' this was a meeting in April 1976 with Victor Fainberg, a deported Russian dissident who had spent five years in Soviet prison hospitals after being pronounced insane for denouncing the Warsaw Pact invasion of Czechoslovakia. This meeting, and the article which prompted it – Fainberg's vivid documentation of his experiences in the magazine *Index on Censorship*[3] – affected Stoppard deeply and, although correspondences between the hero of *Every Good Boy Deserves Favour* and Fainberg are not precise, the play takes for its central character a dissident who is similarly imprisoned in the same cell as a genuine lunatic. In consequence, the play's comedy works within a brutally serious situation for the first time in Stoppard's work.

Stoppard's lunatic, Ivanov, is a triangle-player haunted by an imaginary symphony orchestra and incarcerated in the interests of public security. The dissident Alexander is a man who has protested against the incarceration of sane dissidents in psychiatric hospitals and has for that reason been incarcerated in a psychiatric hospital – in the interests of *state* security. By an improbable coincidence, the two men share the same name: Alexander Ivanov. Positioned on a second acting platform (each of the three acting areas is isolated from the other two by the on-stage orchestra) is the office of the hospital doctor in charge of the two men, who acts under instructions from a superior officer, a colonel. On the third platform is Alexander's[4] young son Sacha, in a schoolroom with his teacher. We learn that Alexander was previously held in one of the tougher, 'special' hospitals and has now been transferred to this more lenient civilian hospital as the result of a hunger strike which almost led to his death. Here, however, still refusing to bargain with the authorities and recant his 'slander', he starts a second hunger strike and the authorities retaliate by using Sacha as a emotional lever. When even the boy's appeal to his father's filial instincts fails, the colonel promptly resorts to a trick. Having deliberately ensured that the two men are sharing the same cell, he proceeds to mis-identify them on purpose during an official assessment of the progress of their treatment, satisfying himself, with little difficulty, that Ivanov holds no slanderous views about the hospitalisation of sane men and that Alexander hears no orchestra playing inside his head. He then duly orders both men's release, thereby freeing the lunatic and depriving Alexander of the hard-earned release – or the martyrdom – which his defiant hunger strike might have secured.

The various stages in the genesis of *Every Good Boy Deserves Favour* are wittily outlined by Stoppard in his introduction. First came an invitation from André Previn (a close friend) to create in conjunction with him a play for actors and a symphony orchestra.

> Mr Previn and I agreed early on that we would try to go beyond a mere recitation for the concert platform, and also that we were not writing a piece for singers. In short, it was going to be a real play, to be performed in conjunction with, and bound up with, a symphony orchestra. As far as we knew, nobody had tried to do anything like that before. (p. 5)

In other words, Stoppard's concern was to eschew any suggestion of opera or stage musical and to keep his actors functioning as actors throughout, while at the same time ensuring that the orchestra was more than a lavish attendant spectre. The orchestra is thus established, at least at first, as a figment of Ivanov's crazed imagination. He conducts it (and plays the triangle in it), but no-one else within the play can hear a single note. Since almost *any* music might have fulfilled this merely dramatic rôle, however, Previn sought to extend it in other ways by providing commentary, rich in pastiche, on the dramatic action, rather in the manner of a film score, highlighting particularly significant moments and linking scenes together. Unfortunately, though, the relationship of his music to the dramatic content seemed, in performance, to be generally slight; only the short, plaintive refrain sung by young Sacha (the only piece of song in the play) created any strong sense of unity between the music and the stage action and the intended 'commentary' rôle of the music often had the opposite effect of diffusing the dramatic force.

*Every Good Boy Deserves Favour* is not the first Stoppard play featuring two prisoners in a cell. In an unpublished early play, *The Gamblers*, performed by students in Bristol in 1965, he brings together two condemned men in a cruel volte-face situation where one is to die and the other to be reprieved. (In a wry comment some years later, Stoppard quoted an agent who had sadly remarked, on seeing the script, that *all* young writers seemed to be writing first plays about people in condemned cells![5]) The novel feature of *Every Good Boy Deserves Favour* lies in the uneasy combination of a comic madman with an injured innocent, which makes genuine conversation of any kind practically impossible:

| | |
|---|---|
| *Ivanov:* | What is your instrument? |
| *Alexander:* | I do not play an instrument. |
| *Ivanov:* | Percussion? Strings? Brass? |
| *Alexander:* | No. |
| *Ivanov:* | Reed? Keyboard? |
| *Alexander:* | I'm afraid not. |
| *Ivanov:* | I'm amazed. Not keyboard. Wait a minute –flute? |
| *Alexander:* | No. Really. |
| *Ivanov:* | Extraordinary. Give me a clue. If I beat you to a pulp would you try to protect your face or your hands? Which would be the more serious – if you couldn't sit down for a week or couldn't stand up? I'm trying to narrow it down, you see. Can I take it you don't stick this instrument up your arse in a kneeling position? |
| *Alexander:* | I do not play an instrument.   (p. 17) |

Stoppard's plays are full of fraught conversations between characters on oblique tacks, variously occasioned by lapses of attention, accidental misunderstandings or sheer stupidity. On this occasion, an unusual kind of technical problem is created, since the division between comedy and seriousness is so clearly delineated by the different characters. The crucial question is whether within this grim setting, the inhumanity of which Stoppard is clearly concerned to condemn, the comedy alleviates the indictment or, like Lear's Fool, intensifies it. When George Riley 'interrogates' the innocent Brown, a complete stranger in his local pub, Brown functions merely as a stooge in a riotously funny episode. In *Travesties*, in contrast, Stoppard evades creating a similar problem with Lenin, his sole serious creation, by keeping him largely separate from the other characters. In *Every Good Boy Deserves Favour* he sometimes gives the impression of trying to steer both these courses. On the one hand, as the quotation above demonstrates, Stoppard has to seek

out the comic potential of the direct encounters between Alexander
and Ivanov if the lunatic is to be a plausible comic creation. On the
other, in order to represent Alexander as a man of dignity and
courage, he needs to isolate him from Ivanov as much as possible; in
the spotlit corner of the cell, for example, with Ivanov all but
forgotten, he delivers an impassive description of his own history,
labelled in the stage directions as 'a sort of solo':

> they arrested a couple of writers, A and B, who had published
> some stories abroad under different names. Under their own
> names they got five years' and seven years' hard labour. I thought
> this was most peculiar. My friend, C,[6] demonstrated against the
> arrest of A and B. I told him he was crazy to do it, and they put
> him back into the mental hospital. D was a man who wrote to
> various people about the trial of A and B and held meetings with
> his friends E, F, G and H, who were all arrested.   (p. 23)

In this vein, without any form of interruptions from the lunatic, the
speech gravely continues to detail the multiplying arrests and
hospitalisations until it culminates in Alexander's own.

The encounters between Ivanov and Alexander in their small,
shared cell are thus dominated by one character or the other,
depending on Stoppard's desire for a 'comic' or 'serious' interlude,
and it is their consultations with the doctor which provide a more
important means of developing their characters. While his approach towards both 'patients' remains broadly consistent, the
enormous difference between their plights ensures that it is seen in a
very different light in each context. With Ivanov, for instance, the
fact that the doctor is a keen violinist proves a considerable
hindrance in his attempts at a cure:

Doctor:   Now look, *there is no orchestra*. We cannot make progress
          until we agree that there is no orchestra.
Ivanov:   Or until we agree that there is.
Doctor:   *(slapping his violin, which is on the table)* But there is no
          orchestra. *(Ivanov glances at the violin.)* I have an
          orchestra, but you do not.
Ivanov:   Does that seem reasonable to you?
Doctor:   It just happens to be so. I play in an orchestra
          occasionally. It is my hobby. It is a real orchestra.
          Yours is not. I am a doctor. You are a patient. If I tell
          you you do not have an orchestra, it follows that you

do not have an orchestra. If you tell me you have an orchestra, it follows that you do not have an orchestra. Or rather, it does not follow that you do have an orchestra.  (p. 21)

This exchange is a beautifully contrived piece of comedy, full of double-dealing logic but in fact making sense. When addressed to Alexander, however, similarly circuitous logic has a very different effect:

*Doctor:*  The idea that all the people locked up in mental hospitals are sane while the people walking about outside are all mad is merely a literary conceit, put about by people who should be locked up. I assure you there's not much in it. Taken as a whole, the sane are out there and the sick are in here. For example, *you* are here because you have delusions that sane people are put in mental hospitals.

*Alexander:*  But I *am* in a mental hospital.

*Doctor:*  That's what I said. If you're not prepared to discuss your case rationally, we're going to go round in circles.  (p. 27)

This neatly brings out the full weight of the oppressive system in which the dissident is caught. Alexander's fate rests solely in his own hands: the circle can only be broken if he acknowledges his so-called schizophrenic delusions before the Examining Commission which is to meet shortly. Such a recantation would, of course, involve him in complicity with his oppressors, would authenticate their methods of 'treatment' and, above all, would deny his earlier victory in the 'special' hospital. So in the face of this doctor who dares to call his defiance 'stupidity', he hurls the details of his previous barbaric treatment: being locked in a barred cell, beaten and humiliated by male nurses, injected with a variety of debilitating drugs, bound with wet canvas which dried and tightened, leaving him unconscious. Finally he went on hunger strike:

And when they saw I intended to die they lost their nerve. And now you think I'm going to crawl out of here, thanking them for curing me of my delusions? Oh no. They lost. And they will have to see that it is so.  (p. 29)

Determined to continue to demonstrate the unconquerability of his spirit, Alexander then embarks on a second hunger strike.

There is, nonetheless, one sensitive area which the doctor, with a veiled threat, can quickly uncover:

> What about your son? He is turning into a delinquent.
> (*Doctor plucks the violin EGBDF*)
> He's a good boy. He deserves a father. (p. 29)

If reason cannot persuade Alexander, then there are other weapons available, as this pun on the musical *aide de memoire* of the title so clearly demonstrates. The state can fail to break his spirit, but his ten-year-old son, who has never known his mother, and whose vulnerability Alexander feels so strongly, is the innocent victim of this struggle. When duly brought in to persuade his father to break his hunger strike, Sacha is unable to understand that he is impelling him towards what is, on Alexander's terms, ignominious defeat. The son's argument thus becomes the state's:

> Sacha: Tell them lies. Tell them they've cured you. Tell them you're grateful.
> Alexander: How can that be right?
> Sacha: If they're wicked how can it be wrong?
> Alexander: It helps them to go on being wicked. It helps people to think that perhaps they're not so wicked after all.
> Sacha: It doesn't matter. I want you to come home.
> Alexander: And what about all the other fathers? And mothers?
> Sacha (shouts): It's wicked to let yourself die! (p. 35)

The child's plangent appeal is moving for the simplicity and directness of its emotion. But in the repressive and divisive system under which they live, father is set against son, unable to convey to the boy the reason for his apparent determination to starve himself to death. In its widest sense the obligation he feels towards his conscience is shown to be a concern for the silent suffering of all his innocent fellow countrymen and women. For like John Proctor in Miller's *The Crucible*, he sees in 'confession' the twin implications of self-defeat and the betrayal of his comrades, known and unknown, in the common fight against injustice and tyranny. At the heart of Proctor's awful heroic determination to die on the gallows is a victory that his wife's iron faith can recognise and lean on for her own support: 'He have his goodness now. God forbid I take it from

him!'⁷ Should Alexander die, there will be no such solace for Sacha:
either father or son must be the loser. On this occasion, it is the
father who loses, at the hands of the underhand colonel who ensures
that Alexander's release is not obtained on his own terms. What
Sacha sees as a victory is thus for his father the heaviest of defeats.

Alexander's dilemma – between principle and instinct, between
the natural rights of all individuals and the specific rights of his own
son – is the fulcrum of the entire play and its success is very largely
dependent on the power with which that dilemma is evoked,
intellectually and emotionally, for the audience. Theatrically, the
sense of Sacha's powerlessness is amplified by the way in which he is
isolated in a separate acting area, representing the schoolroom
where he is bullied by the doctrinaire teacher for his sullen refusal to
play the triangle in the school orchestra and constantly harassed by
her curt reminders of his father's rebelliousness. (Stoppard directs
that she be female, presumably to remind us of the mother whom
Sacha has never known.)

| | |
|---|---|
| *Sacha:* | Is this what they make Papa do? |
| *Teacher:* | Yes. They make him copy, 'I am a member of an orchestra and we must play together.' |
| *Sacha:* | How many times? |
| *Teacher:* | A million. |
| *Sacha:* | A million? (*Cries.*) Papa! |
| *Alexander:* | (*Cries.*) Sacha! |
| (*This cry is Alexander shouting in his sleep at the other end of the stage.*) | |
| *Sacha:* | Papa! |
| *Teacher:* | Hush! |
| *Alexander:* | Sacha!   (p. 20) |

By transposing Alexander's fretful dreams with Sacha's schoolroom
tribulations, Stoppard extracts a poignant, if rather heavily sentimental, force from the exchange, heightening the audience's
awareness of the violent contrary pulls which Alexander is
experiencing.

Sacha's revolt from the school orchestra extends the complex use
of this image which Stoppard exploits to draw the various strands
of his play more firmly together. The orchestra has two quite
distinct identities, in fact: first, it represents Ivanov's phantom
orchestra, and, secondly, as emerges in this scene between Sacha
and his teacher, it figures as both a symbol and a physical

representation of the all-powerful Soviet State itself. The longer the play goes on, the more this second rôle eclipses the first. In the opening sequence, the stage directions require the orchestra to tune-up, then, strangely, to *mime* tuning-up; Ivanov then proceeds to play his triangle while the orchestra mimes a performance:

> *Alexander watches this – a man watching another man occasionally hitting a triangle . . .*

> *Then, very quietly, we begin to hear what Ivanov can hear, i.e. the orchestra becomes audible. So now his striking of the triangle begins to fit into the context which makes sense of it. The music builds slowly, gently. And then on a single cue the platform light level jumps up, with the conductor in position and the orchestra playing fully and loudly.* (pp. 15–16)

The audience, deliberately disorientated, is thus put on its guard from the outset, mistrusting both Ivanov's sanity and the rôle which the orchestra is supposedly filling – in each case with some justification. Not only is Ivanov subsequently shown to be insane, but the orchestra's rôle as a manifestation of that insanity is called into question – a process precipitated by the doctor's first entry at the start of the fourth scene. For, in one of Stoppard's enigmatic gearshifts from one plane of theatrical reference to another, he emerges, violin in hand, from the orchestra itself, thereby offering the first hint that the orchestra's rôle may be rather wider. And as the nature of the doctor's rôle becomes clearer and as the orchestra analogy is developed by Sacha and his teacher, the symbolic rôle of the players, and their deliberate positioning at the centre of the stage, becomes ever more plain. With this runs a mounting sense of their sinister control over the action, culminating in the vivid final image of the play as Sacha and Alexander pass up a centre aisle through the midst of the orchestral ranks and out into the darkness beyond, bravely confirmed as outcasts. Despite Alexander's defeat, their separateness and courage are given sharp dramatic emphasis by the surrounding sea of players, now containing not only the doctor but also the teacher and Ivanov – an image with an underlying sense of menace far more tangible than in any of Alexander's cell scenes with the amiably harmless lunatic. For these characters all belong to the world of state conformism which the orchestra now symbolises, and to which Alexander and his son steadfastly refuse to belong. The 'Every Good Boy Deserves Favour' motif, as one of the pillars of musical notation, thus carries another ominous implication: it comes to stand for the rules by which the establishment, the state-orchestra, insists on its right to call each and every tune.

There are, however, two possible objections – one figurative, one practical – to Stoppard's use of the orchestra in this way. The first, and most obvious, is that the beauty of large-scale musical works can *only* be achieved by highly disciplined ensemble work; as a metaphor for the collectivist state, it is decidedly flawed. The second objection is perhaps more serious: it is the uneasiness with which the orchestra apparently exists on two entirely distinct theatrical planes, one phantasmagorical, the other apparently real. The clarity that informs Stoppard's re-ordering of levels of reality in other plays is not in evidence here; there remains the suspicion that Ivanov's rôle, however cunningly contrived, imposes on the orchestra a para-doxical status with logical implications which cannot be neatly resolved. At the same time, one must recognise the paradox that informs the whole play. The doctor's insistence that only *his* orchestra is real, while literally true, is demonstrably false within the dramatic context which frames it – that context being one in which sane men are imprisoned in mental asylums and insane men are set free. The ambiguous function of the orchestra has therefore to be seen in the light of a dramatic situation where the doctor and, in macrocosm, the state he serves are dictating what is real and what is unreal, what is social and what is anti-social, what is sane and what is insane with an intolerant, self-defeating presumption that is, literally, nonsense. The values that hold for Ivanov's case will clearly not hold for Alexander's; yet it is these same distorted standards of judgement which *do* prevail:

*Alexander:*   I have no symptoms, I have opinions.
*Doctor:*      Your opinions are your symptoms. Your disease is dissent. Your kind of schizophrenia does not presup-pose changes of personality noticeable to others. I might compare your case to that of Pyotr Grigorenko of whom it has been stated by our leading psychia-trists at the Serbsky Institute that his outwardly well-adjusted behaviour and formally coherent utter-ances were indicative of a pathological development of the personality. Are you getting the message? (pp. 30–1)

The doctor may only be a pawn in comparison with the colonel who engineers Alexander's ignominious release, but he nevertheless conforms subserviently to the prevailing ideology; psychiatric science, like any other field, can be perverted to fit a corruptly predetermined scheme. His rightful place is precisely where Stoppard places him, among the lowliest ranks of the violins where, though out of the spotlight, he actively contributes to the orchestra's music.

*Every Good Boy Deserves Favour* must finally be regarded as a less than satisfactory piece of dramatic construction by Stoppard's usual, exceptionally high standards. His main interest so clearly hinges on Alexander's plight and dilemma that Ivanov and the largely disappointing level of the humour which surrounds him suffers in proportion, though there is some felicitous wordplay, especially early in the play, and some witty and dext manipulation of logic, chiefly by the doctor. At times, though, the play seems to split neatly into two halves, with Ivanov, his imaginary orchestra and the comedy on the one side, and Alexander, Sacha and the state-orchestra on the other. In part this is due to the failure of the orchestra image to unify these two main strands of the play; in part, too, it is the result of Stoppard's choice for his hero of a deeply serious man without a single funny line in the entire play. The strongest scenes are those in which the play positively blazes with Alexander's presence, especially the slow-paced descriptions of his past torture and of the constant flow of his friends into prisons and mental hospitals; also, despite sentimental tendencies, those in which Stoppard exploits the emotional bond between father and son. The weakest parts are those between characters conceived in incompatible moulds, such as those between Ivanov and Alexander or the single scene in which Ivanov confronts Sacha, who has come to visit his father. Though there is, as always, a fertile technical and linguistic resourcefulness throughout, the play has more power as a moral statement than as an example of Stoppard's dramatic brilliance.

*     *     *

Stoppard has subtitled *Professional Foul* 'A Play for Television', but it may be regarded more usefully as a television *film*, for it differs very sharply from the more or less domestic settings of his earlier work in the medium.[8] Travelling through its sixteen linear scenes we move from the inside of an aeroplane, to a hotel foyer, bedroom and dining-room, to an apartment in Prague, a dark street by the hotel and a conference lecture-theatre, before a final scene on a second aeroplane. Like *Jumpers*, it takes as its hero a middle-aged professor of ethics, Professor Anderson, a Cambridge don who has been invited to attend an international philosophy colloquium in Prague and he provides the almost exclusive dramatic focus, as successive scenes chronicle his visit. On the day of his arrival, he is called on in his hotel room by a former student, Pavel Hollar, a Czechoslovakian who, while working as a cleaner, has managed to complete a doctoral thesis in his free time. Because the thesis would be regarded as deeply subversive by the state authorities, arguing as it does for the natural rights of the individual over the social rules imposed on the citizen, Hollar asks that Anderson pass it to a friend in England in order to have it translated and published. The professor refuses to involve himself in a political issue but agrees to keep the thesis temporarily in case Hollar, who is being closely watched, is arrested with it in his possession. He then attempts to return it the following day, only to discover that Hollar has been arrested on currency smuggling charges and that secret policemen are conducting an exhaustive search of his flat, to his wife's anger and distress. Though Anderson falls under some suspicion, he manages to keep the existence of the thesis undiscovered. On the following day at the colloquium, appalled by what has happened, he then uses it as the basis for his own address, substituting this for his pre-arranged paper and incurring as a result the severe displeasure of the Czech chairman, who surreptitiously instructs the fire alarm to be set off and thereby brings the lecture to an abrupt halt. Finally, Anderson foils an exhaustive customs search at the airport by concealing Hollar's thesis in the briefcase of one of his unsuspecting – and unsuspected – colleagues until they are safely on the plane home.

Intertwined with Anderson's visit to the colloquium and his unexpected involvement with Hollar and the secret police, are a number of other themes which Stoppard weaves into a superstructure as rich and dense as any he has yet created. The first (and most unlikely sounding) of these themes is football; Anderson's chief motive for accepting the invitation to the colloquium is the opportunity it affords him to slip away for a World Cup qualifying match between Czechoslovakia and England. As a result of his detention at Hollar's flat he misses the game, but discovers on his return that an English sports reporter is telephoning his match report from the adjacent hotel room:

There'll be Czechs bouncing in the streets of Prague tonight as bankruptcy stares English football in the face, stop, new par . . .

Make no mistake, comma, the four-goal credit which these slick Slovaks netted here this afternoon will keep them in the black through the second leg of the World Cup Eliminator at Wembley next month, stop . . .

You can bank on it.   (pp. 73–4)

Stoppard seizes the opportunity for parody with typical relish to construct from the ambiguity of 'Czechs' a beautiful satire of soccer journalism at its most crass and clichéd.[9] At the same time he advances a different theme which carries considerable weight, namely the conscious directing, or mis-directing, of language to various intellectual, journalistic, academic or humorous ends. In general, his concern is to create a broad-based contrast throughout the film between simplicity and sophistication.

This contrast is most clearly illustrated in the philosophical forum and the colloquium is launched in suitably obtuse fashion with a hilarious contribution from an American professor possessing the entirely appropriate name of Stone, whose subject is the confusion which can arise in ordinary language from the ambiguity of such common words as 'well':

I ask you to imagine a competition when what is being judged is table manners. John enters this competition and afterwards Mary says, 'Well, you certainly ate well!' Now Mary seems to be saying that John ate *skilfully – with refinement*. And again, I ask you to imagine a competition where the amount of food eaten is taken into account along with refinement of table manners. *Now* Mary says to John, 'Well, you didn't eat very well, but at least you ate well' . . .

clearly there is no way to tell whether Mary means that John ate abundantly but clumsily, or that John ate frugally but elegantly. Here we have a genuine ambiguity. To restate Mary's sentence in a logical language we would have to ask her what she meant. (p. 62)

Stone's intention is to plot the frontiers of a logical language and Stoppard ridicules the notion with evident glee: Stone's last sentence beautifully and comprehensively deflates the portentous content of all that has preceded it, and the satire is lovingly multiplied by the introduction of three simultaneous translators who become increasingly lost in the professor's merciless coils of deliberate ambiguity. As in *Jumpers*, Stoppard's verbal skills feast on the everyday language of philosophical discourse: its cautious step-by-step logic, the regular use of improbable or extreme examples, the refusal simply to accept what may seem perfectly obvious – all provide boundless opportunities for parody, just like, at the other end of the spectrum, the snappy, metaphor-sodden journalese of sports reporters. In both cases, the task of imitation is so inviting precisely because the normal flow of speech is so strictly suborned to pre-ordained sets of rules which can be as capable of obscuring the truth as of revealing it. Hence our sense of delight in the hotel dining room that evening when McKendrick, the second British speaker at the colloquium, leans over to tell his American colleague, who has a hearty appetite but awful table manners: 'You eat well but you're a lousy eater.' (p. 76) This is emphatically a visual joke, depending for its effect on the audience *previously* digesting the sight of the large American speaking 'with his mouth full of bread, cake, coffee, etc., and being generally messy about it' (p. 77). Like so many of Stoppard's best lines, it picks up an earlier, half-forgotten thread and caps it with malicious delight.

Stone's address raises an appropriate scepticism about the value of the colloquium as a whole by exposing the grand obviousness beneath the pompous sophistry, but the subsequent contributions of McKendrick and Anderson are of much greater importance. The contrast between their characters is revealing; where the Cambridge professor is a quiet, well-mannered and rather ethereal kind of intellectual, his colleague from Stoke is an altogether 'rougher kind of diamond' (p. 43), given lines such as 'What do you think the chances are of meeting a free and easy woman in a place like this?' (p. 76) and getting (in one scene) uproariously drunk. These differences are reflected in their lines of argument in the colloquium, through which Stoppard uncovers the 'play of ideas' that is the kernel of *Professional Foul*. Since Anderson's abortive attempt to get to the football international coincides with McKendrick's address, Stoppard frees himself from the obligation to present three lengthy solo performances from the conference lectern. Instead, the hotel dinner table provides both Anderson and the audience with a chance to catch up on McKendrick's contribution as he outlines to Anderson and a third British colleague, Chetwyn, his 'admittedly audacious' application of what he calls the 'catastrophe theory', and his firm belief in the relativity of lines of 'moral' and 'immoral' behaviour:

*McKendrick:* They're the edges of the same plane – it's in three dimensions, you see – and if you twist the plane in a certain way, into what we call the catastrophe curve, you get a model of the sort of behaviour we find in the real world. There's a point – the catastrophe point – where your progress along one line of behaviour jumps you into the opposite line; the principle reverses itself at the point where a rational man would abandon it.

*Chetwyn:* Then it's not a principle.

*McKendrick:* There aren't any principles in your sense. There are only a lot of principled people trying to behave as if there were.

*Anderson:* That's the same thing, surely.

*McKendrick:* You're a worse case than Chetwyn and his primitive Greeks. At least he has the excuse of *believing* in goodness and beauty. You know they're fictions but you're so hung up on them you want to treat them as if they were God-given absolutes.

*Anderson:* I don't see how else they would have any practical value –

*McKendrick:* So you end up using a moral principle as your excuse for acting against a moral interest. It's a sort of funk – (*Anderson, under pressure, slams his cup back on to its saucer in a very uncharacteristic and surprising way. His anger is all the more alarming for that.*)

*Anderson:* You make your points altogether too easily, McKendrick. What need have you of moral courage when your principles reverse themselves so conveniently? (p. 78)

This lengthy exchange needs quoting in full because it contains the essence of the philosophical or moral argument on which the action turns; for it is McKendrick's theory, despite Anderson's sharp reaction to it, which holds the key to the professor's dilemma whether to help his former student or not.

Anderson's belief in the intractability of moral principles is at least one of the causes of his initial reluctance to help Hollar. When the young Czech outlines his request, the professor's response is that of the perfect gentleman:

> *Anderson:*  Oh, Hollar . . . now, you know, really, I'm a guest of the government here.
> *Hollar:*  They would not search you.
> *Anderson:*  That's not the point. I'm sorry . . . I mean it would be bad manners, wouldn't it?
> *Hollar:*  Bad manners?
> *Anderson:*  I know it sounds rather lame. But ethics and manners are interestingly related. The history of human calumny is largely a series of breaches of good manners . . . Perhaps if I said correct behaviour it wouldn't sound so ridiculous. You do see what I mean. I am sorry.  (p. 54)

As soon as he realises the political implications of Hollar's thesis, Anderson's reaction is to hedge the responsibility which is being thrust upon him. As he does so, the gulf between the professor's apologetic and evasive theorising and his ex-student's thesis, born of bitter experience, becomes increasingly apparent:

> *Hollar:*  The ethics of the State must be judged against the fundamental ethic of the individual. The human being, not the citizen. I conclude there is an obligation, a human responsibility, to fight against the State correctness. Unfortunately, that is not a safe conclusion.
> *Anderson:*  Quite. The difficulty arises when one asks oneself how the *individual* ethic can have any meaning by itself. Where does *that* come from? In what sense is it intelligible, for example, to say that a man has certain inherent, individual rights? . . .
>
> *Hollar:*  I mean, it is not safe for me.  (p. 55)

Anderson does not connect with Hollar's earnestness, only with the argument he advances, discussing it with the polite equanimity of a cocktail party conversation. His habitual language leads him in one direction; Hollar's fervent literalism points in another. Before long, however, Anderson has begun to answer the kind of questions he poses with such quizzical detachment at this stage.

The professor's complacency is first shaken by the events in Hollar's apartment when he goes to return the thesis. Five men are conducting a meticulous search in eerie silence, scrutinising papers, drawers, the spines of books, the insides of a radio set, even the fluff from a carpet sweeper. He is detained for some time, feeling increasingly flustered by the insidious and oppressive atmosphere in the flat and by Mrs Hollar's evident distress, until a sixth man who speaks English arrives:

*Man 6:* So you came to Czechoslovakia to go to the football match, Professor?

*Anderson:* Certainly not. Well, the afternoon of the Colloquium was devoted to – well, it was not a condition of my invitation that I should attend all the sessions. I was invited to *speak*, not to listen. I am speaking tomorrow morning.

*Man 6:* Why should I know Hollar visited you at the hotel?

*Anderson:* He told me he was often followed.

*Man 6:* Well, when a man is known to be engaged in meeting foreigners to buy currency –

*Anderson:* I don't believe any of that – he was being harassed because of his letter to Husak –

*Man 6:* A letter to President Husak? What sort of letter?

*Anderson (Flustered):* Your people knew about it –

*Man 6:* It is not a crime to write to the President –

*Anderson:* No doubt that depends on what is written.

*Man 6:* You mean he wrote some kind of slander?

*Anderson (Heatedly):* I insist on leaving now.   (p. 71)

Remembering the brutal treatment which Alexander suffers for his 'slander' in *Every Good Boy Deserves Favour*, it comes as no surprise when one of the searchers claims to have found a parcel of dollars wrapped in a bundle of old newspapers under the floorboards, justifying the trumped-up charges. Appalled and scared by the situation, Anderson acts with commendable wile in managing to keep the thesis hidden in his briefcase, but is sufficiently shaken to reject the chance of seeing what remains of the football match and returns instead to the refuge of his hotel room.

The unnerving events of the afternoon are the basic cause of Anderson's uncharacteristic fierceness when McKendrick outlines his catastrophe theory that same evening. For in weighing his obligations to his generous hosts against those to the oppressed Hollar, Anderson is in the throes of a moral dilemma which makes McKendrick's detached theorising seem sterile in comparison. Events have roughly jettisoned him from the comfortable and familiar confines of the world of theory into the fierce, testing world of practice, where, ironically, McKendrick's premises, which he so opposes in theory, help to determine his subsequent behaviour. In his predicament, he senses that the plane may be tilting to the point at which the line of supposedly 'immoral' action replaces the 'moral' line. After his outburst, he is chastened:

> I'm sorry . . . you're right up to a point. There would be no moral dilemmas if moral principles worked in straight lines and never crossed each other. One meets test situations which have troubled much cleverer men than us.  (p. 79)

Unknown to his colleagues, Anderson is, of course, in such a 'test situation' himself.

As in *Every Good Boy Deserves Favour*, this central dilemma has emotional as well as intellectual roots, although they here point towards the same course of action. The emotional leverage on the hero is again provided by a young boy, Hollar's son, also named Sacha and also aged ten. Unlike his namesake in *Every Good Boy Deserves Favour*, he seems old enough to avoid inducing a cloying sentimental reaction, though young enough to be less than able to cope with the situation into which his father's abrupt arrest has plunged him. Together with his mother, whose stoical distress Anderson has already witnessed in the flat, he comes to find Anderson in the hotel that same evening; in a nearby park he then tries to explain the position in broken English:

| | |
|---|---|
| *Anderson:* | Did he return home last night? |
| *Sacha:* | No. He is arrested outside hotel. Then in the night they come to make search. |
| *Anderson:* | Had they been there all night? |
| *Sacha:* | At eleven o'clock they are coming. They search twenty hours. |
| *Anderson:* | My God. |

| | |
|---|---|
| *Sacha:* | In morning I go to Bartolomesskaya to be seeing him. |
| *Mrs Hollar:* | *(Explains)* Police. |
| *Sacha:* | But I am not seeing him. They say go home. (p. 80) |

The boy's ungrammatical but clear message is all the more forceful within the context of a work where other characters are constantly scrutinising and playing with language for their own ends – the soccer journalists, Professor Stone, Anderson himself on several occasions and the whole philosophical fraternity. Here, without any kind of false sophistication and without resorting to too obviously sentimental devices, Stoppard creates one of the plainest, most direct and most moving encounters in any of his plays, rivalled only perhaps by the Sophie scenes in *Artist Descending a Staircase* and moments in *The Real Thing*. Anderson's sympathetic response to the child's plight, and his mother's, confirms how far his stance has shifted as, with a new bravery, he rejects the child's offer to pass the thesis to another loyal friend at the congress, convinced that he himself is capable of doing more. The scene ends with the boy sobbing at the contemplation of his father's fate, on a note of sobriety and poignancy comparable to the ending of *Every Good Boy Deserves Favour*, but made infinitely more powerful by the keen sense of felt reality invested in it by Stoppard's prevalent naturalism. Here, too, the mood is not an end in itself and is soon dispelled by the urgency and determination with which Anderson is newly charged. 'Mrs Hollar,' he finally declares, 'I will do everything I can for him.' (p. 82)

.Summoning the kind of moral courage which the philosophers have blithely discussed over dinner, and borrowing a typewriter from the journalist next door, Anderson works into the night on an entirely new paper, based on Hollar's argument. At the colloquium session on the following morning, he drops his pre-announced title, 'Ethical Facts and Ethical Fictions', and launches into a paper discussing 'the conflict between the rights of individuals and the rights of the community' (p. 87), to the dismay of the Czech officials. Before releasing the fire alarm to quench this revolt, the chairman does his best to appeal to Anderson's gentility:

| | |
|---|---|
| *Chairman:* | Pardon me – Professor – this is not your paper – |
| *Anderson:* | In what sense? I am indisputably giving it. |

| Chairman: | But it is not the paper you were invited to give. |
| Anderson: | I wasn't invited to give a particular paper. |
| Chairman: | You offered one. |
| Anderson: | That's true. |
| Chairman: | But this is not it. |
| Anderson: | No. I changed my mind. |
| Chairman: | But it is irregular. |
| Anderson: | I didn't realize it mattered. |
| Chairman: | It is a discourtesy. |
| Anderson (*Taken aback*): | Bad manners? I am sorry. (pp. 87–8) |

The echo of Anderson's own words to Hollar at their first meeting completes the transformation of the professor's attitudes. Though he is subsequently cut off by the fire-bell and the room is cleared, Anderson's point is clearly made and he further ensures that Hollar's own message is not lost by concealing the thesis in McKendrick's briefcase. By his twin revolt, Anderson thus supports McKendrick's catastrophe theory to which his initial reaction was so hostile; his own behaviour has switched to the nominally 'immoral' plane. It is, indeed, with something suspiciously close to smugness that he confesses his subterfuge to his outraged colleague:

| Anderson: | I'm afraid I reversed a principle. |
| McKendrick: | You utter bastard. |
| Anderson: | I thought you would approve. |
| McKendrick: | Don't get clever with me. Jesus! It's not quite playing the game is it? (p. 93) |

Despite his colleague's understandable indignation, Anderson has played by McKendrick's rules, and won.

This final exchange between the two men as the aeroplane taxis on the runway before taking them home, is quite deliberately phrased in terms of game-playing. For throughout the play Stoppard has pursued a witty and clever analogy between game-playing and the professor's involvement with Hollar and his family. Anderson's decision to accept the invitation to the colloquium because it coincides with the football international is not exactly 'playing the game'. Nor is it the first occasion on which he has trespassed on foreign hospitality of this kind, as he reveals in the hotel lift when, by coincidence, he meets two members of the English team before the match:

Anderson:     I see from yesterday's paper that they've brought in
              Jirasek for Vladislav.
Broadbent:    Yes, that's right. Six foot eight, they say.
Anderson:     He's not very good in the air unless he's got lots of
              space.
Broadbent (*Looks at him curiously*): You've seen him, have you?
Anderson:     I've seen him twice. In the UFA Cup a few seasons
              ago . . . I happened to be in Berlin for the Hegel
              Colloquium, er, bunfight. And then last season I
              was in Bratislava to receive an honorary degree.
              (pp. 58–9)

In a minor but revealing way, this indicates the manner in which
Anderson is prepared to bend the rules of behaviour expected of him
when it suits his passion for football. He is also livid when the police
search of Hollar's flat looks like delaying his arrival at the match –
until he has taken full stock of the situation.

What happens in Hollar's flat is, as we have seen, the turning
point of the play. While the security men conduct their search, the
football international is being relayed over a radio and the spirit in
which this is played is very significant. When the first of
Czechoslovakia's four goals comes from a penalty after Broadbent
has crudely brought down one of the Czech forwards, Man 6
interrupts his questioning of Anderson to express his disgust at the
English tactics:

Man 6:        Broadbent – a bad tackle when Deml had a certain
              goal . . . a what you call it? – a necessary foul.
Anderson:     A professional foul. (p. 71)

A professional foul is, of course, *not* necessary and runs quite against
the spirit in which sport should be played. But, moments later, the
Czechs commit their own professional foul on Hollar, by pretending
to uncover the foreign currency in order to lay false charges against
him. Later that night, Anderson discovers McKendrick unwisely,
and somewhat drunkenly, preaching ethics to Broadbent whose
response is to lay him out with his fist. The philosopher has,
however, touched on a very important point. In pillorying what he
calls the 'yob ethics' of football – with throw-ins consistently claimed
by both sides, with 'crowing self-congratulation' following every
goal and with the professional foul becoming an accepted part of the
game – he is demonstrating how fair and unfair, moral and immoral

can be two faces of the same game. In other words, football is merely a further proof of the validity – or the moral rottenness, depending on one's point of view – of McKendrick's precious catastrophe theory. He appears to be oblivious of this inconsistency and he could not be more wrong with a friendly side-swipe aimed at his colleague:

> Anderson is one of life's cricketers. Clap, clap. (*He claps in a well-bred sort of way and puts on a well-bred voice.*) Well played, sir. Bad luck, old chap.    (p. 85)

For Anderson himself becomes guilty of a similar professional foul by changing the topic of his colloquium paper and smuggling Hollar's thesis through the customs. The penalty against Broadbent sets the England football team firmly on the road to defeat, but Anderson's foul is a far greater gamble which not only succeeds but at the same time repays the foul play of the Czech authorities. Anderson's 'tactics' are finally and most conclusively vindicated by the fate of Chetwyn, the shadowy third member of the trio of British philosophers, after customs officials discover that he has hidden letters to Amnesty International and the United Nations, gathered from Czechoslovakian contacts during his stay. Though the letters are quite legal, their bearer is detained and does not join his colleagues on the plane. Like Anderson, he has surreptitious motives for visiting the colloquium, but by playing to the conventional rules, within a country which patently does not, he is caught.[10]

*Professional Foul* is not a piece of simple didactic writing. It is, on the contrary, as accomplished a work as any Stoppard has yet given us, passionate, technically immaculate and replete with the fast, witty humour of the mature Stoppard. Like many of his earlier plays its thrust is thoroughly moral and, like *Jumpers*, its central argument is expressed by the direct philosophical discourse working hand in hand with the momentum of the plot. There is, indeed, a close relationship between the arguments which Anderson finally advances at the colloquium and those rehearsed in the mirror by George Moore. George, it will be remembered, is seeking philosophical justification for his instinctive belief in ethical absolutes. He refuses to accept the comprehensive relativity of value-concepts insisted on by the Logical Positivists and having rejected both Christian and Platonic absolutes of goodness, beauty and truth, he strives to produce a sound substitute which maintains the same essential spirit. Anderson similarly appeals to a sense of natural, instinctive values in a paper delivered with remarkable clarity in view of its relative brevity (a further example of simplicity triumphing over sophistication). As an example, he takes the idea of justice:

> A small child who cries 'that's not fair' when punished for something done by his brother or sister is apparently appealing to an idea of justice which is, for want of a better word, natural. And we must see that natural justice, however illusory, does inspire many people's behaviour much of the time. As an ethical utterance it seems to be an attempt to define a sense of rightness which is not simply derived from some other utterance elsewhere. (p. 90)

Anderson admits the concept's 'illusory' characteristics, but, as he declares in his opening remarks:

> I will be defining rights as fictions acting as incentives to the adoption of practical values; and I will further propose that although these rights are fictions there is an obligation to treat them as if they were truths. (p. 87)

Unlike *Jumpers*, no attempt is made to probe the ultimate causes of this sense of natural values; the professor's concern is rather to relate his philosophical premises to practical situations. Like his rôle, the speech moves from theory to practice and he goes so far as to invoke Articles 28 and 32 of the Constitution of Czechoslovakia, guarantees of the individual citizen's freedom, in an attempt to extract the *sine qua non* of human rights and to raise these above the secondary rules of communities. In short, the whole paper is an attempt to expound and elaborate on the premise to which Hollar introduced him, that: 'There is a sense of right and wrong which precedes utterance'. (p. 90) Stoppard does not resolve the seemingly impossible problem of expressing the belief in a natural sense of right, or justice, or both, in such terms as to satisfy modern philosophers in their post-Platonic, post-Christian wilderness. But, as in *Jumpers*, he insists that it is not a problem with which logic alone is concerned: the practical implications of these values within a given social context are just as important. And here the sense in which *Professional Foul* represents a step forward becomes most clear, for where Stoppard

used George Moore primarily to entrench himself against materialist philosophy, he places Anderson in a more positive position,
advocating his belief in certain fundamental individual values and
visibly putting them into practice. He does so, admittedly, by
breaching other standards, but only under pressure from a far
greater moral imperative; as he tells Professor Stone, 'the important
truths are simple and monolithic'. (p. 63)

Yet what is finally most impressive about *Professional Foul* is not
the argument which Stoppard advances, but the character of
Anderson which he creates as a living fulfilment of it. For the first
time in any of his plays, Stoppard brings to life a character in which
there is authentic development in the course of the play.
Rosencrantz and Guildenstern, George Moore, Henry Carr and
Alexander in *Every Good Boy Deserves Favour* are, for all their vividness,
conceived in singular terms; however refined and stylish their
human faces, they are all developments of an *idée fixe*. Even Riley's
final resolution to visit the employment exchange is only part of a
recurrent cycle of contrition, soon forgotten as often as it comes
round again; even the chameleon-like Player is consistently
chameleon-like. In *Professional Foul* Stoppard takes the unprecedented step of tackling a character in whom he conceives a dynamic
process – that of a growth towards greater enlightenment – and he
resolutely follows the steps of that growth as the camera's eye tracks
Anderson through his eventful weekend. It is not the unprecedented
naturalism in itself which impresses, but the appropriateness of the
convention's intimacy and human attention for this study of the
active growth of an individual's moral awareness, and though
Anderson is less amusing, less colourful and less theatrical than some
of his predecessors, with none of their intrinsic style or eccentricity,
he is one of the most humane and complete characters that
Stoppard has created. His humanity and conviction, coupled with
the clarity and balance of the 'play of ideas', make *Professional Foul*
an extraordinary *tour de force*.

                    *          *          *

Taken together, *Every Good Boy Deserves Favour* and *Professional Foul*
represent a distinct but not drastic advance in Stoppard's work, in
particular a new readiness to take a definite stand on certain
political issues. His characterisation, partially in response to these
new pressures, simultaneously becomes more rounded and naturalistic, especially in the television film. However, concern with serious

issues is not so novel a feature of Stoppard's work as the critical response to these plays has sought to suggest. 'It is significantly different from most of his previous work'[11] wrote Henry Fenwick of *Professional Foul*. Sheridan Morley called it the first time 'that he has climbed down off the Scrabble board of his own remarkable linguistic talents and tackled a tangible issue'[12] while in *The Times* Michael Church observed that the play 'seemed to suggest that Stoppard himself might be breaking through a creative barrier'.[13] These overstatements may arise from the familiarity and topicality of the subject-matter of the plays: East–West politics strikes home more easily than the ethical implications of logical positivist philosophy, the interrelationship of politics and art and the vicissitudes of fortune among the minor characters of Shakespearean tragedy. Where Stoppard's attitude towards his subject does differ is not in the underlying seriousness of his approach, only in the greater clarity with which his own viewpoint is expressed, in the keen sense of indictment built into the dramatic form. In comparison with the swift, intellectual mêlée of *Travesties*, as much vaudeville as discourse, *Every Good Boy Deserves Favour* and *Professional Foul* offer a steadier, more impassioned view of their chosen subjects, in which the plays themselves become acts of protest, expressions of the author's own moral outrage. The success of these plays, especially *Professional Foul*, has provoked a more widespread recognition of Stoppard as a serious writer, but the formula – of integrating argument into an effective, entertaining and adventurous dramatic form – has remained consistent.

# 11 The Road to Kambawe

In the New Year's honours list of 1978 Tom Stoppard's outstanding work in the theatre for more than a decade was recognised by the award of the C.B.E. In July of the same year came the London opening of *Despair*, Fassbinder's film adaptation of Nabokov's novel, featuring Stoppard's screenplay (his second for the cinema)[1] and on 8 November *Night and Day*, his fourth full-length stage play, opened at the Phoenix Theatre in a production by Peter Wood starring Diana Rigg and John Thaw. Like *The Real Inspector Hound* ten years earlier, this was commissioned and mounted by the commercial impresario Michael Codron. The production enjoyed a 15-month run and again earned Stoppard an *Evening Standard* Best Play award. In common with all its full-length predecessors, it then opened on Broadway, in November 1979.

We saw in the last chapter how the critics enthused about the filmic naturalism of *Professional Foul*; now, however, they showed themselves more ambivalent towards a play which suggested a move into the kind of stage naturalism which all Stoppard's previous work in that medium had, in one way or another, seemed to repudiate. Michael Billington, for example, concluded that *Night and Day* was

> a play that shows Stoppard espousing a cause without sacrificing any of his verbal dexterity and one to see, delight in and debate about till the small hours of the morning.[2]

Bernard Levin, on the other hand, found it 'a deeply disappointing play' with 'some horribly clumsy preaching, stiff with caked earnestness' and roundly declared:

> Mr Stoppard has put his viewpoint before his drama, and thus sacrificed the effect of both.[3]

Both review snippets emphasise that *Night and Day* is, once again, a serious 'play of ideas', though the erstwhile formula of its 'marriage' 'with farce or even high comedy'[4] appears to have been set aside. As Stoppard told Ronald Hayman in 1976:

> A lot of things in *Travesties* and *Jumpers* seem to me to be the terminus of the particular kind of writing which I can do. I don't see much point in trying to do it again.[5]

And *Night and Day*, certainly, is not in this vein. Indeed, for all its intermittent verbal felicity and wit, it is still less of a comedy than *Professional Foul* and more visibly than ever *une pièce à thèse*, structuring within its linear plot a lively discussion of modern-day journalism – its practical workings, its ethics and the whole question of the constraints and freedoms within which it operates.

The play is set within the fictitious African state of Kambawe, where reporter Dick Wagner (an Australian) and photographer George Guthrie, two leading journalists from the up-market British paper the *Sunday Globe*, have arrived to cover a rebellion against the government led by one Colonel Shimbu. It has one setting: the garden, verandah and one room of the house of Geoffrey Carson,[6] a prominent English businessman who lives just outside Jeddu (where the President's forces are massing for a counter-attack) and who has a telex machine, a host of influential connections in the country and a wife called Ruth with whom Wagner happens, improbably, to have spent the night in a London hotel at the end of the previous week, after they met by chance at the Kambawe Embassy. An anonymous 'special correspondent' has meanwhile scooped the world by obtaining an exclusive interview with Shimbu and sending it to the *Globe*, and Wagner's jaundice is exacerbated when Carson eventually arrives with the self-same 'special correspondent' – a youthful reporter called Jacob Milne who now has *another* scoop on the go – an exclusive report on how Shimbu's forces have secretly attacked and captured Carson's mines, up-country at Malakuangazi. The friction intensifies when Wagner learns that Milne left his last job after being blacked by his colleagues for refusing to join their union and he swiftly files a complaint to his Union Branch Secretary before Milne wires again. Guthrie and Milne then leave on the following day with a safe pass to drive back to Malakuangazi by jeep, both to catch 'the action' and to pass back to Shimbu the President's reply to his secret request for peace talks. (Carson is acting as the middle-man in this traffic, which is why he and Milne were allowed to leave the captured mines at all.) Wagner stays behind because, after an innocent tip-off from the Carsons' young son Alistair, he concludes that Carson is actually staging the talks at his house that night and he sneaks back to scoop an interview of his own, with President Mageeba. They are interrupted by the sudden return of Guthrie. The President's reply never reached Shimbu and Milne is dead, shot when they were within sight of the mines amidst confused crossfire among the government's own troops. Mageeba leaves, but before Wagner can wire home his story, a telex from London pre-empts him: Milne's copy has been blacked, there is an all-out strike and no paper will appear the following day. Ruefully, Wagner wires an obituary paragraph to Milne's old paper instead and, when Carson and Guthrie have left, is about to fall back into bed with Ruth as the play ends.

Stoppard's characters and plot are original creations but behind them lurks one distinct, though shadowy, literary antecedent, that of Evelyn Waugh's satiric novel *Scoop* (1933). There are no direct borrowings from the book and no hint of the kind of structural relationship that, say, *Rosencrantz* has with *Hamlet* or *Travesties* with *The Importance of Being Earnest*, yet something of the spirit of Waugh's novel is omnipresent in *Night and Day*, not least in their common setting of British reporters out-scooping each other amidst civil war in a fictitious East African republic. Stoppard himself used Waugh's unlikely hero, William Boot, as a pseudonym for some of his own pieces for the magazine *Scene* in the early sixties; now, Boot offers a limited but discernible parallel with the character of Milne. Both are about twenty-three years old,[7] relatively naïve youngsters, inexperienced in the ways of the high-flying foreign press corps and both get their big stories more as the result of good fortune than professional judgement. Each plot also turns on the relationship between two quite separate scoops – though in this case it is Wagner who offers the parallel when, like Boot, he appears to have been scooped by a rival journalist's exclusive interview with the rebel leader. But each then proceeds to get his own, still better scoop by staying behind as the other journalists travel up-country in pursuit of the rebels' story. Boot, alone in the capital, discovers that the President has been placed under house arrest by a Russian-inspired junta led by a member of his own military staff, Wagner, that the President is planning a crucial, secret rendezvous with his rival.

Comparisons between the play and novel cannot be sustained beyond passing points of resemblance such as these. Like Waugh, though, Stoppard uses his African setting as little more than a convenient backdrop. As Michael Billington says, 'Stoppard is less concerned with African politics than with libertarian principles.'[8] Just as Ishmaelian politics are more or less tangential to Waugh's savagely funny indictment of the crude and competitive workings of Fleet Street, so Kambawe politics are only marginally involved in the 'play of ideas' which is Stoppard's central interest in *Night and Day*. This has its core in the plot – in the irony (unparalleled in *Scoop*) which hoists Wagner on his own union card petard and robs him of his scoop – and is embellished and fleshed out at points throughout the play by an intermittent debate on the theories and practices of journalism. This contest between rival schools of thought provides the play with its closest link with *Travesties*; in short, it follows the 'Art Debate' in that play with the 'Press Debate' in this. Ronald Hayman's suggestion that

> the plays of Tom Stoppard are above all the plays of a man who enjoys arguing with himself and crystallising the contradictions into characters[9]

though written with earlier plays in mind, is more true than ever of *Night and Day* and highlights Stoppard's instinctive tendency to create characters whose primary rôle is as the spokesman or woman for a particular point of view. This can, of course, mean that the debate seems to matter rather more than the debaters, especially in *Travesties* where the rival viewpoints on art and revolution are despatched in a brilliant sequence of verbal tennis-court volleys which is far stronger than the characters themselves. As Jim Hunter says,

> The strip-cartoon simplification of the characters doesn't matter – it may even help – when the balloons which come out of their heads are so eloquent.[10]

When the structure is as naturalistic as in *Night and Day*, however, 'strip-cartoon' characters cannot work. Their three-dimensionality becomes of quintessential importance and any suspicion that they existed primarily for the sake of their puppet-rôles in Stoppard's debating chamber could damage the integrity of the entire play. It is therefore revealing to note that when Penelope Mortimer asked Stoppard in 1977 about his next work in the pipeline, he replied:

> I'd like to write a play about journalism, but I don't want to write about what it's like to be a journalist, I don't want to write a play about Life in A Newspaper Office.[11]

Since he chooses to work realistically, however, what we must be able to believe, irrespective of the play's setting, is that these characters might indeed work in a newspaper office, or run a mining consortium or even, in the president's case, a country. It must be as fully rounded dramatic creations that they contribute to any 'play of ideas' which emerges.

Joan Fitzpatrick Dean, pursuing the link with *Travesties*, attempts a summary of this debate in her suggestion that 'In *Night and Day*, journalists rather than artists must face the question of their responsibility to society'.[12] In fact, Stoppard tends to see the equation from the other end. For him, the single most important responsibility of any society is that it should permit and preserve freedom for its journalists. The question of the journalists' own responsibilities is of secondary importance. As he told Melvyn Bragg in a television interview: 'I am passionate about this (press freedom). It's the one thing that separates a free society from an unfree one.'[13] This concern is integrally related to the concern he exhibits in his two previous plays over the removal of other kinds of freedom – the imprisonment of dissidents in mental hospitals in the Soviet Union or their arrest on trumped-up charges in Czechoslovakia. In common with these plays, and to a greater extent than in *Travesties*, Stoppard's own views emerge unmistakably in *Night and Day*, though, given the debate structure, they are not simply invested in a single character. His three journalists all carry some degree of authorial endorsement and it is clear that even Wagner is respected for his toughness and professionalism. Milne comes closest to epitomising Stoppard's essential belief when he declares to Ruth:

> A free press, free expression – it's the last line of defence for all the other freedoms . . .

> No matter how imperfect things are, if you've got a free press everything is correctable, and without it everything is concealable.  (pp. 58, 60).

But Guthrie also reiterates a broadly similar view at the end of the play, when *he* tells Ruth:

I've been around a lot of places. People do awful things to each other. But it's worse in places where everybody is kept in the dark. It really is. Information is light. Information, in itself, about anything, is light. That's all you can say, really. (p. 91)

This principle, then, which Stoppard and at least two of his main characters fully endorse, provides the didactic axis of the play.

It is important, however, to note the very considerable differences between these two characters. Guthrie's view is derived from the lesson of long years of experience, while Milne's is a strongly held, idealistic belief. Stoppard extends this comparison as far as he can. Milne is green, boyish and more than a little gauche. He dresses for the drive back to the mines in an army-style khaki shirt with epaulettes and a camouflage-coloured bush hat – until the exasperated Guthrie makes him change. He is not even concerned at losing face by admitting the sheer luck which led him to his first scoop, when some of Shimbu's men chanced to stop the bus he was travelling on. This cheerful naïvety is part of Milne's charm, and it is certainly this to which Ruth so visibly warms, but it also leads him to his death when he gets into the kind of dangerous situation which, unlike Guthrie, he does not understand. As Guthrie knows, once the shooting has started, the only thing to do is to dive for cover:

I shouted to Jake to run and I got fifty yards and when I looked back he's in the driving seat trying to turn the jeep round. He got it round, and then he was hit. Knocked him into the back seat. I should have looked after him better. (p. 87)

This is no simple martyr's fate, for Stoppard makes it clear that it results as much from Milne's inexperience as from his bravery. As such it shows the effort he makes to avoid turning Milne into a simple, idealistic young hero. But he succeeds only partially in this aim and the critic Benedict Nightingale does not seem excessively harsh when he concludes:

I do not know if Stoppard expects us to wince when we hear that Milne has been killed by unruly troops, but I suspect he does. Alas, the moment passes with a massive shrug – because he is more a set of principles, a series of excited and enthusiastic arguments than a young man cut down in his prime.[14]

Guthrie, by contrast, who has a much less important strategic rôle in the play, emerges as a far more believable creation, largely because Stoppard makes no attempt to define him in black-or-white terms or to involve him in the major debates within the play; he comes over simply as a good professional photographer with a healthy self-regard (bordering on arrogance) and a clear instinct for danger. It is important to note, for instance, the way in which he is rattled when Carson first provides them with the jeep:

*Guthrie:*    Wagner said a car.
*Carson:*    What's the difference? Car, jeep. This isn't a trip for a family saloon.
(*Guthrie is very angry and upset, but still controlled.*)
*Guthrie:*    A family saloon is neutral. A jeep is a target. Listen – I know the game. I know the edge on every hand I'm dealt. It was the same in the Congo, Angola, Somalia. And it's the same here. (p. 62)

This reference to his past wars is one of several pointers to the egotism which colours Guthrie's character, especially alone with Wagner, when the two old pros miss no opportunity to impress each other:

*Guthrie:*    One time in Hué I was in a dug-out with Larry Barnes and . . . . (p. 25)

*Wagner:*    By the time that Paki press officer handed it out with an embargo my story was in London. . . .
I mean, I *cracked* that story, Gigi. (p. 27)

*Guthrie:*    Remember what that Yank admiral said to Malcolm Browne that time in Saigon. . . . (p. 89)

How much they *are* impressed is, of course, another matter. Wagner admits at one point that 'nobody is impressed by reporters except other reporters' (p. 31) and Stoppard implies throughout that this is just a somewhat tedious habit of self-aggrandisement in which all journalists indulge. Even Milne, though, who makes such a refreshing contrast to the hacks in some respects, is overwhelmed at meeting Guthrie:

Guthrie? – Christ. I thought your Lebanon pictures were just – . (p. 35)

He, on the other hand, does not impress either of them at all, especially on the several occasions on which he exposes his ignorance of the world in which they move. He doesn't know what the word 'pigeon' means in their metaphorical jargon. He admits that his scoop was posted to London by one of Shimbu's men and took a week to arrive. And he even mistakes young Alistair's little Kodak camera for Guthrie's own when he sees him putting a film in it for the boy. Such touches provide some amusing comedy and some convincing development of naturalistic interrelationships between the three characters, but however engaging the audience may find Milne's innocence, they are likely to appreciate Guthrie's reservations at the prospect of driving back to Malakuangazi with him:

> *Milne:*    I never thought I'd be on a story with you.
> *Guthrie:* Me neither.  (p. 37)

Most of the differences between these two men end up working, like this wry comment, to Guthrie's advantage.

Milne and Guthrie are, as we have seen, at least united behind the assertion that 'information is light', but Stoppard presents two characters within his naturalistic framework who offer opposing perspectives to this principle. The most obvious of these is President Mageeba, a dictator who rules Kambawe by undisguised military force. Just prior to his arrival in the second act, Carson offers an insight into the true nature of the 'republic' over which he presides, warning Wagner that

> journalists here get hung up by their thumbs for getting his medals wrong  (p. 72)

and adds:

> I think Mageeba isn't going to let Shimbu secede anywhere except into a ditch and at breakfast time when he sees Shimbu hasn't fallen for it, he's going to go in with air-strikes and tanks. (p. 73)

The shoot-out near the mines which leads to Milne's death also shows how disturbingly indisciplined his troops are, but Stoppard does not develop his profile of the rival causes beyond the barest essentials. The African war is less important in its own right than as an opportunity to highlight a dictator in pursuit of the same kind of ruthless political repression as Lenin in *Travesties*:

> We want to establish and we shall establish a free press, free not simply from the police, but also from capital, from careerism, and what is more, *free from bourgeois anarchist individualism!* ( *Travesties*, p. 85)

Lenin demonstrates a truth that Stoppard emphasises throughout *Night and Day*, that control of the media is an essential tool of government repression, whether it comes in the guise of Soviet communism or lies in the whims of an African despot. At this point both extremes meet, and the comparison with *Travesties* becomes concrete when, with deceptive pleasantness, Mageeba describes to Wagner the problems he encountered with Kambawe's old English-language paper:

> At the time of independence the *Daily Citizen* was undoubtedly free. It was free to select the news it thought fit to print, to make much of it or little, and free to make room for more and more girls wearing less and less underwear. (p. 84)

His solution was devastatingly simple:

> *Mageeba:* From the ashes there arose, by public subscription, a new *Daily Citizen*, responsible and relatively free. (*He leans towards Wagner.*) Do you know what I mean by a relatively free press, Mr Wagner?
> *Wagner:* Not exactly, sir, no.
> *Mageeba*: I mean a free press which is edited by one of my relatives.
> *(He throws back his head and laughs. Wagner joins in uncertainly.)* (pp. 84–5)

Seconds later, Mageeba's underlying brutality is bared as he raps Wagner on the head with his metal-tipped cane, releasing his contemptuous fury on the representative of the paper which has given such prominence to his rival's traitorous, secessionist views.

This vivid, aggressive exchange is the only violent scene in any Stoppard play outside the string of playfully dead bodies in *Hound, Jumpers, Artist Descending* and *The Boundary*, and the ironic deaths of

Thumper the hare and Pat the tortoise in *Jumpers*. Even Rosencrantz and Guildenstern do not visibly die, despite their poignant intimations of their mortality. Mageeba's violence is symptomatic of the authentic, rounded nature of his character. For what is most impressive about him is the conviction he carries as a real-life creation, incomparably greater than that of Lenin in *Travesties* and far more developed than Stoppard's 'Press Debate' necessarily demands. Though not on stage for long, he conveys the sense of a genuinely powerful man and the menace behind his seemingly cool, polite restraint is powerfully conveyed as we watch him toy with the ingratiating Wagner:

*Mageeba:* You would give me equal space?
*Wagner:* Oh – absolutely –
*Mageeba:* That's very fair. Isn't it, Geoffrey? Mr Wagner says I can have equal space.
*Wagner:* And some space is more equal than others. I think, sir, I could more or less guarantee that an interview with you at this juncture of the war would be treated as the main news story of the day, and of course would be picked up by newspapers, and all the media, round the world.
*Mageeba:* What war, Mr Wagner?
*Wagner:* Sorry?
*Mageeba:* Kambawe is not at war. We have a devolution problem. I believe you have one, too. (p. 78)

Wagner is trying hard to keep up, but he has fatally underestimated the fury which Milne's article has provoked and as Mageeba runs rings round him, their tense, highly dramatic encounter provides some of the finest naturalistic writing in the play, or, indeed, in any of Stoppard's work.

The second threat to the free flow of information which Stoppard illustrates is the kind of collective action which Wagner, the tough union man, epitomises by preventing his young colleague's story from reaching the printed page. It is worth noting Guthrie's equivocal rôle over this. He cannot at first believe that Wagner's threat is serious:

*Guthrie:* You're kidding.
*Wagner:* No, I'm an officer of the *Globe* chapel.

*Guthrie:*   That doesn't make it your responsibility.
*Wagner:*    That's right. Let Hammaker fight it out with Battersby
             at branch level.   (p. 43)

But although he has just demonstrated his opinion of Branch
Secretary Battersby in another context ('I went on something with
him once . . . bloody useless reporter'), Guthrie does not back
Milne either and opts for a safe, cynical position on the fence.
Stoppard, of course, is rather less neutral as both the eventual
*dénouement* of his plot and his generally sympathetic treatment of
Milne testify, but when he sends Milne in on the counter-attack, he
expresses his position with unusually shrill rhetoric:

*Wagner:*   Is it your principle to betray your fellow workers when
            they're in confrontation with management?
            *(Milne can't believe this. He almost laughs.)*
*Milne:*    Come again?
*Wagner (Furious):* Don't patronize *me*, you little berk.
*Milne:*    I'm sorry – I was just taken aback. I never got used to
            the way the house Trots fell into the jargon back in
            Grimsby – I mean, on any other subject, like the death
            of the novel, or the sex life of the editor's secretary, they
            spoke ordinary English, but as soon as they started
            trying to get me to join the strike it was as if their brains
            has been taken out and replaced by one of those little
            golf-ball things you get in electric typewriters
            . . . 'Betrayal' . . . 'Confrontation' . . . 'Management'
            . . . My God, you'd need a more supple language than
            that to describe an argument between two
            amoebas.   (p. 39)

The heavy contrivance of this exchange provides the strongest possible
contrast with the subtle dialogue between Mageeba and Wagner.
Depending on the audience's own prejudices, it is also capable of
working contrary to Stoppard's intentions and in the opposite
direction from his plot, in Wagner's favour rather than Milne's.
Perhaps, however, this is merely indicative of the way in which
Stoppard (who once dreamed of a similar career to Wagner's for
himself)[15] strives to be at least moderately fair to the rival point of
view. He makes it clear, for instance, that Wagner is acting
according to principle as well:

I believe that a newspaper, although it is a business, is too important to be merely somebody's property. And I'm not talking about protecting my job but my freedom to report facts that may not be congenial to, let us say, an English millionaire. (p. 82)

By admitting the integrity of this opposing standpoint, Stoppard demonstrates the healthy plurality of viewpoints within his debate. Which represents the greater danger to the press's essential freedom: the owners or the unions? Mageeba's example highlights the potential dangers inherent in narrow ownership, but Stoppard's real concerns do not lie in Kambawe. It is in Fleet Street that the *Globe* is brought to a standstill by the union's stance against Milne and in Fleet Street that Stoppard feels the unions to be a greater threat than the proprietors. Any doubts about the firmness of his stance on this issue are removed by two vigorous arguments over the operation of the Press within Britain. The first, towards the end of the first act of the play, is with Milne and the second, during the Mageeba interview, is with Wagner, but the catalyst and opponent in each case is Ruth.

Ruth's contribution to these two arguments cannot be properly considered without first understanding the essential distinction which separates her from all the other characters. Put simply, Stoppard presents her in two discrete guises: inside the action, conventionally, as a provocative catalyst, and outside it, in a largely self-reflecting commentary rôle. The first presents us with a woman of vivacious high spirits who compensates for her relatively peripheral rôle in the action by directing some trenchant sarcasm at the journalists' various pretensions: She is lively, combative and independent. In her second, inner voice, which Stoppard calls 'Ruth' (in inverted commas in the published text, to emphasise the distinction), she bares the character's private thoughts and a very different picture emerges – of a bruised and lonely person much given to cynical introspection and imaginative peregrinations, harbouring images of a fantasy life which offers the kind of romance that Carson and Kambawe cannot. Glimpses of the inner life which thus counterpoints Ruth's gay facade are evident from the outset when she switches into melancholy bursts of song – first 'Night and Day' itself, then the Beatles' classic 'Help!' – which the other characters cannot hear. At this point Ruth begins to suggest a resemblance to Dotty in *Jumpers*, but the comparison fades as play and character gather increased momentum, leaving only her occasional flickers of emotional longing as reminders of Dotty's fixation on the remote, romantic moon. Instead, we find the rôle of 'Ruth' becoming less Freudian 'id' than 'superego'. First, battling with her conscience, she rehearses a confession of her infidelity with Wagner while her husband takes a phone call; then, when Mageeba arrives, the dialogue shuttles frantically between the two Ruths as her inability to avoid putting her foot in it is nicely satirised:

| | |
|---|---|
| *Mageeba:* | Please forgive this late hour. |
| *Ruth:* | It's never too late – welcome . . . we're night birds here. |
| *Mageeba:* | How gracious . . . I, too, sleep very little. |
| *Ruth:* | (*Gaily*) Well – uneasy lies the head that – |
| *'Ruth':* | (*Loudly*) Idiot! |
| *Ruth:* | I mean the sheer volume of work must be enormous, the cares of State, and – |
| *'Ruth':* | Shut up, you silly woman – |
| *Ruth:* | May I introduce Mr Richard Wagner? (p. 75) |

In such ways our access to Ruth's inner life is expanded beyond the bounds of a simple 'asides' technique to illuminate the conflicts and divisions within her complex personality.

It is, however, in the dramatisation of Ruth's contrasting relationships with the journalists who descend on her house that the technique comes into its own. Half-seriously, she exposes her sexual boredom right at the start of the play: 'You're a reasonable looking sort of chap, Guthrie. How would you like to take me away from all this?' (p. 21) This self-addressed remark is mere passing playfulness, but her involvement with the other two journalists is far more developed. What Stoppard broadly sets up is an emotional alliance between Ruth and Wagner on the one hand and 'Ruth' and Milne on the other. Wagner holds little attraction for her, but her verbal battles with the hard-boiled Australian show them trading insults with obvious relish and suggest an element of horse-play which makes it not only unsurprising but entirely credible that at the end of the hectic night's events, close to despair and exhaustion, she should give him a resigned re-call to her upstairs quarters: 'I want to be hammered out, disjointed, folded up and put away like linen in a drawer.' (pp. 93–4) The imagery of a physical skirmish is entirely appropriate since love does not begin to enter into the calculations of either party. Wagner is an opportunist, an entirely unromantic man whose career – and the egotism it embodies – is far more important to him than any woman could be. He thus draws out the cynical, pragmatic side of Ruth's nature – in stark contrast to the gentle, idealistic yearning she develops for Milne during their first, brief meeting at the end of the first act and in the more elaborate scene of seduction which opens the second.

During the first act it is not altogether clear what aim Stoppard's 'dual rôles' technique is serving, beyond expanding Ruth into a much more fully realised character than her fellows. At the start of the second act, however, comes one of his cherished pieces of theatrical gamesmanship designed to jolt the audience from one set of expectations into another – the technique epitomised in *The Real Inspector Hound*. *Travesties* demonstrated his fondness for using such devices immediately after his interval break, by re-starting the play outside Carr's consciousness with Cecily's lecture on Lenin, and *Night and Day* now furnishes a further example. What we *think* we are watching as the lights go back up is a scene of growing affection between Ruth and Milne after he has returned in the jeep, late in the evening:

*Ruth:* It's nice that you've got us to come back to.
*Milne:* Yes – a line to London on tap – one couldn't ask for more. Oh – and present company included, of course.
*'Ruth':* Help.
*Milne:* Well, I expect you'd like to go to bed.
*'Ruth':* I'm over here.
*Milne:* I've got a piece to write.
*'Ruth':* To hell with that. (p. 65)

What it in fact turns out that we are watching is an elaborate Stoppard hoax, a scene running for nearly ten minutes which, like the brief asides in the first half, actually features 'Ruth' and not Ruth throughout. In other words, it is purely imaginary. The series of deceptive darts into 'Ruth' at the start of the scene are the ruses by which Stoppard beguiles us into thinking his first act convention is being continued, so that when Milne goes back out into the garden at the end of the scene and Ruth, unfastening her dress, walks out after him, naked, the seduction seems complete. Immediately prior to this, however, Ruth has flopped into a sofa largely concealed from view – and when Carson walks in moments later, she suddenly arises to ask him for a cigarette. Ruth, in fact, has never left the sofa:

it is 'Ruth', her fantasy *doppelgänger*, who has pursued Milne into the garden. Stoppard has slipped into a new convention in which the double has finally materialised, disappearing into the darkness in search of an illusory love affair which is more impossible than even she knows, since, with heavy irony, Milne is by this time already dead. The 'real' Ruth meanwhile stays in the well-lit lounge, crystallising the opposed images of the title and, as dawn approaches, lets Wagner back into her bed. In the real world of sex, like that of journalism, Stoppard implies that compromise and expediency are always likely in the end to triumph over principle.

Unfortunately, largely because Milne *does* represent principle so strongly within the play's schema, unresolved undercurrents seem to run through both his scenes with Ruth – the 'real' scene and the 'unreal' one. They suffer in part from the kind of emotional awkwardness that we have previously observed in the more direct encounters in Stoppard's earlier plays. The awkwardness is, of course, partially Milne's own, as he has already demonstrated dealing with Wagner and Guthrie, but it also derives from the dramatic mismatch of these would-be lovers, from the fact that Milne is so much less fully realised as a character than Ruth. Hunter's defence of him:

> anyone unusual enough to be worth writing about may risk not being immediately credible. Most of us, after all, have our doubts about Hedda Gabler[16]

is not in the least convincing. Hedda is an enigma – and is meant to be. Milne, on the other hand, is so unenigmatic, so steadfast and so principled that he simply fails to come fully to life. He is far more of a *talkative* creation than a *felt* one, especially at the point in their 'real' scene together when Ruth finally tests the water:

> *Ruth:* Hungry?
> *Milne:* Starving.
> *Ruth:* Then let's eat.
> *Milne:* I'm sorry I talked so much.
> *Ruth:* No, I like you to talk.
>     (*She looks at him steadily, too long for his comfort*)
> *Milne:* Thanks very much for having me here. I'll go and sort myself out.
>
> (*Milne goes into the lighted house. Ruth stays in the dark*) (pp. 61–2)

Ruth's sense that Milne is too good for her world is thus confirmed. Only in the parallel world of 'Ruth' (reinforced by another image that contrasts the rival 'realities' of light and dark) could he love her, and even when she spirits him there in the second act, he (or her evocation of him) warns that they are meeting in a world in which there is 'No day or night, no responsibilities, no frictions, almost no gravity.' (p. 67) It is, ultimately, a vacuum world (as Ruth secretly acknowledges) and its unreality is beautifully caught as Stoppard finally splits Ruth from her double. Yet in the end, the scene's absorbing technical skill is stronger than its emotional conviction and Hunter's claim that it is 'the most painful in Stoppard: a whispered walk along nerve-endings'[17] seems decidedly over-generous. Ruth's nerve-endings are certainly involved, but because they are ruffled and disturbed by a rather blank young man in whom we cannot ever fully believe, her sense of pain or, indeed, of *love*, never quite materialises.

The schematic pattern by which Stoppard brings out the contrasts within Ruth's personality through her emotional involvement with the two journalists is perhaps over-neat, but there is, especially with Wagner, a considerable degree of authenticity. Her exchanges with the two men within Stoppard's 'Press Debate', on the other hand, are very much less convincing as she directs torrents of vitriol at journalists in general and Fleet Street ones in particular. Benedict Nightingale catches the essence of the problem with his gentle complaint that Ruth has 'an organic connection with the journalists, rather less with the subject of journalism'.[18] For a start, the ostensible motive for her bitterness is unconvincing. It emerges that Carson is an earl's brother and that in consequence the press took an unhealthy interest in her elopement with him several years earlier:

> . . . there are worse things than being pursued across Shropshire by the slavering minions of a philistine press lord; in fact, it brought Geoffrey and me closer together. I loved him for the way he out-drove them in his Jaguar, and it wasn't his fault at all that the early morning tea in our hideaway hotel was brought in by a Fleet Street harpie. (p.50)

The sardonic eloquence is very much Ruth's own, but the more she generalises her targets, the less convincing it sounds. Her argument with Milne raises mounting suspicions that she is merely being

utilised in the build-up to a set-piece in which he can gloriously
upstage her objections and defend the rôle of the gutter press. At first
he seems largely in agreement with her detestation of the standards
of the British press:

> I know what you mean. They let *me* down too. Arguing with the
> Trots in the reporters room 'The press is the last hope for
> democracy!!' . . . and I'd find I'm thumping my fist on some
> starlet's left nipple. (p. 60)

But this apparent consensus is only preparing the ground for Milne's
subsequent, triumphant riposte:

> Junk journalism is the evidence of a society that has got at least
> one thing right, that there should be nobody with the power to
> dictate where responsible journalism begins. (p. 61)

This sounds an early warning signal that Stoppard's flair for the
points-scoring language of the debating chamber is taking over the
Carsons' verandah. He seeks to use the scene naturalistically by
suggesting that it is Milne's coy, gauche fluency that the bored,
lonely Ruth finds so attractive, but the closer their conversation gets
to the cut-and-thrust of *Travesties*, the more such intimacy is
undermined. At this point, therefore, two objectives are falling short
of the mark: the evocation of a physical and mental attraction
between Milne and Ruth, and the containing of the 'Press Debate'
within authentic naturalistic dialogue.

In Act Two when Ruth swings back into theoretical discussion,
this time with Wagner, the naturalism creaks still further. The
artifice of the set-piece which Stoppard is employing to complete
the debate becomes more apparent than ever:

> *Ruth:*    The whole country is littered with papers pushing every
> political line from Mao to Mosley and back again, and I
> bet even Allie could work out for himself that it is the
> very free-for-all which guarantees the freedom of each.
> You don't have to be a millionaire to contradict one. It
> isn't the millionaires who are going to stop you, it's the
> Wagners who don't trust the public to choose the
> marked card.

*Wagner:* I'm talking about *national* papers. It's absurd to equate the freedom of the big battalions with the freedom of a basement pamphleteer to challenge them.

*Ruth:* You are confusing freedom with ability. The *Flat Earth News* is *free* to sell a million copies. What it lacks is the ability to find a million people with four pence and a conviction that the earth is flat. Freedom is neutral. Free expression includes a state of affairs where *any* millionaire can have a national newspaper, if that's what it costs. A state of affairs where only a particular, approved, licensed and supervised non-millionaire can have a newspaper is called, for example, Russia.

*Mageeba:* Or, of course, Kambawe.  (p. 83)

Mageeba's presence reminds us how uneasily this sequence slots into the middle of his interview with Wagner. Even allowing for the drinks Ruth has put away before her outburst, she is visibly slipping out of character into mouthpiece. The speech is superbly written, subtle and persuasive, and the views she expresses in it are broadly consistent with her character. The difficulty is its contextual inauthenticity, in the formal jarring of conventions which it generates. It is a different matter when Ruth steps outside the action into 'Ruth', but when such an astonishingly fluent homily trips from her lips while she is supposedly playing by the same rules of naturalism as the other characters, it can scarcely fail to lose her some of the precious credibility which she has previously established. As Irving Wardle says of Ruth:

> She is an invented goddess in a real world and her artificiality colours the surrounding action, so that for part of the time we are watching not characters, but ambulatory attitudes.[19]

The same, as we have already observed, is largely true of Milne and one cannot help concluding that Stoppard works so hard to clinch victory in the 'Press Debate' that he incurs organic damage to the characters who are supposed to be on his side.

How much does this matter? Is it merely pedestrian to complain that the play is not entirely consistent with its self-imposed, untypically traditional principles? The problem is that naturalism is a convention which demands just such a fierce discipline. It stands or falls by the wholeness with which it is sustained. In the play with which we might most nearly compare it, the more ruthlessly naturalistic *Professional Foul*, the only comparable set-pieces which Stoppard permits himself actually take place in the lecture theatre. Elsewhere, the illusion of authenticity is maintained with remarkable steadfastness and made all the more convincing by the visible development of the central character, Anderson. In *Night and Day*, there is no dynamic growth of this kind; with the exception of Milne, who is dead, all of the characters end at more or less the same point at which they began. None of them has changed his views about anything important by the end of the play. It is true that the workings of the linear plot have meshed with stunning clarity at the end with the thrust of Stoppard's arguments; yet precisely because of the beauty of this pattern, the additional 'Press Debate', with its thunderous, rhetorical energy, often seems an excessive, spoiling intrusion. The problem with Ruth is a similar one, since her privileged dual rôle suggests that she does not altogether belong in such a naturalistic play at all, but the bonus is that she nevertheless emerges as its most complex and fully realised creation – indeed, as the most successful female in any of Stoppard's plays. Kenneth Tynan quotes, with some justification, Derek Marlowe's view that Stoppard 'can't create convincing women. His female characters are somewhere between playmates and amanuenses. He simply doesn't understand them.'[20] That was substantially true in 1977. But in 1978 Ruth arrives, the first of his female characters to have any real sense of flesh and blood – and sexuality; the first character, too, to carry Stoppard's experimentation with theatrical conventions into a new dimension of psychological exploration. In consequence, it is particularly paradoxical that this single fascinating character should, since she has no real equal in the play, emerge in many respects as more of a revelation than *Night and Day*.

# 12 Back to Farce

For this last main chapter I have brought together two further short works which Stoppard created for Inter-Action, *Dirty Linen* (first performed in 1976) and *Dogg's Hamlet, Cahoot's Macbeth* (first staged in 1979), together with the 'adaptation' *On the Razzle*, which opened at the National Theatre in 1981. What unifies them (in sharp contrast to *Professional Foul* or *Night and Day*) is their over-riding comic playfulness; the first and last draw more strongly on the classic tradition of farce than any of Stoppard's other plays, and all three show a return to the kind of slender, stereotyped characterisation methods of *After Magritte* or *The Boundary*, where the streams of verbal humour are of paramount concern.

*Dirty Linen* was written as one of a series of plays called 'The American Connection' presented at the Almost Free Theatre, London, by the Ambiance Lunch-Hour Theatre Club to commemorate the United States' Bicentennial celebrations in 1976. Ed Berman, the director of Inter-Action (the theatre's parent body), invited plays with some form of American connection from Stoppard, Edward Bond and John Arden and Margaretta D'Arcy for the first part of the season. For his contribution, Stoppard characteristically seized on the fact that Berman, an expatriate American, had just applied for British nationality and made this the starting point of his play, which Berman himself directed. As a further compliment to Berman, the production opened on 6 April, the actual date of his naturalisation! The original players included Edward de Souza, Richard O'Callaghan, Stephen Moore and the marvellously doddery Richard Goolden. With two initial changes of cast, the play then transferred to the Arts Theatre for a run of evening performances which commenced on 16 June 1976 and ran for over four years – the longest London run of any of Stoppard's plays.

The play dealing with Berman's naturalisation is not, however, called *Dirty Linen*. It is *New-Found-Land*, a semi-independent play sandwiched between the two parts of *Dirty Linen* (which has become the shortened title of both plays). The relationship between the two arises from their shared setting, a Parliamentary Committee Room in the Palace of Westminster. In *Dirty Linen* a Select Committee of MPs gathers there to conduct a meeting on the subject of Moral Standards in Public Life[1] and when they temporarily disperse at the summons of the division bell, it is occupied by two Home Office civil servants looking for a free room in which to discuss Berman's naturalisation request before it is approved by the Home Secretary. With their arrival *New-Found-Land* begins, and when they in turn are ejected by the returning MPs, *Dirty Linen* resumes. *New-Found-Land* can therefore be seen as a digression which Stoppard inserts in order to fulfil his duty to his nominal subject, 'The American Connection'[2] – especially since, with a beautiful sense of tautology, *New-Found-Land* is *itself* a stream of digressions in which each official embarks in turn on largely irrelevant tales, the first about Lloyd George and the second about a train journey across the United States. With a gleeful lack of respect for his purported subject reminiscent at times of Laurence Sterne, Stoppard shows a readiness to follow any path that offers opportunities for comic capital.

Berman first set up Inter-Action in 1968 as an umbrella organisation for a remarkable range of activities run to stimulate community involvement in the arts. These include the Almost Free Theatre in Rupert Street, Soho; the Fun Art Bus, a touring double-decker putting on shows for both children and adults; and the Dogg's Troupe, the community theatre group for whom Berman writes and produces. Close to Inter-Action's base in Camden (the only purpose-built community arts centre in Britain), he created the Fun Art Farm by turning derelict buildings into a barnyard, stables, indoor riding school and allotments. The relevance of these multifarious activities becomes clear in the bemused exchanges between Bernard, 'a very senior Home Office official' who is practically deaf, and Arthur, 'a very junior Home Office official'[3] when, having established themselves in the Committee Room, they turn to the business in hand. Though he is never mentioned by name, the application is clearly Berman's:

> *Bernard:* Did you say he farms in Kentish Town?
> *Arthur:* Yes.
> *Bernard:* Arable or pasture?

| | |
|---|---|
| *Arthur:* | It does seem odd, doesn't it? |
| *Bernard:* | I imagine that good farming land would be at a premium in North London. Is he prosperous? |
| *Arthur:* | He has an income of £10.50 a week. |
| *Bernard:* | Hardly a pillar of the community, even with free milk and eggs. |
| *Arthur:* | No. |
| *Bernard:* | He is either a very poor farmer indeed, or a farmer of genius – depending on which part of Kentish Town he farms. |
| *Arthur:* | He's not exactly a farmer, I don't think . . . he has other interests. Publishing. And he runs some sort of bus service. |
| *Bernard:* | Publishing and buses? And a farm? Bit of a gadfly is he? |
| *Arthur:* | Yes. And community work. |
| *Bernard:* | They all say that.  (p. 58) |

This humorous parade of the many directions of Berman's energies is much more of a tribute than a satire,[4] though by refracting it with characteristic obliquity through the eyes of suspicious Whitehall bureaucrats, Stoppard succeeds in making it extremely funny. But at the end of his benign accolade, it is Stoppard who has the last laugh; the Minister, when he arrives, signs the authorisation without even looking at the papers, with the throw-away remark 'One more American can't make any difference.'  (p. 71)

The 'American Connection' in *New-Found-Land* is sustained by two main strands. There is, firstly, the genial satire occasioned by Bernard's xenophobic die-hard Englishness, including a long-winded 'tribute' in apparent praise of the openness, warmth and self-confidence of Americans – marvellously punctured at the end by his dry remark, 'Apart from that I've got nothing against them.' (p. 60) Here, in miniature, is the masterly reversal of audience expectations which characterises so many of the earlier plays. Secondly, there is Arthur's rhapsodic, trance-like digression as he mentally conjures and describes a coast-to-coast journey across the United States. America is Arthur's 'new-found-land', but as he revels in his chosen images of it, in a stream of ecstatic reverie which commences at the entrance to New York Harbour, it becomes increasingly hard to believe that he can ever have visited the country:

Picture the scene as our great ship, with the blue ribband of the Greyhound of the Deep fluttering from her mizzen, rounds the tolling bell of the Jersey buoy and with fifty thousand tons of steel plate smashes through the waters of Long Island Sound. Ahead of us is the golden span of the Brooklyn Bay Bridge, and on the starboard quarter the Statue of Liberty herself. Was it just poetic fancy which made us seem to see a glow shining from that torch held a thousand feet above our heads? – and to hear the words of the monumental goddess come softly across the water: 'Give me your tired, your poor, your huddled masses, the wretched refuse of your teeming shore . . . ?' The lower decks are crowded with immigrants from every ghetto in the Continent of Europe, a multitude of tongues silenced now in the common language of joyful tears.   (p. 60)

The dream-vision of America as a brave young world is progressively deflated and ridiculed by Arthur's naïve eulogy, a whirling concoction from literary, film and television sources. From the harbour, for instance, it is a short journey to the 'electric marquees' of Broadway where, stepping straight from the nearest musical:

Sailors on shore-leave are doing buck-and-wing dances in and out of the traffic, at times upon the very roofs of the yellow taxis   (p. 61)

and on to Grand Central Station for a deviously routed transcontinental journey which provides a constant flow of comically stereotyped passengers and panoramas. At Chicago, the passengers are all playing poker and smoking cigars as

shirt-sleeved newspapermen of the old school throw in their cards in disgust and spit tobacco juice upon the well-shined shoes of anyone reading a New York paper.   (p. 62)

Heading south, 'thoroughbred stallions' race the train and 'young girls in gingham dresses wave from whitewood fences' before it crosses 'that old green river' the Mississippi, where a familiar figure from literature catches the eye as 'far below, a boy on a raft looks up wistfully at the mournful howl of the Silver Chief' (p. 63). And at New Orleans:

a one-armed white man takes a battered cornet from inside his shirt and picks up the tune with pure and plangent notes. Soon the whole car – Bible salesmen, buck privates from Fort Dixie, majorettes from L.S.U., farm boys and a couple of nuns – is singing the blues into the night.   (p. 63)

This hilarious collection of archetypal figures is an even more extended and ingenious pastiche than Old Carr's pseudo-biographical introduction in *Travesties*. The accuracy with which Stoppard captures the mythic images of America is both funny and utterly destructive of the myth; Arthur's entire journey becomes a parody of the American psyche, a fairytale that crumbles ever further into implausibility. Yet despite the comedy being so emphatically verbal (accompanied only by the spectacle of Bernard falling asleep) and despite the tremendous demands placed on the actor by its sheer length, the constant fertility of the images themselves and the inventiveness with which they are brought together maintains theatrical tension with consummate ease. It is certainly the most accomplished piece of writing in the play and provides a delightfully double-edged tribute to the nation on its Bicentennial Anniversary.

Another kind of satire is provided in *New-Found-Land* by an almost equally long-winded digression of Bernard's describing how, as a youth, he once outwitted Lloyd George, winning a fiver off the Prime Minister when he visited the house of Bernard's parents. It is apparently a story that he regularly tells at every opportunity. Lloyd George bet Bernard that he could see Big Ben from the window of his mother's bedroom. Put to the test, he was duly proved correct.

> 'Bernard' he said, 'I see from Big Ben that it is four minutes past the hour. The £5 which you have lost,' he continued, 'I will spend on vast quantities of flowers for your mother, by way of excusing this intrusion. It is a small price to pay,' he said, 'for the lesson that you must never pit any of the five Anglo-Saxon senses against the Celtic sixth sense.' 'Prime Minister,' I said, 'I'm afraid Welsh intuition is no match for English cunning. Big Ben is the name of the bell, not the clock.' He paid up at once.
> (p. 58)

What Bernard (who then leaves) does not perceive is that he himself has been more seriously outwitted. On his return, the Prime Minister is just letting himself out of the house.

> Nervousness caused me to commit the social solecism of trying to return him his money. 'Keep it,' he said, 'I never spent a better £5.'   (p. 58)

And Bernard has kept the old-style not to that very day. The purpose of the whole episode is, of course, that it enables Stoppard to suggest a mischievously witty reference to the familiar refrain 'Lloyd George Knew My Father', without once stating his implied punchline, but it also roundly complements the genial American satire that it accompanies by poking fun at activities and standards that seem quintessentially British.

Within the context of *Dirty Linen*, however, Bernard's digression performs another distinct function by casting a jocular swipe at the discussion of the moral standards of public figures which is the main play's theme. The concern of the MPs' Sub-Committee is that the reputations of an ever-growing number of Parliamentary colleagues have been jeopardised by a mysterious woman under circumstances well documented by the national papers. What is worse, the Committee members considering what action to advise in the face of this onslaught are themselves not above suspicion. A new strike at the weekend by the *femme fatale* is reported in the morning copy of the *Daily Mail*:

> On the day the Select Committee on Moral Standards in Public Life is due to reconvene I ask – was it wise for one of the members to be seen holding hands under the table with a staggeringly voluptuous, titian-haired, green-eyed beauty in a West End restaurant at the weekend? And if so, was it modest to choose the Coq D'Or?   (p. 28)

The onus is thus on each MP on the Committee to prove that he is not the Member in question. It transpires, however, that no less than five of the six committee members have dined with this 'staggeringly voluptuous, titian-haired green-eyed beauty' at various stages of the weekend! Furthermore, the very lady in question, Miss Maddie Gotobed, has now turned up as Clerk to the Select

Committee, despite possessing a rather less than thorough grasp of basic secretarial skills! The stage is therefore set for a riotous farce of misfiring cover-ups as the embarrassed MPs, arriving in turn for the meeting, make furtive attempts to return incriminating underwear to their clerk and seek to ensure that she obliterates from her mind all the details of their weekend encounters.

Stoppard's intention throughout is to satirise the obsessive secrecy and hypocrisy to which this kind of situation gives rise. The chairman, Withenshaw, starts the proceedings by producing a draft report endorsing the principle that members' personal lives 'must stand in an exemplary relationship to the behaviour of the British people generally' (p. 35) – qualified by a string of amendments abusing the press. This is duly supported by all the Committee members except Cocklebury-Smythe, who happens to be a journalist. Such an approach, however, implicitly demands one set of values for those in the public eye and another for those out of it, thereby condemning the all-too-human men who are drafting it. Maddie cannot understand this, and plainly tells them so:

*Maddie:* People just don't care what M.P.s do in their spare time, they just want them to do their jobs properly bringing down prices and everything.
*Withenshaw:* Yes, well . . .
*Maddie:* Why don't they have a Select Committee to report on what M.P.s have been up to in their *working* hours – that's what people want to know. (p. 35)

Later she reiterates her point more forcibly:

*Maddie:* The press. The more you accuse them of malice and inaccuracy, the more you're admitting that they've got a right to poke their noses into your private life. All this fuss! The whole report can go straight in the waste-paper basket. All you need is one paragraph saying that M.P.s have got just as much right to enjoy themselves in their own way as anyone else, and Fleet Street can take a running jump.
*Withenshaw:* Miss Gotobed, you may not be aware that the clerk traditionally refrains from drafting the report of a Select Committee. (p. 41)

The late arrival of French, the sixth, unblemished member of the
Select Committee, goes some way towards explaining why the
others do not readily adopt Maddie's advice. The shrill self-
righteousness of his manner, superbly pilloried by Stoppard, sends
shivers of fear down their several spines:

> All right! Cards on the table! I didn't want to be the one to bring
> this up, but I rather expected to learn on arriving here today that
> one of the number – I except Mrs. Ebury, of course – had seen fit
> to resign from this Committee. I refer to the paragraph in today's
> *Mail*.   (p. 48)

It is worth noting that Stoppard does *not* except Mrs. Ebury, the one
female member of the committee; a clandestine encounter with
Maddie behind the blackboard makes it clear that she, like all her
male colleagues except French, has something to hide. Not one of
them, however, is prepared to contest French's schoolmasterly
insistence that 'this is going to teach them a lesson they'll never
forget' (p. 52) and it is left to Maddie's persuasive ways to win the
day. When the division bell sounds, and the other Members hasten
down to the floor of the Chamber, she asks French to direct her to
the ladies' cloakroom. What passes there can only be guessed at (!)
but after the Committee has reassembled, French reveals an abrupt
change of heart. Prompted by Maddie, he proposes a new resolution
defending MPs' rights to pass their social hours however they please,
which all present then unanimously adopt. To confirm the true
nature of his conversion, French meanwhile inadvertently mops his
brow with Maddie's knickers.

   *Dirty Linen* first appeared when the press exploration of Jeremy
Thorpe's alleged relationship with Norman Scott was beginning,
culminating in Thorpe's resignation as leader of the Liberal Party
and subsequent trial.[5] At the same time reporters in the United
States were exposing the way in which certain members of Congress
were bestowing perks on secretarial staff in return for sexual favours.
Yet the play was actually completed well before either of these
events became headline news and, as Stoppard modestly insisted,
the simultaneous emergence of these stories was quite coincidental.[6]
Maddie's straightforward view appears to reflect Stoppard's own,
recalling Milne's assertion in *Night and Day* that 'Junk journalism is
the evidence of a society that has got at least one thing right' (p. 61),
but the idea is treated almost from the start as a truism and the

eventual conclusion merely summarises the evident ridiculousness of the MPs' furtive attempts to cover up their tracks.

Stoppard pillories this obsessive secrecy with a general tone of mischievous, smirking sexuality and an armoury of carefully selected farcical devices: disappearing clothes, hasty cover-ups in mid-sentence, misfiring missives and desperate and hilarious attempts to preserve dignity on all sides. At the same time his critical awareness is constantly employed in creating the means to distance us from these mechanics. There is a mocking obviousness behind his puns – like the mounting pile of Maddie's drawers in her desk drawer, or the briefs which Withenshaw accidentally fishes from his briefcase. Other devices are so heavily mannered and deliberately executed that they underline their own crassness with pointed humour: Maddie's undressing by layers as her skirt, blouse and slip 'accidentally' come off in the hands of successive committee members; the overtly manipulated sequence of interruptions when McTeazle returns for his bowler hat just as Cocklebury-Smythe is imploring Maddie not to give him away, with Cocklebury-Smythe seconds later doing exactly the same to him; the charade of miscarrying notes passed to Maddie by Withenshaw and McTeazle, which culminates in Maddie's loud announcement 'I'm sitting on your slip' to the assembled committee when she mistakes one such message for a written amendment! Above all, the sense of selfconscious, dramatic contrivance emerges, as in *Travesties*, in the regular use of an action-freezing technique; each time a committee member glances at one of the pin-ups in the popular newspapers, Maddie herself assumes a simultaneous pin-up pose on the stage and the action is briefly and provocatively frozen.

In all these instances of theatrical and verbal manipulation, Stoppard parades the obviousness of his techniques with enormous relish in order to engage the audience's complicity in his theatrical game-playing – an approach quite distinct from that of conventional farce, where the author seeks to engage the audience's sympathy in his characters' embarrassments and misfortunes. As a result, Stoppard's play can perhaps be seen as a parody of the farce as practised, say, by Feydeau or Travers or Rix, and invites comparison with the kind of generic satire found elsewhere in Stoppard's work: in *The Real Inspector Hound* with the thriller form, for example, or even in *New-Found-Land* with a wide range of familiar American stereotypes. In each case a variety of telling details are accurately observed, only to be drawn into a richly ironic frame as Stoppard gently mocks or exposes the ridiculousness of his subject: the vainly distorted self-image of America, the crass mechanics of the thriller, or here, the furtive naughtiness of the farce.

The play's language, with its streams of punning, game-playing and elaborate verbal patterns (surpassing even *The Boundary*), its *Travesties*-like mimicry of Wildean style, its parody of rival newspaper styles (as in *Night and Day*) and its opening section, a conversation conducted entirely in snippets of foreign languages (an idea probably borrowed from the 'nonsense' language with which *Travesties* opens), constantly serves to further this deliberate sense of festive contrivance. Stoppard makes no concessions to character development so as to leave himself the greatest possible freedom to push their asides, innuendoes and slips of the tongue quite beyond the bounds of plausibility. As Cocklebury-Smythe gazes at Maddie's cleavage, for example, his words to his colleagues are submerged beneath a deluge of lewd thoughts:

> McTeazle, why don't you go and see if you can raise those great tits – boobs – those boobies, absolute tits, don't you agree, Malcolm and Douglas – though good men, of course, useful chaps, very decent, first rate, two of the best, Malcolm and Douglas, why don't you have a quick poke, peek, in the Members' Bra – or the cafeteria, they're probably guzzling coffee and Swedish panties, Danish . . . .   (p. 22)

Maddie's unlikely surname serves as a further contribution to the lecherous atmosphere and, elsewhere, sentences abruptly change direction in mid-course to enable furtive verbal messages to be conveyed to her in hushed undertones or because an intruder briefly enters. The most elaborate examples occur early in the play as the Members arrive for the meeting and try to erase from Maddie's memory any potentially incriminating details. An uproarious confusion results from the array of like-sounding restaurant names as Stoppard constructs a linguistic maze in which even the ever-willing Maddie becomes hopelessly entangled:

> *Cocklebury-Smythe:*  All right – tell you what – say you had *break-fast* at Claridges, *lunch* at the Coq D'Or, and had *dinner* at Crockford's. Meanwhile I'll stick to –

*Maddie (concentrating harder than ever)*:

Claridges, Coq D'Or, Crockford's. Forget Crockford's, Claridges, Coq D'Or. Remember Claridges, Coq D'Or, Crockford's. Remember Claridges, Coq D'Or, Crockford's. Claridges, Coq D'Or, Crockford's, Claridges, Coq D'Or, Crockford's.

*Cocklebury-Smythe:* But not with me.

*Maddie:* Not with you. Not with Cockie at Claridges, Coq D'Or, Crockford's. Never at Claridges, Coq D'Or, Crockford's with Cockie. Never at Claridges, Coq D'Or, Crockford's with Cockie.

*Cocklebury-Smythe:* Wait a minute. *(Rapidly)* The best thing is forget Claridges, Crockford's and the Coq D'Or altogether.

*Maddie:* Right. Forget Claridges, Crockford's, Coq D'Or – forget Claridges, Crockford's, Coq D'Or –

*Cocklebury-Smythe:* And if anyone asks you where you had lunch on Friday, breakfast on Saturday and dinner last night, when you were with me, tell them where you had dinner on Friday, lunch on Saturday and breakfast yesterday.

*Maddie:* Right! *(Pause. She closes her eyes with concentration.)* *(Rapidly.)* The Green Cockatoo, The Crooked Clock, The Crock of Gold – and Box Hill. (pp. 23–4)

The multiplying verve and relentless contrivance of such scenes serve to confirm Michael Billington's suggestion that the play's 'cumulative effect is of language being sent on a roller-coaster ride'.[7]

The hiccup in the roller-coaster ride lies, of course, in the strange relationship between *Dirty Linen*, with its genial social satire, and *New-Found-Land* with its cascade of allusions and digressions. This 'hiccup', however, is rather pleasurable, providing as it does a fine illustration of Stoppard's habitual upending of traditional the-atrical convention. Instead of following the MPs to a new scene when the division bell sounds (as might have been anticipated),

Stoppard provides dramatic continuity through the room itself. This would not be unusual were it not for the fact that Bernard and Arthur do not have the faintest connection with the Sub-Committee. They are, so to speak, taking part in a quite different play and the MPs' return therefore provokes alarming uncertainty as the two groups of occupants contest the available space! Although the committee members were present first, the Home Secretary (who has now joined the two civil servants) reminds Withenshaw that he is the senior member present: 'Yes, well, I'm sorry to pull rank on you, Malcolm – but I've got to deal with a very sensitive and difficult case –.' (p. 70) In the event, *Dirty Linen* is salvaged by the return of the clerk:

> Maddie (*to Home Secretary*): Hello, what are you doing here?
> Home Secretary:     How do you do? My name's Jones. (*To Withenshaw*) As I was saying, you must have the room, of course. *Noblesse oblige* –.    (p. 70)

The naturalisation form is hastily signed and the Home Secretary, Arthur and Bernard depart, enabling *Dirty Linen* to run its course. Before Stoppard neatly rounds off both pieces, however, he permits himself one final twist: Withenshaw's secret missives to Maddie have been on paper the same size as an old-style £5 note. When Bernard approaches Withenshaw, seemingly about to repeat his Lloyd George story, and declares 'Take a look at this – there's quite a story behind it' (p. 71), Withenshaw tears it up in guilty haste, not recognising what it really is or, as a result, the sentimental attachment it has for the crestfallen old man. He provides in the process the play's only moment of pathos and a rare connecting thread between the detail of the two plays – alongside the Home Secretary's guilty recognition of Maddie and Withenshaw's passing, cryptic remark: 'Yes, I once took a train journey right across America...but that's another story.' (pp. 31–2) Perhaps here, in the midst of a pair of plays packed to the seams with digressions of so many kinds, is the untold story of the *real* 'American Connection'!

\*              \*              \*

*Dogg's Hamlet, Cahoot's Macbeth* is, as the title this time acknowledges, another amalgam of two distinct plays, though their history is a good deal more complicated. The first part is, in Stoppard's words, a 'conflation'[8] of two earlier short pieces – *Dogg's*

*Our Pet*, commissioned for the opening of Inter-Action's Almost Free
Theatre in Rupert Street and premiered there in December 1971,
and *The (15-Minute) Dogg's Troupe Hamlet*, written ('or rather edited'[9])
for presentation on an Inter-Action double-decker playbus, but first
performed as a 'platform' presentation at the National Theatre in
1976.[10] The conflated play, with *Cahoot's Macbeth* newly added, was
first staged by Ed Berman (Professor Dogg is his pseudonym) and
his British American Repertory Company, featuring actors and
actresses of both nationalities, in May 1979 at the University of
Warwick Arts Centre in Coventry. Short runs at other British
theatres followed, including a brief season at the Collegiate Theatre
in London from the end of July, before the play was taken to the
United States in a rare example of co-operation between the actors'
unions on both sides of the Atlantic.

What separates *Dogg's Hamlet* most decisively from all of
Stoppard's other work is the fact that much of it is not written in
English, but in 'Dogg language', an at first mysterious tongue in
which sound and meaning appear to be utterly divorced from each
other. 'Brick', it transpires, means 'here'; 'block' means 'next' and
'slab' means 'thank you'. As Stoppard explains in his Preface, the
idea from which he derives his language is to be found in the work of
the innovative linguistic philosopher, Ludwig Wittgenstein. One
can think of very few playwrights (perhaps, indeed, only one!) who
might conceive the idea for a new play while reading the
*Philosophical Investigations*, yet it was during his thorough immersion
in philosophy which Stoppard undertook as background work for
*Jumpers* that the idea of *Dogg's Our Pet* took shape. The principles of
Wittgenstein's work are notoriously difficult to summarise. Put
briefly, he moved from upholding that the analysis of language was
our only reliable guide to discovering the true nature of the world
(not an unconventional view as such, but one which had very
considerable influence – not least on the fledgling Logical Positivists
of the Vienna Circle – when set down in his *Tractatus* in 1921/22) to
a far more radical position in which, contrarily, he decisively
separated the structure of language from the structure of the
perceivable world. In his seminal *Philosophical Investigations* (published posthumously in 1953), as Bartley suggests in a useful
monograph:

Human language, embedded in human conduct, is taken as the
starting point for an investigation which no longer àssumes that

the exploration of human language gives access to reality, but rather proposes that human language, as a *projection* of the mind rather than a picture of the world, in a sense *creates* reality.[11]

Wittgenstein stresses that all systems of language are man-made, that none is manifestly superior to any other and that it is the theory-forming habits implicit within these systems which colour all our observations. To this end he takes as an example a team of builders and explores the various theoretically possible meanings that their calls such as 'block!', 'slab!' or 'pillar!' might have, thereby demonstrating that it may *not* be the purpose of these words to evoke images and that senses other than simple descriptions of the building materials might be thus conveyed. His intention is to show the limitations of the theory of language-learning advanced by St Augustine in his *Confessions*, which suggested that a child acquires language when a man points at an object and states its name; according to Wittgenstein, this works

> as if the child came into a strange country and did not understand the language of the country; that is, as if he already had a language, only not this one.[12]

He establishes that Augustine's premise could only be true of very primitive linguistic forms and proceeds to examine the far more complex fabric of modern-day language.

It is this specific example of the team of builders, taken from the first few pages of the *Philosophical Investigations*,[13] which Stoppard develops in creating a situation where Easy the lorry driver (like Augustine's child) discovers that all the other characters are using a language with different (and usually contrary) senses from his own and it is the comic confusion engendered by their misfiring attempts at communication which provides the core of the play. The ramifications of Wittgenstein's argument are entirely serious but, unlike *Jumpers*, Stoppard's treatment is essentially playful. In presenting Dogg language to Easy, and to the audience, he erects as few barriers as possible. The language's structure, syntax, rhythms and intonations are thus broadly the same as English. Only the *sense* of the words is altered, so as to provide some lively, if often rather schoolboyish humour. This may, however, be appropriate in one sense, since the play's setting is a prep. school on speech day, to which Easy (the only non-Dogg speaker) brings his lorry-load of wood to assemble a platform for the prize-giving ceremony and the schoolboys' performance of *Hamlet* which is to follow it. The other main characters are Dogg, the headmaster, a small group of schoolboys, chiefly Abel, Baker and Charlie (the alphabetical naming emphasises their slenderness as individual characters)[14] and the dignified Lady who is guest of honour for the afternoon and whose main speech provides the most extended and slapstick example of Dogg language in action:

> Sad fact, brats pule puke crap-pot stink, spit; grow up dunces crooks; rank socks dank snotrags, conkers, ticks; crib books, cock snooks, block bogs, jack off, catch pox pick spots, scabs, padlocks, seek kicks, kinks, slack; nick swag, swig coke, bank kickbacks; . . . frankly can't stick kids.   (p. 28)

Here, with great obviousness but almost equal hilarity, Stoppard uses the thin 'disguise' of Dogg language to send up the speaker's stiff-necked propriety with a welter of crudely onomatopoeic syllables which point a meaning diametrically opposed to that which she intends.

As the play opens, the audience's first response – not an uncommon feature of a Stoppard play! – is disorientation, soon followed by a hunt for the 'correct' meanings of the Dogg language vocabulary:

> *Empty Stage*
> Baker:  *(Off-stage)* Brick!
> (*A football is thrown from off-stage left to off-stage right. Baker receiving ball*) Cube.
> (*Abel enters . . . with microphone and stand which he places down stage. The microphone has a switch.*)
> Abel:  *(into the microphone)* Breakfast, breakfast . . . sun – dock – trog . . .
> (*He realises the microphone is dead. He tries the switch a couple of times and then speaks again into the microphone.*) Sun – dock – trog – pan – slack . . .
> (*The microphone is still dead. Abel calls to someone off-stage.*) Haddock priest!   (p. 15)

Unlike the Lady's speech (which rather bends Stoppard's self-imposed rules), the members of the audience have to translate these exchanges for themselves in order to keep up with the play. In rough-and-ready terms, this proves to be a simple enough affair. 'Brick' means 'here', 'cube' means 'thank you', 'breakfast' means 'testing', 'sun, dock, trog' is a sequence of numbers (one, two, three) and 'haddock priest' means 'the mike is dead'. The audience's task here and throughout the play is eased very considerably by the explanatory visual context which Stoppard provides to help place the 'wrong' words into the 'right' context. It quickly emerges, for instance, that 'git' means 'sir'. 'Cretinous pig-faced, git?' (note the interrogation) sounds like an insult, but when it is addressed respectfully to Dogg by young Abel, the headmaster looks at his watch and answers with the correct time. The context is equally self-defining when the three boys, examining their packed lunches, propose various swaps of their sandwiches or when Charlie starts singing to the tune of 'My Way':

> Engage congratulate moreover state abysmal fairground.
> Begat perambulate this aerodrome chocolate eclair found.
> Maureen again dedum-de-da ultimately cried egg.
> Dinosaurs rely indoors if satisfied egg.   (p. 19)

Here the crucial clue is musical and even the rhyme scheme plays an important rôle. When Charlie then turns on his radio, the pace and intonations of the speaker's voice make it clear that we are listening to the day's football results, even if the teams' names are themselves indecipherable:

> Cabrank dock, Blanket Clock quite; Tube Clock dock, Handbag dock; Haddock Clock quite, Haddock Foglamp trog; Wonder quite, Picknicking pan.   (p. 25)

In all these cases, the clarity and familiarity of the context is such that the meanings are virtually unmistakable.

Sharing our confusion, of course, is Easy. When Abel asks *him* for the time ('Cretinous pig-faced, git?'), he gets an undeserved thick ear for his troubles. And when Easy offers an amiable 'Afternoon squire' to the headmaster he soon gathers, to his cost, that this means 'Get stuffed, you bastard'. As might be anticipated, though, the mutual confusion is at its greatest when the boys form a chain to help him construct the speech-day platform:

Dogg:    (*Calling out to Abel loudly – shouts*) Plank! (*To Easy's surprise and relief a plank is thrown to Baker who catches it, passes it to Charlie, who passes it to Easy, who places it on the stage. Dogg smiles, looks encouragingly at Easy.*)

Easy:    (*Uncertainly, calls.*) Plank!
(*To his surprise and relief a second plank is thrown in and passed to him the same way. He places it.*)
Plank!
(*A third plank is thrown in and positioned as before. Confidently, calls.*) Plank!
(*A block is thrown instead of a plank.*)    (p. 21)

And so it continues, occasionally as Easy intends, usually as he does not, since 'plank' in Dogg language means 'ready'! At the same time, he (like the audience) gradually pieces together one or two of the more basic meanings of Dogg and by the start of the boys' production of *Hamlet* he is able to demonstrate his growing grasp of the jargon by introducing it over the microphone: 'Hamlet bedsocks Denmark. Yeti William Shakespeare' (p. 38). As Cahoot says later, in the second play, 'You don't learn it, you catch it' (p. 74) – which is one of the crucial points that Wittgenstein is concerned to make. Learning, as he sees it, is more a process of 'tuning in' to the correct structures than of acquiring by rote (though this can in due course achieve the desired result). The process of learning Dogg is designed to make this very point, since its assimilation is more comparable with learning a technical jargon than a foreign language.[15]

By this point, readers unfamiliar with *Dogg's Hamlet* may well be wondering what this elaborate 'rival' system of language is all in aid of. Stoppard says:

The appeal consisted in the possibility of writing a play which had to teach the audience the language the play was written in. (*Preface*, p. 8.)

This invites a clear comparison with the 'puzzle' plays which we have previously examined. Dogg language, in this case, presents the puzzle which the audience must 'solve', and it is by no means surprising that rather than a mysteriously dead body or an incomprehensible sequence of sounds on a tape, Stoppard should on this occasion use an entire language system, to be deciphered like a code. For codes, jargons, clichés and other non-conversational language forms have exerted a continual fascination for him, from the clashing speech modes of *Lord Malquist and Mr Moon* or the thriller clichés of *Hound* to the football writers' jargon in *Professional Foul* or the deluge of restaurant names in *Dirty Linen*. A still clearer parallel might be drawn with *Rosencrantz*, in which the language of *Hamlet* introduces a decidedly alien note each time it swirls in to take over the stage. It may, indeed, have been this dramatic device which suggested to Stoppard how excitingly his truncated *Hamlet* might be accommodated within a context of Dogg language, for since the Shakespeare language is the first sustained English that we hear in the play, the effect is to undercut all of its archaisms or dissimilarities with our contemporary idioms. Coming after a prolonged exposure to the often banal and mainly monosyllabic Dogg language, Shakespeare thus sounds more like a breath of spring air than ever!

The version itself, which the schoolboys perform immediately after the prizegiving, is a remarkably ingenious compression, extracting only the most 'essential' exchanges of Shakespeare's play to create ten lightning-fast scenes in which all 'extraneous' descriptions, explanations or poetic embellishments are removed and where cut-outs of the sun and moon flick up or down to suggest night or day. Minor characters such as Rosencrantz and Guildenstern are naturally omitted, together with the second Gravedigger, Reynaldo (Polonius's servant), Voltimand and Cornelius (the ambassadors to Norway) and the Players, who are reduced to hand-puppets. Some half-dozen speeches are re-attributed to aid continuity (Hamlet, for instance, usurps from Marcellus the line 'Something is rotten in the state of Denmark'), but the fidelity to Shakespeare's words is otherwise absolute, with no interpolations and no speeches taken far out of their true sequence:

(*Enter Ghost above the wall built of blocks*)
Hamlet: Angels and ministers of grace defend us! Something is rotten in the state of Denmark! Alas, poor ghost.
Ghost: I am thy father's spirit.
Revenge his foul and most unnatural murder.
Hamlet: Murder?
Ghost: The serpent that did sting thy father's life
Now wears his crown.

*Hamlet:* O my prophetic soul! My uncle? *(Exit Ghost. To Horatio.)*
There are more things in heaven and earth
Than are dreamt of in your philosophy.
*(Exit Horatio.)*
(pp. 33–4)

All the main threads of the plot emerge intact, and far more of the spirit of Shakespeare's play survives than one might have anticipated. The *reductio ad absurdum* exercise is, however, taken to its logical extreme in two further separate versions: in Dogg's prologue, a sketchy resumé of key lines from the play, cleverly tailored to resemble the typical generalities of a headmaster's speech, and in a final two-minute 'encore' in which almost the same number of characters rush on and off-stage but with their speeches desperately truncated. This version, conducted in breathless haste, palpably lacks the coherence of the 15-minute version, despite the dexterity with which Stoppard assembles it and is included simply for the frenetic comedy which it generates.

Comedy, in fact, is the guardian angel that presides over all of *Dogg's Hamlet*, whether in its Wittgenstein-inspired language games or its equally playful compression of Shakespeare's most familiar masterpiece. The same cannot be said of its integrated companion piece *Cahoot's Macbeth*. Its centrepiece is another cleverly scaled-down Shakespearean classic that comes near to rivalling the compact precision of Stoppard's mini-*Hamlet*. Yet the setting of the mini-*Macbeth*, a living-room in the Prague flat, offers the starkest of contrasts with the English prep. school of the first play. We are back in the terrain of *Professional Foul*, in an illiberal, post-Dubcek Czechoslovakia which systematically clamps down on dissent of all kinds, in the company of a group of persecuted, out-of-work actors who are mounting a reduced-scale production of *Macbeth* in the homes of friends and sympathisers. As Stoppard explains in his Preface, the play's origin lies in a real-life version of *Macbeth* presented with a 'Living-Room Theatre' group during the summer of 1978 by the persecuted playwright Pavel Kahout,whom Stoppard met on his visit to Prague in 1977 and to whom the play is dedicated. This production featured Kahout himself in some minor rôles and Pavel Landovsky as Macbeth, with other parts played by well-known actors who had similarly fallen foul of the authorities. Stoppard retains these two names in his version (though he insists that they are not in any sense intended as portraits) to authenticate the factual basis of the idea, while at the same time fictionalising other details. Chief among these is the invented character of the Inspector who interrupts the performance on two occasions, firstly delivering a stern warning of possible repercussions, and secondly physically attempting to put a stop to the proceedings.

Yet although the Inspector personifies a police-controlled state whose oppression is only too real, Stoppard presents him as an essentially comic creation, striving to highlight the paradoxes of the repressive system in the most humorous light possible. Under the Inspector's deadpan, but discernibly tongue-in-check questioning, it soon emerges that the plight of the actor Landovsky is akin to that of Hollar in *Professional Foul*:

| | |
|---|---|
| *Inspector:* | Who are you, pigface? |
| *'Macbeth':* | Landovsky. |
| *Inspector:* | The actor? |
| *'Macbeth':* | The floor cleaner in a boiler factory. |
| *Inspector:* | That's him. I'm a great admirer of yours, you know. I've followed your career for years. |
| *'Macbeth':* | I haven't worked for years. |
| *Inspector:* | What are you talking about? – I saw you last season – my wife was with me . . . |
| *'Macbeth':* | It couldn't have been me. |
| *Inspector:* | It *was* you – you looked great – sounded great – where were you last year? |
| *'Macbeth':* | I was selling papers in – |
| *Inspector:* | (*Triumphantly*) – in the newspaper kiosk at the tram terminus, and you were wonderful! I said to my wife, that's Landovsky – the actor, isn't he great?' |

(p. 54)

The irony here is neatly balanced between dismay and comedy in a manner reminiscent of *Every Good Boy Deserves Favour* and, moments later, another echo from the same source is caught as the Inspector starts to quiz 'Lady Macbeth' with the same kind of circular, pseudo-logic which characterises the violin-playing Doctor:

| | |
|---|---|
| *Inspector:* | Could I have your autograph, it's not for me, it's for my daughter – |
| *'Lady Macbeth':* | I'd rather not – the last time I signed something I didn't work for two years. |

| | |
|---|---|
| *Inspector:* | Now, look don't blame *us* if the parts just stopped coming. Maybe you got over-exposed. |
| *'Lady Macbeth':* | I was working in a restaurant at the time. |
| *Inspector:* | (*Imperturbably*) There you are, you see. The public's very funny about that sort of thing. They don't want to get dressed up and arrange a baby-sitter only to find that they've paid good money to see *Hedda Gabler* done by a waitress.  (p. 55) |

It becomes clearer by the minute that whereas the reduction of *Hamlet* is pure Stoppard fun, the reduction of *Macbeth* is a brutal necessity – the only conceivable means of presenting the play in *any* form under the pressures of the Czechoslovakian police state.

Kahout's *Macbeth* apparently ran for about 75 minutes. Stoppard's version, which is not based on Kahout's, remains (like his *Hamlet*) selectively true to Shakespeare's text, retains all the main characters in its cast, and runs for perhaps rather less than half of this, though its precise length is difficult to gauge on account of the Inspector's lengthy interventions. These interventions, however, are dovetailed with beautiful, ironic appropriateness into the unfolding action, the first coming immediately after the murder of Duncan, with all the weight of a prophecy:

| | |
|---|---|
| *Macbeth:* | I have done the deed. Didst thou not hear a noise? |
| *Lady Macbeth:* | I heard the owl scream and the crickets cry. (*A police siren is heard approaching the house. During the following dialogue the car arrives and the car doors are heard to slam.*) |
| *Macbeth:* | There's one did laugh in's sleep, and one cried 'Murder!' One cried 'God bless us!' and 'Amen' the other, (*Siren stops*) As they had seen me with these hangman's hands.  (p. 52) |

With further irony, the inspector then raps at the door to coincide, with exquisite timing, with the rapping that wakens the Porter and leads to the discovery of the murder. His jocular manner is not altogether unlike the Porter, either, and also shares many charac-

teristics with Stoppard's previous stock policeman – Hound, Foot in
*After Magritte* and Bones in *Jumpers* – not least in the way he comes
remarkably close to a stand-up comic at times:

> *Hostess:*  I'm afraid the performance is not open to the public.
> *Inspector:*  I should hope not indeed. That would be acting
> without authority – acting without authority! – you'd
> never believe I make it up as I go along.  (p. 56)

The absence of a corpse, of criminal activity or indeed of criminal
intent of any kind provides the crucial distinction which sets him
apart from these wholly comic forebears, however, for it is the
Inspector himself who is the oppressor in *Cahoot's Macbeth*. When he
declares, for instance, 'If I walk out of this show, I take it me with
me' (p. 56), the jocularity of his manner strikes a discomforting
balance with the sinister intentions which underpin it and there is a
particularly unnerving sense of implied threat when he turns to the
state's concept of subversive activity:

> The chief says he'd rather you stood up and said 'There is no
> freedom in this country', then there's nothing underhand and we
> all know where we stand. You get your lads together and we get
> our lads together and when it's all over, one of us is in power and
> you're in gaol. That's freedom in action. But what we don't like is
> a lot of people being cheeky and saying they are only Julius
> Caesar or Coriolanus or Macbeth. Otherwise we are going to
> start treating them the same as the ones who say they are
> Napoleon. Got it?  (p. 60–1)

Culture *can*, of course, be just the kind of liberating force that the
police department realises, as Stoppard deftly demonstrates by
developing to maximum effect the ironic parallels between
Scotland under the tyrant Macbeth and Czechoslovakia under the
tyrannical secret police. When the Inspector returns a second time,
his approaching siren is used to still more devasting effect:

> *Macduff:*  Bleed, bleed, poor country!
> *(Police siren is heard in distance)*
> *Malcolm:*  It weeps, it bleeds, and each new day a gash is added
> to her wounds.

*Macduff:*　O Scotland, Scotland!
　　　　　　O nation miserable,
　　　　　　With an untitled tyrant, bloody-sceptred,
　　ˎ　　　When wilt thou see thy wholesome days again?
　　　　　　See who comes here.
　　　　　　(*Siren stops*)
*Malcolm:*　My countryman; but yet I know him not. (*Inspector enters.*)　(p. 72)

Their 'countryman' then attempts to bring the curtain down by force, since the actors have ignored his earlier warning and resumed their performance. (The flat is bugged, so the police are fully aware of everything that is said or done, even in their absence.) But in the interim Easy has arrived unexpectedly with his lorry-load of wood, speaking fluently in Dogg language; in the face of the Inspector's second assault on their production, the actors abruptly decide to switch *en masse* into Dogg in order to press ahead to Shakespeare's conclusion and the tyrant's final downfall:

(*Lady Macbeth wails and cries off-stage. Messenger enters.*)
*Messenger:* Git! Margarine distract!
*Macbeth:*　Dominoes et dominoes et dominoes,
　　　　　　Popsies historical axle-grease, exacts bubbly fins crock
　　　　　　lavender.　(p. 77)

Refusing to admit defeat, the Inspector and his comic sidekicks Boris and Maurice start using Easy's slabs to build a wall across the front of the performing area, to cut the actors off from the audience, but before they can finish Macbeth is duly slain and Malcolm crowned – to a final, defiant fanfare from which Stoppard's moral clearly reverberates: that however hard the authorities might combat dissent and drive it underground (into other languages even!), it can never be obliterated from the human spirit.

　In the end, the curious admixture of comic and serious intentions within *Dogg's Hamlet, Cahoot's Macbeth* is strongly reminiscent of the unequal struggle between similar elements in *Every Good Boy Deserves Favour*. Stoppard's intention seems not so much the creation of a tragi-comic mood (*Rosencrantz*, of all his plays, comes closest to this), but more the reconciliation of these separate elements within an enfolding dramatic unity. And here, as in *Every Good Boy*, the serious and comic elements are for the most part kept skilfully apart. Our unease only becomes apparent when they encroach into each other's 'territory'. The Inspector, for instance, though he is a superbly developed comic creation, emerges as far and away the play's most attractive character; despite all that he stands for, he is an almost lovable comic villain and, as Hunter suggests:

> one almost worries more at the end about what the Inspector is going to say to his chief than about the future of the hounded actors.[16]

Equally, Stoppard's audacious comic stroke in having the Czech actors switch into Dogg language completes his *Macbeth* and links the two plays with all his customary ingenuity, but the vehicle by which it is achieved – Easy's improbable arrival in Prague – strains our credulity to the very limit and tips the delicate balance he has carefully struck between frivolity and seriousness so firmly in the former direction that it diminishes the true plight of the dissidents in a way in which neither of his 1977 plays do. Thus, although there is an enormous amount to enjoy in both *Dogg's Hamlet* and *Cahoot's Macbeth*, their enforced yoking to each other imposes a colossal sense of strain. The scope of *Dirty Linen* and *New-Found Land* is altogether more slender, but the delightfully effective 'marriage' of its two virtually unconnected playlets cannot but emphasise by comparison the shotgun wedding that bonds together the other pair of plays.

*                    *                    *

*On the Razzle* opened at the National Theatre's Lyttleton auditorium on 22 September 1981 in a production by Peter Wood starring Dinsdale Landen, Felicity Kendal, Ray Brooks and Michael Kitchen. Based on Johann Nestroy's Viennese comedy *Einen Jux will er sich machen* (He's Out for a Fling), it is the fourth play which Stoppard adapted from a foreign language original, following productions of Slawomir Mrozek's *Tango* (1966), Lorca's *House of Bernarda Alba* (1973) and Schnitzler's *Undiscovered Country* (1979).[17] While these three adaptations have great colloquial and dramatic fluency (especially *Undiscovered Country*), all are more or less faithful renderings, in an English idiom, of the literal translations from which Stoppard worked and cannot, in consequence, really be considered as part of his own canon. On the evening of the opening of *Bernarda Alba*, for instance, he told Michael Leech:

I don't know any Spanish at all. Lorca has already decided what the play is about and how it works. I think of myself as an adaptor.[18]

It is because *On the Razzle* is *not* adapted in this same spirit that it is discussed here; for with this play, the 'adaptation' has become something altogether freer, balanced mid-way between an adaptation and a complete re-working. In Stoppard's own words:

this text is not really a translation of Nestroy's play in the strictest sense. My method might be compared to cross-country hiking with map and compass, where one takes a bearing on the next landmark and picks one's way towards it: a method which would not have done when I was turning Schnitzler's *Das Weite Land* into *Undiscovered Country*.[19]

Consequently, though the story outline, the characters and something of the spirit of Nestroy's play remain clearly visible, Stoppard's distinctive stamp is far more in evidence than in his other adaptations.

There is a special precedent for the more liberal reshaping of this play. For a start, Nestroy's tale of a day out in Vienna is itself a considerably expanded version of the little known one-act farce *A Day Well Spent* by the English playwright John Oxenford, first performed in 1835 (the city in this case being pre-Victorian London). In its turn, *Einen Jux* (first performed in 1842) was liberally reshaped by the American playwright Thornton Wilder, first into *The Merchant of Yonkers*, a Broadway flop of 1938, and subsequently, with minimal re-writing, into *The Matchmaker*, first staged at the Edinburgh Festival in 1954.[20] Wilder's sentimental farce follows Nestroy's broad storyline, but switches the action to New York, renames nearly all of the characters and introduces one important new one, Dolly Levi – the 'matchmaker' of the title – who is angling to land an advantageous marriage for herself. *The Matchmaker*, in turn, provided the inspiration for Michael Stewart and Jerry Herman's musical *Hello Dolly!* (Broadway, 1964; Drury Lane, 1965), which makes Mrs Levi a still more central character. It is to these five extant versions, then, from three different countries, that Stoppard adds *On the Razzle*.

His play is far closer than Wilder's to Nestroy's original. Working from a literal translation by Neville and Stephen Plaice, he keeps the same characters, retaining their original names, and most of the plot. Wilder, in his preface, compares his version to Nestroy's stressing that it is

> all 'about' quite different matters. My play is about aspirations of the young (and not only of the young) for a fuller, freer participation in life.[21]

Stoppard's preface duly declares that

> Wilder's temperament, which serves *The Matchmaker* so well, made gentler and more dignified use of the original than I intended, while, furthermore, his adaptation of the plot was rather more free than anything I had in mind.[22]

Stoppard's aim, he avows, was to follow Nestroy's 'prime concern to make the tale as comic an entertainment as possible' (p. 7). This, clearly, was never Wilder's intention, since he introduces moral considerations at several points as a deliberate counter to the farcical spirit, nowhere shown more clearly than in the speeches of self-justifying sermonising made by one character or another at key points in each of the four acts. Thus Malachi the servant (Melchior in Nestroy and Stoppard) finds himself 'obliged' in the third act to explain in a lengthy aside why he does not intend to keep a purse he has just found on the restaurant floor and Dolly, in the final act, defends her intention of marrying the well-to-do grocer Vandergelder (Zangler in Nestroy and Stoppard) as if addressing her late husband's 'spirit'. The tone of this speech, like much of the play, strives for something of the worldly-wisdom of Shakespearean comedy:

> Yes, we're all fools and we're all in danger of destroying the world with our folly. But the surest way to keep us out of harm is to give us the four or five human pleasures that are our right in the world – and that takes a little *money*![23]

This typifies the moralising, defensive posture which Wilder strikes throughout his comedy. Stoppard has no such guilt at the shamelessly farcical thrust of his. He makes no attempt to 'civilise' or 'humanise' his farce and underplays or excises those tendencies in this direction encountered in *Einen Jux*, including the three comic song sequences commenting on aspects of everyday morality which Nestroy created for Weinberl (originally his own rôle). James Fenton in *The Sunday Times* complained, with some justification, that 'one important typical feature of Austrian comedy is lost' as a result, but in declaring that Stoppard shows 'complete misunderstanding of the dynamics of the plot'[24] he both overstates his objections and fails to allow for the kind of new version at which Stoppard is aiming. That aim, moreover, once recognised and accepted in all its singularity, is carried out with an absolute mastery of the farce idiom; in its breathtakingly engineered mechanics and its often dizzying verbal game-playing, *On the Razzle* is the equal not only of any of Stoppard's own previous work, but of any British farce of recent memory.

The storyline of *On the Razzle*, which has three main threads, is simply told. Zangler, the country town grocer, is travelling to the city (Vienna) to secure his hoped-for marriage to Madame Knorr, who runs a milliner's shop. He is simultaneously trying to foil the attentions which Sonders, a suitor, is paying to his ward and niece, Marie, and aims to despatch her to the safe keeping of his sister-in-law, Miss Blumenblatt. Zangler's newly promoted shop assistants, Weinberl and Christopher (Christopherl in *Einen Jux*) meanwhile close the shop and secretly embark on a day-long fling in the city. As chance (patron deity of the farce) would have it, they are forced to conceal themselves from Zangler in his fiancée's hat-shop, then obliged to take Madame Knorr and her friend Frau Fischer out for a slap-up meal at the very restaurant where Marie and Sonders are dining, having eloped, and where Zangler arrives in hot pursuit of them! A complex system of near-misses and disguised exits ensues, with all the characters finally arriving at Miss Blumenblatt's flat. Zangler now suspects that Weinberl and Christopher are 'on the razzle' but they successfully hide from him and by travelling home undetected on the roof of his coach, manage to be back in the shop first, defraying his suspicions and concentrating his mind on his bride-to-be. Sonders, disguised as the coachman, is exposed but abruptly learns that he has come into a fortune, and he and Marie are permitted to marry. Weinberl, however, chances his arm rather too far; unlike Nestroy's original, he fails to win the rich widow, Frau Fischer.

Stoppard's main innovation is to bring the characters of Nestroy's play into both the broad tradition of English farce and a terrain that is distinctly his own. Zangler provides the clearest illustration of this. His rôle in Nestroy's play is largely that of a blustering, impatient task master and comic butt. (Wilder follows in this broad direction, but also takes him closer to a miserly stereotype.) Stoppard, as might have been at least half-expected, turns him into a delightful blunderer, a paradigm of confusion, getting nearly everything wrong and spraying spoonerisms and malapropisms into the comic air with confetti-like ease. From his first encounter with Sonders, the scene is set for a deluge of linguistic confusion:

*Sonders:*   Marie must be mine!
*Zangler:*   Never! She is a star out of thy firmament, Sonders...

           Do you suppose I'd let my airedale be hounded up hill and–my heiress be mounted up hill and bank by a truffle-hound–be trifled with and hounded by a moun-tebank?! Not for all the tea in China! Well, I might for all the tea in China, or the rice–no, that's ridiculous–the preserved ginger then–no, let's say half the tea, the ginger, a shipment of shark-fin soup double-discounted just to take it off your hands–

*Sonders:*   All you think about is money!
*Zangler:*   All I think about *is* money! As far as I'm concerned, any man who molests Marie might as well have his hand in my till!   (pp. 10–11)

As the action progresses, and as Zangler's patience shrinks, other characters try to help him fish for the right phrases, such as Weinberl, when asked to mind the shop in his employer's absence:

*Zangler:*   I'm sending Marie away for a few days. You'll have to manage the while the till . . . No–
*Weinberl:*   To while the time...
*Zangler:*   No!
*Weinberl:*   The till the while?
*Zangler:*   That's the boy   (pp. 23–4)

or the cook, when instructed to watch out for Sonders:

*Zangler:*   Marie's window is open! God in Himalayas!–If I keep having to come back I'll miss the parade. I told you not to let Marie out of your sight.

| | |
|---|---|
| *Gertrud:* | You told me to find Weinberl and tell him— |
| *Zangler:* | Don't tell me what I told you—search her room, perhaps he's got my ward's behind between his knees and raped her backwards—no— |
| *Gertrud:* | —got back behind your niece and ward's drapes— |
| *Zangler:* | No! |
| *Gertrud:* | Got behind your back and in your niece's wardrobe. |
| *Zangler:* | That's the boy.  (p. 38) |

Zangler's ancestry clearly includes Brenda, the delightfully improbable lexicographical assistant in *The Boundary*, the various MPs who prompt and coax Maddie into 'correct' versions of the restaurants she has visited in *Dirty Linen*, and also Henry Carr. The words 'That's the boy' are established as a catch-phrase which pulls Zangler's sense back onto the rails, rather in the same way as Carr's erratic memory is frequently tugged back into line. This kind of linguistic confusion, so beloved of Stoppard, is not derived from Nestroy's Zangler at all, though the catch-phrases of other characters are originally his, particularly Melchior's perpetual use of the word 'classic!' and Marie's insistent refrain 'It's not proper!' Nestroy's strong Viennese dialect and his highly idiosyncratic use of language do, nevertheless, provide a precedent of sorts for Stoppard's playful trails of verbal chaos; he has, for instance, been described by one critic as 'untranslatable, even into German'![25]

It is also significant that Stoppard elects to move the action forward from mid-century to turn-of-the-century Vienna, since this enables him to create a plausible sense of style in the genteel late Victorian mould, previously cultivated with such panache in *Lord Malquist* and *Travesties* (though one is set in 1965 and the other in 1917!). The social order is again one in which waiters are wiser than customers (Weinberl has no idea how to order a meal in the rather posh restaurant) and servants are conspicuously smarter than their employers:

| | |
|---|---|
| *Zangler:* | You have never been sacked? |
| *Melchior:* | Technically, yes, but only after I have let it be known by subtle neglect of my duties that the job has run its course. |
| *Zangler:* | That's very considerate. |

> *Melchior:* I don't like to give offence by giving notice–in a servant
> it looks presumptuous.
> *Zangler:* That shows modesty.
> *Melchior:* Your humble servant, sir.  (p. 15)

The echoes of Crouch, the wrily philosophical servant in *Jumpers*, or
Bennett, the politically astute 'servant' in *Travesties*, are distinctive.
So too are the echoes of suave Wildean polish, emerging in some
splendid epigrams such as this, from the endangered Weinberl:

> Thank heavens! Now you can see that my friend and I are the
> innocent victims of a police force the like of which would explode
> the credibility of a comic opera.  (p.65)

And earlier, when Weinberl tries to pass himself off as Frau Fischer's
new husband (to her astonishment), a series of beautifully clipped
exchanges ensue:

> *Mrs Fischer:* My husband has a very individual way of dealing
> with the banalities of ordinary time – I expect we'll
> be engaged next week and exchange cards the week
> after.
> *Mme Knorr:* Isn't she priceless?
> *Weinberl:* I expect you think I'm rather presumptuous.
> *Mrs Fischer:* No, I wouldn't say you were presumptuous.
> Presumption one has encountered before.
> *Weinberl:* Well, a little forward.
> *Mrs Fischer:* A little? You're in danger of meeting yourself
> coming back.  (p. 41)

The slightly over-formal dialogue, with just sufficient hints of
nineteenth-century manners and syntax, is most effective in evoking
a touch of period flavour to which English audiences can effortlessly
relate.

At the same time, Stoppard's festive wordplay, selfconsciously
parading its own contrivance, evokes the kind of carnival atmosphere in which some fairly broad sexual innuendo can be comfortably and inoffensively accommodated. This runs intermittently
(and usually unconsciously!) through Zangler's speeches, as we
have already seen, but it is also employed with particular gusto in
expanding two of Nestroy's walk-on characters into splendid minor

comic creations. The coachman, wholly nondescript in *Einen Jux*, becomes a man who, every so often, becomes ablaze with sexual obsession:

*Coachman:* I'm sorry, your honour! – my apologies! – please disregard it. I'll be all right now.
*Zangler:* Are you quite sure?
*Coachman:* Oh yes. These attacks never last long.
*Zangler:* What sets you off?
*Coachman:* Thinking about buttocks, sir.
*Zangler:* Well, can't you keep your mind off them?
*Coachman:* I'm a coachman.  (p. 48)

Moments later, however, on hearing that Miss Blumenblatt has a French maid, he becomes almost uncontrollable again. This maid, Lisette – equally nondescript in *Einen Jux*, and not explicitly French – turns out to be longing for a man to steal her heart, and when the coachman duly arrives, it is a clear case of lust at first sight:

(*The Coachman turns his attention to Miss Blumenblatt but Lisette stops him.*)

*Lisette:* Wait! (*She leaps up and kisses him firmly on the mouth.*) At last!
*Coachman* (*Highly gratified*): Are you a goer?
*Lisette:* I am a goer! You have horses?
*Coachman:* I have the finest pair of chestnuts of any coachman in the city. (*Lisette half swoons in his arms.*)
(*Bewildered*) What did I say?
*Lisette* (*Reviving*): My window will be open. Get up with me on your high horse.  (pp. 63–4)

The barely controllable coachman and maid then retire to the kitchen, from which Lisette, progressively *déshabillé*, progressively unstable on her feet, emerges each time a new arrival rings the doorbell. This, naturally, recalls Maddie's gradual undressing in *Dirty Linen* and is, in one form or another, an almost essential ingredient of contemporary farce. This particular relationship, however, is not merely the pretext for introducing some rumbusti-

ous sex-play into contexts from which it would be otherwise absent;
Stoppard uses it in the very next scene to untangle a vital strand of
his plot. In Nestroy's play, Sonders is simply captured in pursuit of
Marie in Madame Blumenblatt's garden. In Stoppard's, the
coachman sneaks up a ladder to Lisette's room, only to be
overpowered by Sonders, who then dresses up in his livery and,
unsuspected, drives home the coach in which Zangler is travelling
with his supposedly 'rescued' niece!

This is one of several adjustments to the storyline that Stoppard
makes. It would be tedious and unrewarding to catalogue the
variations between his version and *Einen Jux*, but a few specific
comments are illuminating. Among the strands not in Nestroy's
original is the running joke about Tartan capes which, besides
setting up a string of witty puns (there is 'plum Macduff' on the
restaurant menu; the 'tartan fad' is 'plaid out', and so forth), adds
both colour and familiarity to the frequent disguises in over-sized
cloaks and capes called for by the action. As Zangler explains:

> Vienna has been over-run with Scottish capes, kilts, tam-o'-
> shanters, Royal Stuart pencil cases and highland flingery of every
> stripe since the town lost its head over the Verdi *Macbeth*. In my
> opinion it's a disgrace.  (p. 37)

Other new threads Stoppard introduces include a mysterious (and
perhaps anachronistic) romantic pen-friendship which Weinberl is
conducting under the name of 'Scaramouche' with 'Elegant And
Under Forty' – who turns out, improbably, to be Frau Fischer! –
and the mischievous link he provides between Miss Blumenblatt's
lost love and Madame Knorr's past. In Nestroy's version,
Blumenblatt was actually deserted, years before, by her lover;
Stoppard's character has merely spent her life pining for a man who
once sat opposite her on a horse-tram in the Bahnhofstrasse:

| | |
|---|---|
| *Lisette:* | What happened to 'im, Madame? |
| *Miss Blumenblatt:* | He jumped off between stops and I never saw him again. But it was still love, and it was still separation. I'll never forget the pain as he rolled out of my sight for ever!  (p. 63) |

Later, when she meets her brother-in-law's intended for the first time, their conversation idly drifts to the subject of Madame Knorr's *first* husband:

| | |
|---|---|
| *Mme Knorr:* | Oh yes, *he* had two left feet, poor Alfred . . . |
| *Miss Blumenblatt:* | What happened to him? |
| *Mme Knorr:* | He got knocked down by a horse-tram in the Bahnhofstrasse. (p. 72) |

Could it have been the same man? This typically, furiously neat minor link (reminiscent of the ironic twist at the heart of *Artist Descending a Staircase*) is casually upturned, only to be left tantalisingly in the air.

A more important innovation is the way in which Stoppard begins and ends the action inside Zangler's shop, which never figures in Nestroy's play (nor, indeed, in Wilder's). Once again, this demonstrates his concern to leave out no possibilities for multiplying the farcical effects. Nestroy's opening scene takes place in Zangler's house behind the shop and the action returns there at the end when Weinberl and Christopherl catch a burglar (acting in league with Zangler's former servant) to earn their boss's beaming approbation. Stoppard, who cuts these burglary scenes, chooses instead to focus on the shop itself, using to the full an array of built-in gadgetry such as an old-fashioned cashier's cage, fed by wire canisters from the counters, a trapdoor, a large cupboard and a shute for delivering sacks of flour and similar provisions to the shop floor. All of these are employed with typical ingenuity. During the first act, Zangler catches Sonders sending secret love missives down the wires to Marie (the cashier) and Sonders and Marie mistake Weinberl for Zangler when all three hide in a cupboard. In the last scene, which in Stoppard's play hinges to a far greater extent on the race for home between Zangler and his two assistants, the devices enable Christopher to arrive via the trapdoor and Weinberl via the flour shute, just in the nick of time! Such contrivances are typical of those used throughout the play, many (but by no means all) of which are taken from *Einen Jux*. Elements of disguise, assumed identities and confused identities are constantly interchanged, while jangling spurs, a tailor's dummy, swing doors, a folding screen, a ladder, a bedroom window and a coach roof all have significant rôles to play.

The frenetic, dual concentration on verbal and mechanical acrobatics is never slackened. In the process no serious statement of any kind emerges from the play (not even one comparable to the truism at the heart of *Dirty Linen*) and none of the characters is developed more than peremptorily. What matters is the on-rushing comic feast. *On the Razzle* is Stoppard's least serious play and at the same time one of his most accomplished.

Although *On The Razzle* is an adaptation, then, it offers far more points of comparison with Stoppard's 'original' work than one might have anticipated. The process of working from another play, is, of course, scarcely new to him. Back in 1974, while working on *Travesties*, he admitted to *Theatre Quarterly*:

> I have enormous difficulty in working out plots, so actually to use *Hamlet*, or a classical whodunnit, or another play (which I'm afraid I've just done again) for a basic structure, takes a lot of the pressure off me.[26]

The remark naturally holds true of *Travesties*, in which *The Importance of Being Earnest* provides a crucial rudder, but it is still more revealing in the context of *On the Razzle*. For although at least partially belied by the ingenuity with which Stoppard *complicates* Nestroy's plot, it shows how a more or less ready-made structure of plot and characters enables him to turn his almost undistracted attentions to injecting his raw materials with the greatest possible comic invention. According to Hunter, the play amounts to Stoppard's 'homage to the farce tradition'.[27] This is clearly more apt a description of *On the Razzle* than of *Jumpers* or *Travesties* or *Dirty Linen*, although all of them draw strongly at times on the rich traditions of nineteenth and twentieth century farce, but 'homage' is not perhaps quite the right word since, as in *Dirty Linen*, a mischievous current of farcical parody continually bubbles throughout the play. The same relentlessly tongue-in-cheek theatrical self-consciousness which produces the ingenious enmeshing of two virtually unrelated plays in *Dirty Linen* and *New-Found-Land* and, less happily, in *Dogg's Hamlet* and *Cahoot's Macbeth*, and which is such a constant feature of all Stoppard's work, is once again in firm control.

# 13  Conclusion

No more than an interim assessment can be made of a writer in his mid-forties who is still writing fairly prolifically and whose work covers such a diverse range. As if to emphasise both these facts, Tom Stoppard produced two very different new plays at the end of 1982. *The Real Thing* opened at the Strand Theatre on 16 November, in a production again directed by Peter Wood which starred Roger Rees and Felicity Kendal.[1] Dedicated by Stoppard to his wife Miriam, and easily his most personal play to date, it tackles a subject from which in the past he has notoriously shied away, namely love. Taking as his two central characters, Henry, a drily unemotional and at least semi-autobiographical playwright, and Annie, an actress, he enquires whether love and marriage can ever be truly compatible, and after conducting us through their initial affair (while each is married to someone else), their marriage and their subsequent love entanglements, finally answers his question in the affirmative. Writing in *Punch*, Sheridan Morley averred that

> When they come to write the textbooks on Tom Stoppard, if they haven't already started, this is the play that's going to give them the most trouble since it fits almost no preconceived notion of the kind of playwright he is thought to be.[2]

This is not altogether true. The subject-matter of the play admittedly leads us into new terrain, both because of its intrinsic emotional content and because Stoppard's treatment of it is less a survey of possible social and moral viewpoints (à la *Travesties*), more a genuine-hearted exploration of the value of love through the experiences of his two central characters. Structurally, however, *The Real Thing* offers a mixture of broad naturalism and subversive artifice closely akin to *Night and Day* and, as in that play, the admixture is not wholly felicitous. Stoppard has never been at his best as a conversational playwright and in this carefully structured sequence of conversational exchanges, some direct and fraught, others elliptical and cynical, his comic energies are again kept under severe rein. There are scenes of considerable ingenuity, shuttling between the world of Henry's plays and that of his 'real' life, and a number of splendidly witty exchanges (nearly all of them in the first half of the play), but no moment between Annie and Henry, the two characters whom Stoppard intends us to care passionately about, is ever as poignant or as 'real' as the painful realisation by Max, Annie's first husband, that he has lost her forever. The intensity of this early scene carries the same sharp dart of anguish as Sophie's death in *Artist Descending* after her love affair has turned so sour. It brings to mind the remark, echoed in one form or another in so many literary or dramatic contexts, that 'love is an experience that can *only* be experienced, not explained' – which is how Tarkovsky puts it in his haunting, enigmatic film, *Solaris*.[3] For although Stoppard's extraordinary agility at handling ideas and explanations does not let him down in *The Real Thing*, it often seems to be offering only a small part of the 'real' story.

    *The Dog It Was That Died* offers, in marked contrast, a gloriously unresolved confusion between layers of 'reality'. This splendid, playful radio comedy (Stoppard's first venture into the medium for ten years) was broadcast on 9 December 1982 as one of the commissions marking the sixtieth anniversary of the BBC. Among a distinguished cast were Charles Gray, Dinsdale Landen, Penelope Keith and Kenneth Cranham, with delightful cameo roles from John Le Mesurier, Betty Marsden and Stephen Moore. The producer was John Tydeman. Once again, the play has a puzzle at its core. Before leaping off Chelsea Bridge, Q6's long-standing double agent Rupert Purvis posts a mysterious letter full of wild accusations to his superior, Giles Blair. Aided (and hindered) by Hogbin, his suspicious policeman colleague from Q9, Blair imperturbably attempts to make sense of it. In the process of this unravelling – as in *Artist Descending* and its other radio predecessors – the play makes elaborate and ingenious use of the medium. Blair's country home, for instance, is a bastion of eccentricity full of rare clocks, which he collects, and donkeys, which his wife nurses. Purvis's dramatic suicide bid backfires when he lands – as chance would have it – on a passing barge, killing the bargee's dog but only breaking his own legs. (This is the imaginative aural sequence with which the first scene ends.) And when Blair visits Purvis in a rest home, he discovers a host of mysterious doctors, matrons and patients (liberally confused with

one another) mowing lawns, clambering into cupboards or potter-
ing up stone staircases in search of belfry bats! These, and other
opportunities for delightful sound effects, make a substantial
contribution to the prevailing comic atmosphere. Purvis's subsequent, successful suicide, however, is not a laughing matter and a
distinctly sombre tone is introduced at those points when he sadly
tries to recall on which side his loyalties are 'real' and on which false,
and what his years loyally spent passing information of doubtful
value between East and West can really have added to either cause.[4]

I want in this concluding chapter to consider three key issues
which run throughout all the plays previously considered and which
both *The Real Thing* and *The Dog It Was That Died* continue to
illuminate. The first of these is the adventurousness with theatrical
form which is so characteristic of Stoppard's work, in sharp contrast
to the vast majority of his contemporaries. When *Rosencrantz and
Guildenstern are Dead* first bared the influence of Beckett, many critics
were eager to align him with the Theatre of the Absurd; even in
*Rosencrantz*, though, the debt to *Godot* is less significant than the
play's ingenious and original structure, dovetailing the uncertain-
ties of the courtiers' apparent plight with the fixed and familiar
certainties of *Hamlet*, and the passing of time has made it ever
clearer that only here is Stoppard's debt to Beckett any stronger
than a shared sense of dramatic boldness. It is this kind of
adventurousness (and, broadly, this alone) that he drew from the
Absurd, an adventurousness subsequently captured in his fascinating succession of ingenious, artfully patterned structures which
break decisively with established practice, whether on stage or on
radio. In *If You're Glad I'll Be Frank*, for instance, Gladys's clock-like
existence is imaginatively intensified by counterpointing her apprehensive thoughts with her regulated repetition of the passing
minutes. Here, and to a lesser extent in *Albert's Bridge*, Stoppard is
attempting not merely to depict characters with eccentric sensibilities, but to express those sensibilities in terms of his own
dramatic structures, so that it is the distorted perceptions of
Rosencrantz, Guildenstern, Albert or Gladys, rather than the
authenticity or 'realism' of these characters, which seem to control
the shape and tone of each play. Even the most 'realistic' of Stoppard's
early characters, George Riley in *Enter a Free Man*, is sufficiently
anarchic in his eccentricity to put the predominant naturalism
under considerable pressure, so that the characters who conform to
it – such as Linda and Persephone – never really come to life.

The patterning which Stoppard substitutes for naturalism becomes still clearer in those subsequent plays in which some form of puzzle or mystery provides the axis around which the characters and actions are arranged. Thus in *The Real Inspector Hound* the working out of the plot of a detective thriller determines the shape of all the multiple, seemingly discrete layers of the action; thus too in *Artist Descending a Staircase* a complex, pyramidic series of flashbacks through time is triggered off by the discovery of Donner's corpse and the search for explanations of the ambiguous sounds caught on a tape recorder. In these plays, as in *The Boundary* or *Dirty Linen* or *The Dog It Was That Died*, the absence of detailed characterisation, the heart of naturalistic drama, is at once apparent; in its place there is a high degree of structural organisation running on well-oiled rails to furiously neat resolutions – the murder mysteries are solved; Rosencrantz and Guildenstern, Albert, Brenda, Purvis, Birdboot and both Moons (in the novel and *Hound*) die, and Maddie completes her obsessive round of parliamentary seductions. In the lighter plays, these frameworks are so meticulously wrought that they virtually provide their own justification, especially in *After Magritte*, which is assembled only to be slowly taken apart, brick by brick, before being reassembled in a different, equally improbable guise. Yet in the major plays, where the dramatic structures house much more ambitious comedies of ideas, this kind of unifying format is no less in evidence. *Hamlet* in many senses provides the key to the 'puzzle' within *Rosencrantz*. *Jumpers* is constructed on the back of a 'whodunnit' mystery. *Travesties* takes unconventional patterning further still; one of the most architecturally complex plays ever written in the English language, it is a marvellously free-wheeling discussion of art and politics and war, woven around *The Importance of Being Earnest* in a manner which shows Stoppard reaching new heights of inventiveness.

There is a distinct move towards realism in the majority of the plays after *Travesties*, inevitably accompanied by a reduction in structural originality, though even within these more conventional forms, Stoppard's unfailing inventiveness frequently rebels against the prevailing disciplines. In *Every Good Boy Deserves Favour* the realistic figure of Alexander, the imprisoned dissident, is surrounded by a lunatic, an orchestra and a musical commentary. In *Cahoot's Macbeth* the threatened actors, confronted by a comically manic police inspector building a wall of bricks across their living-room performance area, switch into a half-incomprehensible language none of them has ever heard before! In these relatively minor works, the prevailing eccentricity is sufficiently pronounced to make any objections of structural inconsistency well-nigh irrelevant, but in the two full-length stage plays where Stoppard resorts to far more sustained naturalism – *Night and Day*, which has much in common with the conventional 'well-made' play, and *The Real Thing*, which is far more serial and episodic – there is an intermittent sense that the form is undermined at a number of crucial points. This is more pronounced in the earlier play, epitomised by the lecturettes and dialectic exchanges which Stoppard incorporates in order to provide his 'Press Debate' – interludes which could be accommodated with flair and ease within a *Travesties*-like structure, but which, in this naturalistic context, have a brilliancy and contrived fluency which impair the plausibility of the characters and their setting. *The Real Thing*, freed from this kind of debating chamber structure, resolves rather more successfully the tensions between the humdrum constraints of naturalistically drawn characters and Stoppard's barely quenchable desire to quest beyond such everyday machinations (epitomised by a lengthy conceit which Henry spins out between playing cricket well and writing good plays), but it remains, in the light of his earlier achievements, a relatively unadventurous enterprise in purely formal terms. In consequence, it is to *Professional Foul* that one turns for conclusive proof that Stoppard's instinctive talents need not be hampered by the resort to more naturalistic presentation and a more didactic treatment of specific themes – and it can surely be no coincidence that this, Stoppard's most successful venture into more realistic works, should also prove to be his most singular and disciplined structure. Yet although it is of 'realistic' construction in many important respects (the dynamic movement of Anderson from theory to practice, the authenticity of the settings and humanity of many of the characters), *Professional Foul* has more in common with the cinema than with the stage, and, unlike *Night and Day*, nothing at all in common with the 'well-made play'. In its almost seamless ravelling together of the fortunes of the urbane professor with the repression of his former pupil, the fate of England's football team and the state of modern philosophy in a unified sequence of sixteen scenes, it demonstrates the full powers of Stoppard's ingenuity and intellect once more working hand in hand.

Inseparable from Stoppard's formal inventiveness is a second, constant feature of his work, its ostentatious theatricality. Interviewed by Melvyn Bragg in 1978, he insisted

> I am quite hot on the theatricality of theatre. That's not really the
> tautology it sounds . . .. For me, theatre is not literature. It's an
> event.[5]

It is in this kind of circular self-reference – given particular emphasis
by Stoppard's stress on the performance aspect – that his work is
most recognisably 'Post-modernist'. Naturalism is, in general terms,
an untheatrical form. It eschews deliberate display, seeking both to
minimise the audience's awareness that they are watching a
performance and to maximise their close, felt involvement with the
action taking place on the stage, as though it were a facsimile of life.
In place of this conventional link between the audience and the
playwright's characters, Stoppard substitutes a shared artfulness
between the audience and the playwright himself. Throughout his
work, in consequence, runs a recurrent element of friendly conspiracy and game-playing, involving sudden twists of action,
deliberate shifts of convention, abrupt flashbacks through time,
unreliable narration, parody, pastiche and playful reference to such
a wide range of dramatic, literary and historical subjects that
Stoppard seems at times to be staging his own celebration of culture
in all its plurality, with Magritte, Wilde, Beckett, Wittgenstein,
Eliot, Joyce or Shakespeare jostling alongside the more mundane
forms of the 'whodunnit' thriller, or newspaper styles, or popular
love songs (in *Albert's Bridge* and *Jumpers*, as again in *The Real
Thing*). This irrepressible eclecticism makes it extremely difficult to
talk of Stoppard's own 'style', yet what is maintained throughout his
plethora of parodies and travesties and twists and turns is an
unrelenting emphasis on the playwright's theatrical contrivance
and on the nature of performance *per se*.

It is perhaps not surprising, then, that Stoppard's least successful
plays should often be those which are least theatrically adventurous.
In the television play *A Separate Peace*, for instance, the central
character, John Brown, is conceived and written in quite deliberately flat and passive terms because the controlling idea – that
he wants to become a recluse – leads Stoppard away from his
customarily energetic use of character, comedy and language.
Similarly, although *Travesties* is in many senses the apotheosis of
Stoppard's inventiveness, his refusal to integrate Lenin into the
highly theatrical pattern of the rest of the play can seem an
important failure. *Night and Day*, too, lacks the colourful theatrical
vivacity that illuminates all its full-length predecessors; its relatively

prosaic form is a particular disappointment. In contrast, the strongest expression of Stoppard's ostentatious theatricality is found in those plays which treat the nature of theatre as a controlling concept, particularly in the dialogue between 'actors' and 'characters' (with all its disturbing implications) in *Rosencrantz and Guildenstern are Dead* and *The Real Inspector Hound*. Where the former shows in the uncertainty of its 'off-stage' sections how strongly determined its characters' lives are, the latter shows the 'on-stage' reality snowballing beyond its 'natural' confines, playfully engulfing a pair of apparent spectators. Elsewhere, the theatrical self-emphasis is made parasitically: the structure and storyline of *The Importance of Being Earnest* is deftly employed to control the general direction of *Travesties*, while in *Cahoot's Macbeth* the performance of Shakespeare's tragedy is marshalled to provide an ironic commentary on the outside world of police oppression. The artifice of the theatrical process is also stressed and manipulated in *Dirty Linen* and *New-Found-Land*, where the disputed occupancy of the 'room' provides chaotic doubt over which of the two plays is to continue, and in the juggling between 'reality' and 'illusion' in *The Real Thing*, where the first scene, which seems to be introducing us to two of the main characters, turns out to be a scene from the latest play by Henry, which is merely introducing us to his wife and Annie's husband in their 'on-stage' rôles. But although the scene is therefore 'illusion', its relevance to many of the 'real' events in the play is hammered home by later ironic echoes back to this 'text'.

Stoppard's revolt from the realistic tradition through his insistent theatricality is not only confined to his work for the stage: his novel is in several respects a highly theatrical achievement, as are his radio plays and some aspects of his work for television. Theatricality in this context means not 'stagey-ness' as such, but 'the resort to a special grammar of composed behaviour'.[6] Moon's lament in the novel that 'hardly anyone behaves naturally any more' (p. 53) is an aphorism for Stoppard's characters in two distinct senses. First, it is true of a particular strain of polished, pre-composed, stylish characters who seem almost to speak as performers, in inverted commas. The first embodiment of this type is Moon's own opposite, Malquist; later examples include The Player in *Rosencrantz*, Archie in *Jumpers* and Tzara in *Travesties*. (In this respect it is unsurprising that the extrovert, anarchic Tzara, rather than the thinly drawn figure of Joyce, most successfully opposes Lenin's intransigence, not because his arguments are any stronger – Stoppard has far greater natural sympathy for Joyce[7] – but because of his vivid theatrical energy.) This, then is the kind of theatricality which Moon opposes. On the other hand, there is Stoppard's own organisation of *all* his characters into ostentatiously 'composed' edifices, schematised according to highly theatrical principles and governed by his desire to provide as much entertainment as possible for his audiences. Since all of his characters are framed within structural plans less concerned with individual psychology than with highlighting their own flamboyance or pursuing their own trains of argument, none – within this definition – is really any more or less theatrical than any other. This is clearly most true of the relatively undeveloped characters locked into fixed rôles within extravagantly playful dramatic patterns like *After Magritte*, *On The Razzle* or *The Boundary*, but even the more rounded characters such as Alexander in *Every Good Boy* or Ruth and the journalists in *Night and Day* are rooted within contexts making moral and political points that seem far dearer to the author than the characters themselves. At times, of course, their concerns are at one with Stoppard's own, as with George Moore and Anderson in their respective quests for truths, but only with Henry and Annie in *The Real Thing* can it be maintained that the characters indisputably matter to Stoppard as much as the highly schematised, highly theatrical structures which are such a distinctive hallmark of his work.

The third key issue which runs throughout the comedies is the question of how serious they really are. Stoppard himself has insisted that there are two distinct broad strands to his work on several occasions, among them the interview he gave to *Gambit* in 1981:

> I think like a lot of writers I've got a cheap side and an expensive side. I mean rather like a musician might stop composing for a few days to do a jingle for 'Kattomeat' because he thinks it's fun. And I honestly can't believe that because of something that happened to the world or to England I'll never write a 50–minute rompy farce for Ed Berman.[8]

In the light of such comments it might therefore seem a relatively straightforward task to divide his plays into two camps – in the mould of *Dirty Linen* on the 'cheap' side and of *Travesties* on the 'expensive' side. But the process is a good deal more complicated than this because, as Stoppard himself has also stated on more than one occasion;

> In my mind, my plays perfectly express my own being in that they are serious plays, seriously compromised by their own frivolity, or frivolous plays redeemed by their seriousness, according to the audience's own attitude toward them.[9]

The intermingling of these two strands is in evidence from the outset of Stoppard's writing career. Throughout his development, he has maintained a distinct ability, practically unique on the modern British stage, to fuse fertile comic invention with sharp intellectual enquiry. Their 'marriage', as the medieval, Elizabethan and even Shavian theatre amply testify, is far from impossible. Yet for some critics Stoppard's particular treatment of this concept is, frankly, irritating. Philip Roberts, for example, considers that in *Jumpers* and *Travesties*:

> the more disturbing matters . . . are severely diffused by the shifting insistence upon farce which both featherbeds and suffocates them.[10]

In this segregationalist position, he seems unwilling (or unable) to allow Stoppard any room for experimentation across these frontiers. As I have tried to demonstrate throughout this study, I consider this a woefully mistaken attitude. Even a very brief resumé of the clear development of social and moral concerns in Stoppard's writing can lay the ghost of this misconception.

The first point to be stressed is that Stoppard has a vision of life that is, simultaneously, both comic and serious. His early plays (and novel) are characterised by the constant sense that life is comically absurd, but behind all the bizarre and bewildering guises runs the question: how do we cope with existence in such a mad world? The first answer, in a world which cannot be changed by the actions of mere men (a philosophical stance that has its apotheosis in *Rosencrantz and Guildenstern are Dead*), is by retreating from it, and the early plays, taken as a group, are a playfully diverse pot-pourri of various kinds of escapism. Riley takes refuge in hopeless, private fantasies, John Brown retires peacefully to hospital and Gladys and Albert resort to otherworldly perspectives on life. In their opposite ways, Malquist and Moon represent the fullest manifestation of this theme. Behind these eccentricities, however, runs a pronounced sense of disenchantment and alienation, carried to its furthest limits in *Rosencrantz*, where Stoppard most clearly defines the uselessness of wild escape-attempts. His heroes are trapped in a state of perpetual half-enlightenment on the perimeters of the play until finally, without announcement or ceremony, they are eliminated. The sense of human powerlessness has rarely been more vividly captured in any contemporary play, whether serious or comic. The pessimism, however, is not total, since behind the courtiers' seemingly drifting world is a thoroughgoing determinism: the world of *Hamlet*. And although the pattern of *Rosencrantz* is thus susceptible to allegorisation in quasi-religious terms – that God or Destiny's design does exist, however comfortless and obscure its manifestations – this is not its *raison d'être*. Stoppard's viewpoint here, and throughout his subsequent work, is essentially humanist, bound up with the consequences of a *given* determinism, not with an inquiry into the universe's determined or non-determined nature.

This broader view is, however, one of the concerns of Stoppard's next major play, *Jumpers*, in which George's desperate rear-guard action against the logical positivist approach of pragmatism in all things leads him to wrestle with the philosophical concept of a God-given world. Behind his comic doggedness and his inability to find a decisive rockbed for his beliefs lies Stoppard's own debate with himself over the root problem of all humanism: how 'sacrosanct' values can be ultimately justified. The fates of McFee and Archie's other opponents have repercussions which stretch far wider than Stoppard's playfully futuristic world, to embrace the desperate need of any society for moral, social and political values – whether or not such values can ever receive watertight sanction. *Travesties*, though it lacks any decisive synthesis of its controlling ideas (unlike *Jumpers*), reinforces this conviction in its broad-based appeal for tolerance, not only for the artist, but for all society. Quietly, however, *Travesties* is also a turning point in the development away from general themes of determinism, philosophy and art – marked by the dramatisation of Lenin. Stoppard's search, to some extent, is over; his comedy, which turned on the *absence* of values in *Rosencrantz* and *Jumpers*, now switches gently to the attack. There are values to which we must cling, he asserts, and they alone can give us a hold on the madness that is no longer seen as an inalienable fact of the world, but as a product of the *wrong* values.

*Every Good Boy Deserves Favour* removes the arena of debate from a comically futuristic world of materialist orthodoxy or the whirling fragments of memory within Carr's head to the specific, brutal suffering in a modern-day Soviet prison hospital, where the doctor's circuitous use of logic against his patients furthers Archie's conclusive demonstration in *Jumpers* that reason and logic themselves are not beyond abuse. George's stance is valiant but hapless; in *Every Good Boy Deserves Favour*, however, and still more emphatically in *Professional Foul*, the confrontation of such abuses becomes the primary trait of a new strain of Stoppard heroes, whose firmness and resolve are a conclusive demonstration of their creator's own philosophical development. Professor Anderson is fully prepared to commit himself to the kind of humanist ethical proposition on which George ultimately foundered; rather than seeking the foundation stone for his absolute standards, he infers them from within the realm of practical experience. In strict philosophical terms, Anderson's conclusions may seem unexceptional, but in terms of Stoppard's own progress through his plays, they reveal a highly important advance. For where Stoppard left it to his own detective 'sub-plot' in *Jumpers* to provide the final indictment of Archie and his logical positivists, his hero in *Professional Foul* emerges victorious in his own right. There is, in short, a growth from uncertainty to commitment from *Rosencrantz and Guildenstern are Dead* through *Jumpers* to *Professional Foul*, as the slightly sentimental, doubting humanism of the earlier plays becomes grounded in a number of quite unsentimental principles – primarily a deep respect for human life and a devout belief in an individual's freedom of conscience, both derived, in essence, from a philosophical conviction about the nature of all human values. The roots of what increasingly emerges in the form of ostentatious political statement are, therefore, moral and philosophical.

The importance of the political left in the re-emergence of new writing in the British theatre seems to have increased progressively since the 1950s, effectively polarising still further the West End theatre from the 'intellectual' theatre of the new playwrights of the left – Brenton, Hare, Edgar, and above all, Bond. In contrast, Stoppard's position since *Every Good Boy Deserves Favour* has been clearly of the right, especially in his attacks on the repression of individual liberties in Communist countries. A Marxist view would presumably be that Stoppard abandons the nihilism of modernism for a position of conventional bourgeois entrenchment. But *Professional Foul* is, in fact, a powerful demonstration of a central tenet of the socialist dramatist: that man can change his world. Anderson acts from a sense of moral outrage and makes in the process ethical choices which are both brave and admirable. Stoppard is not simply attacking Communism; as he once said when it was suggested that his view represented an interference with the domestic concerns of other states:

> There are certain truths which translate and these truths can be encapsulated in simple sentences and when these truths *have* been encapsulated then there is nowhere to hide.[11]

And it is the insistence on these truths that inspires almost all the plays after *Every Good Boy Deserves Favour* – not only *Professional Foul*, and, in a lighter vein, *Cahoot's Macbeth*, but also the full-length stage plays. *Night and Day*, in its lively championing of the liberty of the individual against a closed shop union framework, presses for the upholding on the home front of the same rights as in other parts of the world. *The Real Thing*, too, despite its narrower domestic plane, is about values – the supreme value of love and what it means in practice, particularly within a marriage. Throughout this development, then, there is a coherent, gradual and utterly serious discussion of human values, presented within the most felicitously imaginative and comic structures which, however untraditional, cannot be valued too highly.

What, finally, are we to make of Stoppard's rôle in our contemporary theatre and of his likely place in its posterity? As a result of his marked individualism in defying traditional structures, in introducing a heightened sense of theatricality and in forging a rare compact between seriousness and comedy, it leaves us most clearly with a dramatist who doggedly defies categorisation, who writes like almost none of his contemporaries and who has, so far, attracted no significant imitators. Nor, perhaps, is he likely to, since he once admitted in an interview:

> if the mixing up of ideas in farce is a source of confusion, well, yes, God knows why I try to do it like that – presumably because I *am* like that.[12]

We are finally left, then, with the playwright himself, with his inventiveness, with his theatricality, with his principles; in short, with his uniqueness. Peter Wood, in a television interview on the eve of the opening of *The Real Thing* roundly declared:

> I can't imagine an English theatre without Tom. I don't know how many of the others are dispensible. He's not.[13]

Peter Wood is not neutral. Peter Wood has directed almost all of Stoppard's stage plays since 1972 and is a close personal friend. But Peter Wood is right.

# Appendix One: The original ending of *Rosencrantz and Guildenstern are Dead*

In the second edition of *Rosencrantz and Guildenstern are Dead*, published in 1968, there are a number of small alterations from the first edition published in 1967. The one major change occurs at the end of the play, which, in the second edition, ends with a slow fade in the course of Fortinbras's speech 'Let four captains bear Hamlet . . . ', taken from the final scene of *Hamlet*. In the first edition, however, the play runs on to encompass a conversation between the two ambassadors freshly arrived from England (there is only one ambassador in subsequent editions), who discuss the royal carnage as follows:

| | |
|---|---|
| *Fortinbras:* | Let four captains |
| | bear Hamlet, like a soldier, to the stage: |
| | for he was likely, had he been put on, |
| | to have proved most royally: and for his passage, |
| | the soldiers' music and the rite of war |
| | speak loudly for him. |
| | Take up the bodies: such a sight as this |
| | becomes the field, but here shows much amiss. |
| | Go, bid the soldiers shoot. |
| | (*The Bodies are picked up: a peal of ordnance is shot off. A dead march begins and continues until the stage is empty except for the two Ambassadors.*) |
| | (*Pause. They move downstage. They stop.*) |
| *Ambassador:* | Hm . . . |
| *2nd Amb:* | Yes? |
| *1st Amb:* | What? |
| *2nd Amb:* | I thought you – |

| | |
|---|---|
| *1st Amb:* | No. |
| *2nd Amb:* | Ah. |
| | (*Pause.*) |
| *1st Amb:* | Tsk tsk . . . |
| *2nd Amb:* | Quite. |
| *1st Amb:* | Shocking business. |
| *2nd Amb:* | Tragic . . . (*he looks in the direction of the departing corpses*) . . . four – just like that. |
| *1st Amb:* | Six in all. |
| *2nd Amb:* | Seven. |
| *1st Amb:* | No – six. |
| *2nd Amb:* | The King, the Queen, Hamlet, Laertes, Rosencrantz, Guildenstern and Polonius. Seven. |
| *1st Amb:* | Ophelia. Eight. |
| *2nd Amb:* | King, Queen, Hamlet, Laertes, Rosencrantz, Guildenstern, Polonius, Ophelia. Eight. |
| | (*They nod and shake their heads.*) |
| | (*Looks about.*) Well . . . One hardly knows what to . . . |
| | (*From outside there is shouting and banging, a Man, say, banging his fist on a wooden door and shouting, obscurely, two names.*) |
| | (*The Ambassadors look at each other.*) |
| *1st Amb:* | Better go and see what it's all about . . . |
| | (*The other nods.*) |
| | (*They walk off together. The Tragedians' tune becomes audible – far away.*) |
| | (*The house lights come up until they are as bright as the lights on the empty stage.*) |

# Appendix Two: List of First Performances

*A Walk on the Water*: Rediffusion Television, November 1963
    revised as *Old Riley Walked The Water*: Hamburg, June 1964
    revised as *A Walk on the Water*: BBC Radio Home Service, November 1965
    revised as *Enter a Free Man*: St Martin's Theatre, London, March 1968
*The Dissolution of Dominic Boot*: BBC Radio Light Programme, February 1964
    revised as *The Engagement*: NBC Television (USA), March 1970
*'M' is for Moon Among Other Things*: BBC Radio 4, April 1964
*The Gamblers*: Bristol, 1965
*If You're Glad I'll Be Frank*: BBC Radio Third Programme, February 1966
*Tango* (adaptation of Mrozek's play, translated by Nicholas Bethell): Aldwych Theatre, London, May 1966
*A Separate Peace*: BBC 2 Television, August 1966
*Rosencrantz and Guildenstern are Dead*: Colston Hall, Edinburgh, August 1966
    revised version: Old Vic Theatre, London, April 1967
*Teeth*: BBC 2 Television, February 1967
*Another Moon Called Earth*: BBC 2 Television, June 1967
*Albert's Bridge*: BBC Radio Third Programme, July 1967
*The Real Inspector Hound*: Criterion Theatre, London, June 1968
*Neutral Ground*: Granada Television, December 1968
*Where Are They Now?*: BBC Radio 4 (Schools Service), January 1970
*After Magritte*: Green Banana Restaurant, London, April 1970
*Dogg's Our Pet*: Almost Free Theatre, London, December 1971
*Jumpers*: Old Vic Theatre, London, February 1972
*One Pair of Eyes* (documentary): BBC 1 Television, July 1972
*Artist Descending a Staircase*: BBC Radio 3, November 1972

*The House of Bernarda Alba* (adaptation of Lorca's play): Greenwich Theatre, London, March 1973

*Travesties*: Aldwych Theatre, London, June 1974

*The Boundary* (with Clive Exton): BBC 1 Television, July 1975

*The Romantic Englishwoman* (screenplay with Thomas Wiseman based on his novel): London première, Plaza One, October 1975

*Three Men in a Boat* (adaptation of Jerome's novel): BBC 2 Television, December 1975

*Dirty Linen and New-Found-Land*: Almost Free Theatre, London, April 1976

*The (15-Minute) Dogg's Troupe Hamlet*: National Theatre, August 1976

*Every Good Boy Deserves Favour*: Royal Festival Hall, July 1977

*Professional Foul*: BBC 2 Television, September 1977

*Despair* (screenplay based on Nabokov's novel): London première, Screen on the Hill, July 1978

*Night and Day*: Phoenix Theatre, London, November 1978

*Dogg's Hamlet, Cahoot's Macbeth*: University of Warwick Arts Centre, Coventry, May 1979

*Undiscovered Country* (adaptation of Schnitzler's play): National Theatre (Olivier), London, June 1979

*The Human Factor* (screenplay based on Greene's novel): London première, Classic, Haymarket, January 1980

*On the Razzle*: National Theatre (Lyttelton), London, September 1981

*The Real Thing*: Strand Theatre, London, November 1982

*The Dog It Was That Died*: BBC Radio 3, December 1982

# Appendix Three: First Major Performances in America

*Rosencrantz and Guildenstern are Dead*: Alvin Theatre, New York –
October 1968
*Enter A Free Man*: Olney Theatre, Maryland – August 1970
*The Real Inspector Hound* and *After Magritte*: Theatre Four, New
York – April 1972
*Jumpers*: Kennedy Center, Washington – February 1974
*Travesties*: Ethel Barrymore Theatre, New York – October 1975
*Dirty Linen/New-Found-Land*: Kennedy Center, Washington – 1976
John Golden Theatre, New York – January 1977
*Every Good Boy Deserves Favour*: Temple University Music Festival,
Ambler, Pennsylvania and Kennedy Center, Washington –
August 1978; Metropolitan Opera House, New York – July 1979
*Dogg's Hamlet, Cahoot's Macbeth*: Kennedy Center – September
1979; 22 Steps Theatre, New York – October 1979
*Night and Day*: Kennedy Center, Washington – October 1979
ANTA Theatre, New York – November 1979
*Undiscovered Country*: Hartford Stage Company, Connecticut –
February 1981 Arena Stage Company, Washington – April 1981
*On the Razzle*: Arena Stage Company, Washington – October 1982
*The Real Thing*: (under negotiation, 1983)

# References

## CHAPTER 1 INTRODUCTION

1. *The Sunday Times*, 6 February 1972, p. 29.
2. *The Observer*, 23 June 1968, p. 26.
3. *New Republic*, 5 January 1980 (quoted by Douglas McMillan in *Gambit*, 10, 37, p. 62).
4. *Critical Quarterly*, Autumn 1978, p. 91.
5. *The Playwright: Tom Stoppard*, broadcast by Thames Television, 28 September 1976.
6. 'Playwrights and Professors', *Times Literary Supplement*, 13 October 1972, p. 1219.
7. Ibid.
8. Raymond Williams, *Drama in Performance*, revised and extended edition (Harmondsworth: Pelican Books, 1972) p. 4.
9. Some of his early, previously unpublished TV and radio plays have, however, now become available. See p. 68.
10. *The Real Thing*, which appeared as this book went to press, is considered briefly in the Conclusion, Chapter 13.
11. Arnold Hinchliffe, *British Theatre 1950/70* (Blackwell, 1974) p. 142. Robert Brustein, *The Third Theatre* (Cape, 1970) p. 153.
12. Ronald Hayman, 'Profile: Tom Stoppard', *The New Review*, vol. I, no. 9 (Dec. 74) p. 15; reprinted in *Tom Stoppard* (Heinemann, 1977) p. 1.
13. Stoppard, 'The Definite Maybe', *Author*, 78, 1967, p. 18.
14. These were published in 1983 with *The Dog It Was That Died*. See p. 68.
15. See John Russell Taylor, *The Second Wave* (Methuen, 1971) p. 99.
16. *The Observer*, 28 August 1966, p. 15.
17. Some ten years later, Tynan wrote his essay 'Withdrawing with Style from the Chaos' which remains the liveliest short introduction to Stoppard's work. Reprinted in *Show People* (Weidenfeld & Nicolson, 1980).
18. Felicia Londré, *Tom Stoppard* (New York: Ungar, 1981) p. 44.
19. According to Stoppard's agent, Kenneth Ewing. See *Show People*, p. 49.


## CHAPTER 2 'STYLE' VERSUS 'SUBSTANCE'

1. Jon Bradshaw, 'Tom Stoppard Non-Stop', *Telegraph Sunday Magazine*, 26 June 1977, p. 30. On the eve of *Rosencrantz*'s London opening he also describes the novel, according to Keith Harper, as 'the best thing he's done', *The Guardian*, 12 April 1967, p. 7.

2. *Introduction Two* (Faber & Faber, 1964) p. 134. All subsequent references are to this edition.
3. 'The Definite Maybe'.
4. See 'Ambushes for the Audience', *Theatre Quarterly*, vol. IV, no. 14, p. 4.
5. *c.f.* 'The Definite Maybe', p. 18.
6. Published by Anthony Blond in 1966, and reprinted by Panther Books (1968) and Faber & Faber (1974). Page references are to this last edition.
7. See below, Chapter 6.
8. T. S. Eliot, *Collected Poems 1909–1962* (Faber & Faber, 1963) p. 14.
9. See p. 127.
10. Conrad, *The Secret Agent* (Harmondsworth: Penguin Books, 1972) p. 147 (and elsewhere).
11. Bradshaw, 'Tom Stoppard Non-Stop', p. 30.

## CHAPTER 3 POST-WAR THEATRE

1. Quoted in Marowitz, Milne and Hale (eds), *The Encore Reader* (Methuen, 1965) p. 40.
2. Tynan, *A View of the English Stage* (Davis-Poynter, 1975) p. 148.
3. Its continuity is persuasively demonstrated by John Russell Taylor in *The Rise and Fall of the Well-Made Play* (Methuen, 1967).
4. Interview with Philip Oakes, *Sunday Times*, 1 January 1976, p. 35.
5. Francis King, *Sunday Telegraph*, 4 February 1979, p. 14.
6. *The Guardian*, 5 May 1980, p. 7.
7. Strindberg, *The Plays*, vol. I, translated by Michael Meyer (Secker & Warburg, 1964) p. 99.
8. M. Esslin, *Brecht: A Choice of Evils* (Eyre & Spottiswood, 1959) p. 127.
9. Lawrence Ryan, 'Bertolt Brecht: A Marxist Dramatist?' in *Aspects of Drama and the Theatre* (Sydney University Press, 1965) p. 102.
10. David Edgar, 'Politics and Performance', *Times Literary Supplement*, 10 September 1982, p. 969.
11. Laurence Kitchin, *Mid-Century Drama* (Faber & Faber, revised edn, 1962) p. 73.
12. Katharine Worth, *Revolutions in Modern English Drama* (Bell, 1972) p. vii.
13. Kitchin, *Mid-Century Drama*, p. 155 ff.
14. Hinchliffe, *British Theatre*, p. 105.
15. Kitchin, p. 81.
16. M. Esslin, *The Theatre of the Absurd* (Harmondsworth: Pelican, 1968) p. 422.
17. A useful short chapter on Handke's work appears in Hayman's *Theatre and Anti-Theatre* (Secker & Warburg, 1979).
18. John Barth, 'The Literature of Replenishment', *Atlantic Monthly*, June 1980, p. 66.

## CHAPTER 4 IN THE OFF-STAGE WORLD

1. *The Sunday Times*, 16 April 1967, p. 49.
2. *The Observer*, 16 April 1967, p. 34.

3. *The Times*, 12 April 1967, p. 8.
4. 'The Definite Maybe', p. 19.
5. Charles Marowitz, who saw this version, describes it briefly in *Confessions of a Counterfeit Critic* (Methuen, 1973) pp. 123–4.
6. Alfred Emmet, letter, *Theatre Quarterly*, V, 17, 1975, pp. 95–6.
7. W. S. Gilbert, *Original Plays*, vol. III (Chatto & Windus, 1920) p. 83. Reprinted in *Plays by W. S. Gilbert*, ed. George Rowell (Cambridge University Press, 1982).
8. *Hamlet*, V.ii.56–62 (New Shakespeare edition, ed. J. Dover Wilson, 1936.) All subsequent references are to this edition.
9. In *Transatlantic Review*, 29, 1968, p. 20.
10. *The Observer*, 16 April 1967, p. 34.
11. *Rosencrantz and Guildenstern are Dead*, 2nd edition (Faber & Faber, 1968) p. 49. All subsequent references are to this edition.
12. John Weightman, 'Mini-Hamlets in Limbo', *Encounter*, July 1967, p. 40.
13. Brustein, *The Third Theatre*, p. 152.
14. Jonathan Bennett, 'Philosophy and Mr. Stoppard', *Philosophy*, vol. 50, 191, 1975, p. 8.
15. Ibid., p. 18.
16. Shakespeare, *As You Like It*, II.vii.139–41 (*Collected Works*, ed. Peter Alexander [Collins, 1951] p. 266).
17. C. J. Gianakaris surely misreads the play in suggesting that they 'allude joyfully to their dual positions as both actor . . . and spectator', 'Absurdism Altered', *Drama Survey*, VII, Winter 1969, p. 56.
18. Elizabeth Burns, *Theatricality: A Study of Convention in the Theatre and in Social Life* (Longman, 1972) p. 11.
19. C. W. E. Bigsby, *Tom Stoppard* (Longman for the British Council, 1976) p. 14.
20. See Ch. 2, p. 23.
21. Weightman, 'Mini-Hamlets in Limbo', p. 40.
22. William Babula, 'The Play-Life Metaphor in Shakespeare and Stoppard', *Modern Drama*, vol. 15, pt. 3, 1972, p. 280.
23. Pirandello, *Six Characters in Search of an Author*, translated by Frederick May (Heinemann, 1954) p. 49.
24. T. S. Eliot, *Collected Poems 1909–1962*, p. 115.
25. *Love's Labour's Lost*, V.ii.847–9 (Arden Edition, ed. Richard David, 1968, p. 176).
26. A. K. Kennedy complains that 'the rhetoric on what constitutes death is both unfelt and unwitty', but Guildenstern's inarticulate hesitancy is surely the whole point. See 'Old and New in London Now', *Modern Drama*, XI, 1969, p. 442.
27. Tynan, *Show People*, p. 85.
28. Tynan points out, with some justification, that Shakespeare's contemporary Robert Greene regaled his lack of originality too, calling him 'an upstart crow, beautified with our feathers', ibid., p. 87.
29. Hinchliffe, *British Theatre 1950/70*, p. 142.
30. Interview with Giles Gordon, *Transatlantic Review*, p. 23.
31. Tynan, *Show People*, p. 83.
32. Though this premise seems reasonable enough, the trail on which it leads Cahn often seems singular to the point of misconception. See *Beyond Absurdity: The*

*Plays of Tom Stoppard* (Farleigh Dickinson U. P., 1979) p. 35. See also Levenson, 'Views from a Revolving Door', *Queens Quarterly*, LXXVIII, 1971.

33. Hunter, *Tom Stoppard's Plays* (Faber & Faber, 1982) p. 149.
34. *The Playwright: Tom Stoppard*, interviewer Benedict Nightingale, Thames Television, first broadcast 28 September 1976.
35. Beckett, *Waiting for Godot* (Faber & Faber, 2nd edition, 1965) p. 59.
36. Ibid., p. 61.
37. Ibid., p. 48.
38. Ibid., p. 85.
39. Emmet, *Theatre Quarterly*, p. 96.
40. Gordon, *Transatlantic Review*, p. 24.
41. *Next Time I'll Sing To You* (Heinemann, 1965) p. 3.
42. Ibid., p. 45.
43. Ibid., p. 9.
44. *The Death of Tragedy* (Faber & Faber, 1963) p. 168.
45. *Collected Poems 1909–1962*, p. 17.
46. See above, p. 20.
47. As he once told Ronald Hayman, 'There are certain things written in English which make me feel as a diabetic must when the insulin goes in. Prufrock and Beckett are the twin syringes of my diet, my arterial system.' *Tom Stoppard*, p. 8.

## CHAPTER 5 ESCAPE ROUTES

1. Gordon, *Transatlantic Review*, p. 21.
2. *The Dog It Was That Died* is considered briefly in the Conclusion, Chapter 13.
3. See above, p. 5.
4. See Tynan, *Show People*, p. 69.
5. This title, according to Stoppard, is derived from a negro prison blues. See *Radio Times*, 6–12 November 1965, p. 25.
6. 'Ambushes for the Audience', p. 5.
7. *The Observer*, 31 March 1968, p. 31.
8. It later transpires that her real name is 'Constance.
9. *Enter a Free Man* (Faber & Faber, 1968) p. 21. All subsequent references are to this edition.
10. 'Ambushes for the Audience', p. 4 and 'The Joke's The Thing' (with Mark Amory) *Sunday Times Magazine*, 9 June 1974, p. 68.
11. Arthur Miller, *Collected Plays* (Gerset Press, 1958) pp. 162, 165.
12. C. W. E. Bigsby seems very wide of the mark when he describes Persephone as 'every bit as compassionate and understanding as Linda in Miller's play', *Tom Stoppard*, p. 8.
13. 'Structure and Intellect', *Plays and Players*, July 1970, p. 17.
14. Alan Durband (ed.), *Playbill Two* (Hutchinson, 1969) p. 108. All subsequent references are to this edition. Reprinted in *The Dog It was That Died and other plays* (Faber & Faber, 1983).
15. *And Did Those Feet?* in David Mercer, *Three Television Comedies* (Calder & Boyars, 1966) p. 100. (Reprinted in *Collected TV Plays*, vol. 2 [John Calder, 1981].)

16. Ibid., p. 112.
17. In *The Second Wave*, p. 99.
18. *If You're Glad I'll Be Frank* (Faber & Faber, 1969) published with *Albert's Bridge*, subsequently issued in a single edition, 1976. All references are to this latter edition.
19. Some lines are virtually duplicated on this theme; compare *A Separate Peace* p. 134 with *If You're Glad*, pp. 23–4, for example.
20. *Albert's Bridge* (Faber & Faber, 1969) published with *If You're Glad I'll Be Frank*. Subsequently issued in a single edition, 1970. All references are to this latter edition.
21. Quoted incidentally in Malcolm Lowry, *Under The Volcano* (Harmondsworth: Penguin, 1963) p. 212.
22. *Queen's Quarterly*, vol. 78, 1971, pp. 431–42.
23. Ibid., p. 435.
24. Ibid., p. 432.
25. *A Resounding Tinkle*, in *New English Dramatists*, vol. II (Harmondsworth: Penguin, 1960) pp. 113–14.

## CHAPTER 6 NUTS AND BOLTS

1. See above, p. 68.
2. Bradshaw, 'Tom Stoppard Non-Stop', p. 30.
3. The others – *Dogg's Our Pet* (1971), *Dirty Linen* (1976) and *Dogg's Hamlet, Cahoot's Macbeth* (1980) – are examined in Chapter Twelve.
4. 'Ambushes for the Audience', p. 8.
5. Ibid., p. 7.
6. Ronald Hayman has suggested that Pinter's years as an actor taught him 'that audiences have a masochistic love of being kept in ignorance, that the puzzle matters infinitely more than the solution'. (*Theatre and Anti-Theatre*, p. 128). Perhaps Stoppard's years as a critic taught him the same?
7. Other ingredients seem to be derived from *Peril at End House* and *The Mousetrap*.
8. *The Real Inspector Hound* (Faber & Faber, 2nd edition, 1970) p. 15. All subsequent references are to this edition.
9. For an account of the genesis of this idea see Stoppard's interview with Janet Watts, *The Guardian*, 21 March 1973, p. 12.
10. *After Magritte* (Faber & Faber, 1971), p. 23. All subsequent references are to this edition.
11. *The Second Wave*, p. 105.
12. It has been suggested by the American critic Wendell V. Harris that the opening scene is modelled on Magritte's painting *L'Assassin menacé*, 'Stoppard's *After Magritte*', *Explicator*, 34, 1976.
13. Brian Crossley recognises that Foot 'like Moon and Birdboot in *Hound*, is drawn into the action he has come to solve', but does not explore the sharply different kinds of assimilation. See *Modern Drama*, XX, March 1977, p. 84.
14. 'Magritte . . . has long been a favourite of mine', *Readers Theatre (News)*, San Diego State University, IV, 2, Spring 1977, p. 3.
15. *Where Are They Now?* published with *Artist Descending a Staircase* (Faber & Faber, 1973) p. 61. All subsequent references are to this edition.

16. First performed in April 1971.
17. *Forget-me-not Lane* (Faber & Faber, 1971) p. 25.
18. The same technique is employed by Peter Shaffer in *Amadeus*.
19. See *Lord Malquist and Mr Moon*, pp. 49–50.
20. Roberts, 'Serious Artist or Siren?', *Critical Quarterly*, Autumn 1978, p. 91.
21. Hunter, *Tom Stoppard's Plays*, p. 154.

## CHAPTER 7 ETHICS ON THE WANE

1. It was also voted Best Play of 1972 by *Plays and Players* magazine.
2. 'Ambushes For the Audience', p. 11.
3. Ibid., p. 8.
4. *Financial Times*, 3 February 1972.
5. See above, p. 68.
6. *The Listener*, 30 September 1976, p. 422.
7. 'A Metaphysical Comedy', *Encounter*, vol. 38, April 1972, p. 45.
8. Bennett, 'Philosophy and Mr Stoppard', pp. 5, 8.
9. *The Guardian*, 4 February 1972, p. 10.
10. 'Ambushes for the Audience', pp. 12, 16.
11. Tynan suggests that the genesis of the play lay in Stoppard's 'fascinated revulsion' from Logical Positivism. See *Show People*, pp. 90–1.
12. Bennett, 'Philosophy and Mr Stoppard', p. 8. A second article in the same journal, 'Jonathan Bennett and Mr Stoppard' by Henning Jensen, reached the same conclusion for slightly different reasons and culminated in the remarkably naïve assertion that, although *Jumpers* 'does contain philosophical issues relevant to the play as a whole, the weakness of its philosophical materials is such as to render it of no philosophical significance *and of little worth as a play*'. [author's italics] (*Philosophy*, 52, 1977) p. 217.
13. Ayer (ed.), 'Sociology and Physicalism', *Logical Positivism* (Allen & Unwin, 1959) p. 282. This collection of essays also contains an extensive and useful bibliography.
14. *A Critique of Logical Positivism* (Gollancz, 1950) p. 31.
15. Quoted, ibid., p. 116.
16. Quoted, ibid., p. 115.
17. *Logical Positivism*, p. 22.
18. *A Critique of Logical Positivism*, p. 22.
19. Ibid., p. 17.
20. *Jumpers* (Faber & Faber, 1972) p. 38. All subsequent references are to this edition.
21. This speech provides perhaps the clearest example of the way in which parts of *Jumpers* are derived from *Another Moon Called Earth*. It is reworked from a similarly apocalyptic (and scarcely less impressive) speech of Penelope's. See *The Dog It Was*, p. 99.
22. Joad, *A Critique*, p. 63.
23. 'A Metaphysical Comedy', p. 45.
24. *Cosmopolitan*, January 1978, p. 31.
25. *Revolutions in Modern English Drama*, p. 104.
26. Hunter, *Tom Stoppard's Plays*, p. 25.

27. Stoppard himself has strangely underestimated his own achievement by denying that his resolution *is* decisive. In the Introduction to *The Dog It Was* (p. 8) he suggests that he 'ended up by trying to make a virtue of not declaring who-dun-it.'

## CHAPTER 8 THE IMPORTANCE OF BEING CARR

1. See above, p. 6.
2. *James Joyce*, (New York: Oxford University Press, 1959).
3. See *Travesties* (Faber & Faber, 1975) preface, p. 12. All subsequent references are to this edition.
4. It is interesting to compare Carr's comically exaggerated self-importance with that of Spike Milligan in *Adolf Hitler: My Part in his Downfall* (Harmondsworth: Penguin Books, 1972), which is also set in the chaos and passion of a World War. (See, for example, p. 34.)
5. *New York Times*, 19 October 1975, II, p. 1.
6. See above, p. 116.
7. See, for instance, Ellmann, *James Joyce*, p. 133.
8. Ibid., p. 409.
9. Ibid., p. 191.
10. Ibid., p. 438.
11. Ibid.
12. Ibid.
13. Ibid., p. 439.
14. Ibid., p. 440.
15. Ibid., p. 459.
16. Ibid., Carr quotes the court verdict (p. 64) which is taken from *The Letters of James Joyce*, ed. Ellmann (Faber & Faber, 1966) vol. II. pp. 421–2.
17. Ibid., p. 459.
18. James Joyce, *Ulysses*, (Harmondsworth: Penguin, 1969), p. 525.
19. Ibid.
20. 'Art versus Life', *Encounter*, September 1974, p. 59.
21. 'The Zealots of Zurich', *T.L.S.*, 12 July 1974, p. 744.
22. Kenneth Tynan has pointed out that this more or less makes sense in French. Others have followed with further untangling attempts. See Tynan, *Show People*, p. 110; Hunter, *Tom Stoppard's Plays*, p. 240; Londré, *Tom Stoppard*, pp. 71–2.
23. Compare Wilde, *Plays*, (Harmondsworth: Penguin, 1954) p. 266.
24. Stanislaus Joyce, *My Brother's Keeper*, quoted Ellmann, *James Joyce*, p. 169.
25. Tynan also complains that Stoppard gets Joyce wrong politically. See *Show People*, pp. 112–13.
26. Only a critic insensitive to theatrical effect could assert that 'of the three figures who dominate this play, only Joyce emerges with stature'. Cahn, *Beyond Absurdity*, p. 140.
27. Wilde, *Plays*, p. 254.
28. Compare Wilde, p. 255.
29. Hauser, *The Social History of Art*, vol. 4 (Routledge & Kegan Paul, 1962) p. 222.

30. Herbert Read, 'Art in Europe at the end of the Second World War,' *The Philosophy of Modern Art* (Faber & Faber, 1952) p. 41.
31. Hauser, *Social History*, p. 219.
32. Adam B. Ulam, *Lenin and the Bolsheviks* (Secker and Warburg, 1966) p. 308.
33. Edmund Wilson, *To the Finland Station* (Macmillan, 1972) p. 534.
34. Ulam, *Lenin*, Introduction, p. viii.
35. Wilson, *Finland Station*, p. xii.
36. Ibid.
37. Ibid., p. 449.
38. 'Ambushes for the Audience', p. 12. Stoppard declared his intention to write about the Russian revolution as early as 1968, in fact. See 'Something to Declare', *Sunday Times*, 25 February 1968, p. 47.
39. 'Ambushes for the Audience', p. 13.
40. Tynan, *Show People*, p. 109.
41. Read, *Modern Art*, p. 46.

## CHAPTER 9 MORE PUZZLES

1. This is most clear in the case of the moon sub-plot in *Jumpers* (see Chapter 7, note 5) and in the duplications between *If You're Glad I'll Be Frank* and *A Separate Peace* (see Chapter 5, note 19).
2. *The Playwright: Tom Stoppard*, a profile with Benedict Nightingale, broadcast by Thames Television, 28 September 1976.
3. *Artist Descending a Staircase* published with *Where Are They Now?* (Faber, 1973) p. 13. All subsequent references are to this edition.
4. One wrily notes that in 1982 the Tate Gallery duly mounted an exhibition called 'Artists and Sound' with some similar characteristics!
5. Compare Tzara in *Travesties*, p. 38.
6. In a letter from Clive Exton to the author.
7. This and all subsequent quotations are based on transcriptions made from a videotape recording of *The Boundary*.
8. This 'Stoppardian' sequence is one of many by Exton.
9. This, according to Exton, is one of the few exchanges which was rewritten together by both authors.
10. *The South Bank Show* with Melvyn Bragg, London Weekend Television, broadcast 26 November 1978.

## CHAPTER 10 EYES EAST

1. 'The Face at the Window', *Sunday Times*, 27 February 1977, p. 33.
2. *Every Good Boy Deserves Favour* and *Professional Foul* (Faber & Faber, 1978) pp. 8–9. All subsequent references are to this edition.
3. See Stoppard's Introduction to the play, p. 6.
4. Stoppard's practice of calling the dissident Alexander and the lunatic Ivanov is followed throughout.
5. 'Ambushes for the Audience', p. 4.

6. Stoppard explains in his Introduction (p. 7) that the figure 'C' is Vladimir Bukovsky, to whom, with Fainberg, the play is dedicated. None of the other figures is identified.
7. Arthur Miller, *Collected Plays*, p. 329.
8. Interestingly, the only real exception is *Neutral Ground*, which also deals with East-West politics. See above, p. 68.
9. According to Tynan, Stoppard often fondly refers to himself as 'a bounced Czech' – *Show People*, p. 46.
10. Chetwyn's trouble at the customs closely resembles Stoppard's own. A petition to the UN calling for all nations to respect 'Prisoner of Conscience' Year and containing the signatures of many prominent Russian dissidents, was taken from the wallet of his colleague Peter Luff of Amnesty International as the two men went through the customs at Moscow Airport. As Stoppard said, 'The petition named no countries. It was merely a generalised plea for prisoners of conscience everywhere, but when it came to the point the KGB hadn't needed to embarrass the Soviet Union by officially confiscating it. They simply stole it.' ('The Face at the Window', p. 33).
11. *Radio Times*, week commencing 1 October 1977, p. 78.
12. *Playbill* (New York), June 1979.
13. *The Times*, 29 September 1977, p. 11.

## CHAPTER 11 THE ROAD TO KAMBAWE

1. Made in English and starring Dirk Bogarde. This followed *The Romantic Englishwoman* in 1975 (co-written with Thomas Wiseman, on whose novel of the same title it was largely based), which starred Glenda Jackson, Michael Caine and Helmut Berger. A third Stoppard screenplay, *The Human Factor*, based on Graham Greene's novel, opened in London in January 1980, directed by Otto Preminger. Its long list of stars included Richard Attenborough, John Gielgud, Derek Jacobi, Robert Morley and Nicol Williamson.
2. *The Guardian*, 9 November 1978, p. 12.
3. *The Sunday Times*, 12 November 1978, p. 37.
4. See above, pp. 116, 140.
5. Hayman, *Tom Stoppard*, p. 135.
6. His name suggests a private Stoppard joke, since he is one of the old boys mentioned in the headmaster's speech in *Where Are They Now?*:

> It is with great pride and pleasure that I am able to announce to you an item of news that has brought great honour to the School – namely that for services to national industry, Geoffrey Carson has been honoured by Her Majesty the Queen with the Order of the British Empire. Congratulations, Carson Minor! (p. 76).

7. *Scoop* (Penguin, 1943) p. 126; *Night and Day* (Faber & Faber, 1978) p. 11. All subsequent references are to this edition of the play.
8. Billington, *Guardian*, p. 12.
9. 'Profile: Tom Stoppard', p. 15.

10. Hunter, *Tom Stoppard's Plays*, p. 27.
11. *Cosmopolitan*, January 1978, p. 39.
12. *Tom Stoppard: Comedy as a Moral Matrix* (University of Missouri Press, 1981) p. 14.
13. 'The South Bank Show', London Weekend Television, broadcast 26 November 1978.
14. *New Statesman*, 17 November 1978, p. 671.
15. 'I wanted to be Noel Baker on the *Daily Mail* or Sefton Delmer on the *Daily Express* – that kind of big-name roving reporter.' 'Ambushes for the Audience', p. 4.
16. Hunter, *Tom Stoppard's Plays*, p. 58.
17. Ibid., p. 210.
18. Nightingale, *New Statesman*, p. 671.
19. *The Times*, 9 November 1978, p. 11.
20. *Show People*, p. 63.

## CHAPTER 12 BACK TO FARCE

1. The idea of setting *Dirty Linen* within the framework of a Parliamentary Select Committee may well be derived from Clive Exton's two-act 1969 comedy, *Have You Any Dirty Washing, Mother Dear*. Published in *Plays of the Year 37* (Elek Books, 1970) pp. 109–91.
2. According to Oleg Kerensky, *New-Found-Land* was not even completed when rehearsals for *Dirty Linen* began. See *The New British Drama* (Hamish Hamilton, 1977) p. 168.
3. *Dirty-Linen* and *New-Found-Land* (Faber & Faber, 1976) p. 54. All subsequent references are to this edition.
4. Stoppard attempts a similar mix in his article on Berman, 'Yes, We Have No Banana', *The Guardian*, 10 December 1971, p. 10.
5. Thorpe and his co-defendants were found not guilty of conspiring to murder Scott, who had alleged that he and Thorpe had once had a homosexual relationship.
6. 'It looks rather more topical now than it did when I was writing it,' he told an interviewer on *Tonight* (BBC 1, broadcast 16 June 1976).
7. *The Guardian*, 13 April 1976, p. 10.
8. Preface to *Dogg's Hamlet, Cahoot's Macbeth* (Faber & Faber, 1980) p. 7. All subsequent references are to this edition.
9. Ibid.
10. Both pieces were eventually published in *Ten of the Best British Short Plays* (Inter-Action Publications, 1979). The title of *Dogg's Our Pet* is an anagram of Ed Berman's 'Dogg's Troupe', who first presented the play.
11. W. W. Bartley, *Wittgenstein* (Quartet, 1974) p. 116.
12. *Philosophical Investigations*, trans. G. E. M. Anscombe, (Oxford: Blackwell, 2nd edition, 1958) p. 16.
13. The example was in fact first used by Wittgenstein in *The Brown Book*, written in English between 1934 and 1936, though this was not published until 1958. See *The Blue and Brown Books*, (Oxford: Blackwell, 2nd edition, 1965) p. 77 ff.

14. Easy did not figure in *Dogg's Our Pet*. Charlie, who becomes an extra schoolboy here, was the non-Dogg speaker – 'some kind of workman or caretaker'. See *Ten of the Best*, p. 82.
15. The process might also be compared to the teasing and provocative article written in an incomplete version of the English language which Paul Jennings recently published in the *Times Literary Supplement* – 'Invenkion; buk necessiki?, *T.L.S.*, 13 August 1982, p. 882.
16. Hunter, *Tom Stoppard's Plays*, p. 204.
17. *Tango* was published by Jonathan Cape in 1968 and *Undiscovered Country* by Faber & Faber in 1980. *Bernarda Alba*, in Stoppard's adaptation, has not been published to date. For details of first performances, see Appendix II.
18. *Plays and Players*, April 1973, p. 37.
19. National Theatre programme note.
20. By coincidence, Stoppard's play was previewed at the Edinburgh Festival in the same theatre, the Royal Lyceum, twenty-seven years later.
21. Preface to *Our Town, The Skin of our Teeth and The Matchmaker*, (Harmondsworth: Penguin, 1962) p. 13.
22. Preface to *On the Razzle* (Faber & Faber, 1981) p. 8. All subsequent references are to this edition.
23. Wilder, *Our Town*, p. 278.
24. *The Sunday Times*, 4 October 1981, p. 43.
25. Stoppard's Preface, p. 7.
26. 'Ambushes for the Audience', p. 8.
27. Hunter, *Tom Stoppard's Plays*, p. 39.

## CHAPTER 13 CONCLUSION

1. The text was published simultaneously by Faber & Faber.
2. *Punch*, 24 November 1982, p. 872.
3. *Solaris* (1972) uses a science-fiction setting in which the character's dead wife is 'revivified' in its own powerful exploration of the 'real'. This quotation is, of course, from the English subtitles.
4. Purvis's desolation, which recalls that of Castle in *The Human Factor*, is one of several strands that seem to hark back to Greene's novel, which Stoppard adapted for the cinema (see p. 283, note 1). *The Human Factor* also involves a dog which gets killed and an elaborate and leaky chain of espionage, counterespionage and counter-counter-espionage.
5. 'The South Bank Show', London Weekend Television, broadcast 26 November 1978.
6. Elizabeth Burns, *Theatricality*, p. 33. See above, p. 51.
7. 'My prejudices were all on Joyce's side'. See Oleg Kerensky, *The New British Drama* (Hamish Hamilton, 1977) p. 169.
8. 'Trad Tom Pops In', *Gambit*, 37, 1981, p. 13. Broadly the same point is made in the quotation from *Theatre Quarterly*, above, p. 115.
9. *Readers Theatre (News)*, San Diego State University, vol. 4, no. 2, 1977, p. 4. Virtual re-statements of this remark have been made on several other occasions, including the *Theatre Quarterly* interview ('Ambushes for the Audience', p. 13) and television interviews with André Previn (broadcast on

BBC 1, 29 May 1977 and Benedict Nightingale ('The Playwright: Tom Stoppard', Thames Television, 28 September 1976). As Stoppard once playfully warned Jon Bradshaw, 'I now have a repertoire of plausible answers which evade the whole truth. . . . There's no point in being quoted if one isn't going to be quotable', 'Tom Stoppard Non-Stop', pp. 30, 34.

10. Roberts, 'Serious Artist', p. 87. A similar point is made rather more gently by Bigsby, *Tom Stoppard*, p. 24.
11. At a symposium organised by Conscience, following a performance of *Every Good Boy Deserves Favour* at the Mermaid Theatre, London, on 10 July 1978.
12. 'Ambushes for the Audience', p. 13.
13. In an interview with Stephen Phillips, *Channel Four News*, 15 November 1982.

# Bibliography

## (a) THE WORKS OF TOM STOPPARD

*Note:* all Grove Press titles listed below indicate publication in the United States of America.

Three short stories in *Introduction 2* (Faber & Faber, 1964)

*Lord Malquist and Mr Moon* (Anthony Blond, 1966; Panther Books, 1968; Faber & Faber, 1974; Grove Press, 1975)

*Rosencrantz and Guildenstern are Dead* (Faber & Faber, 1967; 2nd edition, 1968; Grove Press, 1968)

*Enter a Free Man* (Faber & Faber, 1968; Grove Press, 1972)

*The Real Inspector Hound* (Faber & Faber, 1968; 2nd edition, 1970; Grove Press, 1975)

*Tango*, adaptation of Mrozek's play, translated by Nicholas Bethell (Cape, 1968)

*Albert's Bridge* and *If You're Glad I'll Be Frank* (Faber & Faber, 1969)

*A Separate Peace* in *Playbill 2*, ed. Alan Durband (Hutchinson, 1969)

*Albert's Bridge* (Faber & Faber, 1970; Grove Press, 1977)

*After Magritte* (Faber & Faber, 1971); with *Hound* (Grove Press, 1975)

*Jumpers* (Faber & Faber, 1972; Grove Press, 1972)

*Artist Descending a Staircase* and *Where Are They Now?* (Faber & Faber, 1973)

*Travesties* (Faber & Faber, 1975; Grove Press, 1975)

*Dirty Linen* and *New-Found-Land* (Inter-Action Playscripts (limited edition) 1976; Faber & Faber, 1976; Grove Press, 1976)

*If You're Glad I'll Be Frank* (Faber & Faber, 1976)

*Every Good Boy Deserves Favour* and *Professional Foul* (Faber & Faber, 1978)

*Every Good Boy Deserves Favour* (Grove Press, 1978)

*Night and Day* (Faber & Faber, 1978; 2nd edition, 1979; Grove Press, 1979)

*Dogg's Our Pet* and *The (15-Minute) Dogg's Troupe Hamlet* in *Ten of the Best British Short Plays* (Inter-Action Publications, 1979)

*Dogg's Hamlet, Cahoot's Macbeth* (Faber & Faber, 1980)

*Undiscovered Country*, adaptation of Schnitzler's play (Faber & Faber, 1980)

*On the Razzle* (Faber & Faber, 1981)

*The Real Thing* (Faber & Faber, 1982)

*The Dog It Was That Died and other plays*: (*The Dissolution of Dominic Boot, 'M' is for Moon Among Other Things, Teeth, Another Moon Called Earth, A Separate Peace, Neutral Ground*) (Faber & Faber, 1983).

## (b) ARTICLES BY TOM STOPPARD

'The Definite Maybe', *Author*, 78, 1967

'Something to Declare', *Sunday Times*, 25 February 1968

'Confessions of a Screenwriter', *Today's Cinema*, 3 February 1969

'Orghast' (on Ted Hughes), *Times Literary Supplement*, 1 October 1971

'Yes, We Have No Banana', *The Guardian*, 10 December 1971

'Playwrights and Professors', *Times Literary Supplement*, 13 October 1972

'Dirty Linen in Prague' (on Havel), *New York Times*, 11 February 1977

'The Face at the Window' (on his Moscow visit), *Sunday Times*, 27 February 1977

'But For The Middle Classes' (on Paul Johnson), *Times Literary Supplement*, 3 June 1977

'I stand firm says Czech playwright' (on Havel), *Sunday Times*, 26 June 1977

'Prague: the Story of the Chartists' (on Havel), *New York Review of Books*, 4 August 1977

'Looking-Glass World' (on Havel), *New Statesman*, 28 October 1977


(Numerous early articles and reviews by Stoppard can also be found in the *Western Daily Press*, 1954–8, the Bristol *Evening World*, 1958–62 and *Scene* magazine 1962/63)

## (c) BOOKS WITH CHAPTERS, SECTIONS OR EXTENDED REFERENCES TO STOPPARD'S WORK

John Russell Taylor, *Anger and After* (Methuen, revised edition, 1969)
Robert Brustein, *The Third Theatre* (Cape, 1970)
John Russell Taylor, *The Second Wave* (Methuen, 1971)
Arnold P. Hinchliffe, *British Theatre 1950/70* (Oxford: Blackwell, 1974)
Allan Rodway, *English Comedy: Its Role and Nature from Chaucer to the Present Day* (Chatto & Windus, 1975)
C. W. E. Bigsby, *Tom Stoppard* (Longman, 1976 [enlarged edition, 1979])
Ronald Hayman, *Tom Stoppard* (Heinemann, 1977 [enlarged edition, 1978])
Oleg Kerensky, *The New British Drama* (Hamilton, 1977)
Philip Gaskell, *From Writer to Reader: Studies in Editorial Method*, (Winchester: St Paul's Press, 1978)
Ronald Hayman, *Theatre and Anti-Theatre* (Secker & Warburg, 1979)
Victor L. Cahn, *Beyond Absurdity: The Plays of Tom Stoppard* (Farleigh Dickinson U.P., 1979)
Kenneth Tynan, *Show People* (Weidenfeld & Nicolson, 1980)
Felicia Londré, *Tom Stoppard*, (New York: Ungar, 1981)
Joan Fitzpatrick Dean, *Tom Stoppard: Comedy as a Moral Matrix* (University of Missouri Press, 1981)
Jim Hunter, *Tom Stoppard's Plays* (Faber & Faber, 1982)
Thomas R. Whitaker, *Tom Stoppard* (Macmillan, Modern Dramatists Series, 1983)

## (d) CRITICAL ARTICLES AND INTERVIEWS

*Note:* this list (which is not comprehensive) excludes reviews of *specific productions*. These have regularly included the serious daily and Sunday newspapers, together with a host of weekly, monthly and quarterly magazines, including *Encounter, The Listener, Plays and Players, Drama*, etc.

Keith Harper, 'The Devious Route to Waterloo Road', *The Guardian*, 12 April 1967

John Gale, 'Writing's my 43rd Priority Says Tom Stoppard', *The Observer*, 17 December 1967

Giles Gordon, 'Tom Stoppard', *Transatlantic Review*, 29, 1968

A. K. Kennedy, 'Old and New in London Now', *Modern Drama*, XI, 1969

R. H. Lee, 'The Circle and Its Tangent', *Theoria* (University of Natal, S.A.) XXXIII, 1969

Anthony Callen, 'Stoppard's Godot: Some French Influences on Postwar English Drama', *New Theatre Magazine*, Winter 1969

C. J. Gianakaris, 'Absurdism Altered', *Drama Survey*, VII, Winter 1969

John Russell Taylor, 'Tom Stoppard: Structure and Intellect', *Plays and Players*, July 1970

Jill Levenson, 'Views from a Revolving Door: Tom Stoppard's Canon to Date', *Queens Quarterly*, LXXVIII, 1971

A. J. Ayer, 'Love among the Logical Positivists', *Sunday Times*, 9 April 1972

William Babula, 'The Play-Life Metaphor in Shakespeare and Stoppard', *Modern Drama*, XV, 3, 1972

Barry Norman, 'Tom Stoppard and the Contentment of Insecurity', *The Times*, 11 November 1972

Janet Watts, 'Interview with Tom Stoppard', *The Guardian*, 21 March 1973

Michael Leech, 'The Translators: Tom Stoppard', *Plays and Players*, April 1973

Norman Berlin, '*Rosencrantz and Guildenstern are Dead:* Theatre of Criticism', *Modern Drama*, XVI, 1973

Randolph Ryan (ed.), 'Theatre Checklist no. 2: Tom Stoppard', *Theatrefacts* (published by *Theatre Quarterly*), May–July 1974

Mark Amory, 'The Joke's the Thing', *Sunday Times Colour Supplement*, 9 June 1974

Richard Ellmann, 'The Zealots of Zurich', *Times Literary Supplement*, 12 July 1974

Ronald Hayman, 'Profile: Tom Stoppard', *The New Review*, I, 9, 1974

'Ambushes for the Audience: Towards a High Comedy of Ideas', (Tom Stoppard interviewed by editors), *Theatre Quarterly*, IV, 14, 1974 (Reprinted in *New Theatre Voices of the Seventies*, ed. Trussler, Methuen, 1981)

A. C. H. Smith, 'Tom Stoppard', *Flourish* (Royal Shakespeare Company News-sheet), 1, 1974

Jonathan Bennett, 'Philosophy and Mr. Stoppard', *Philosophy*, L, January 1975

Alfred Emmet, 'Rosencrantz in Embryo' (letter), *Theatre Quarterly*, V, 17, 1975

Clive James, 'Count Zero Splits the Infinite', *Encounter*, November 1975

Wendell V. Harris, 'Stoppard's *After Magritte*', *Explicator*, 34, 1976

Allan Rodway, 'Stripping Off', *London Magazine*, XVI, August/September 1976

Anon, 'Tom Stoppard', *Readers Theatre (News)* (San Diego State University), IV, 2, Spring 1977

Lucina P. Gabbard, 'Stoppard's *Jumpers:* A Mystery Play', *Modern Drama*, XX, March 1977

Henning Jensen, 'Jonathan Bennett and Mr. Stoppard', *Philosophy*, LII, April 1977

Jon Bradshaw, 'Tom Stoppard Non-Stop', *Telegraph Sunday Magazine*, 26 June 1977

John Barber, 'Tom Stoppard at a terminus', *Daily Telegraph*, 4 July 1977

Brian M. Crossley, 'An investigation of Stoppard's 'Hound' and 'Foot'', *Modern Drama*, XX, March 1977

Clifford D. May (with Edward Behr), 'Master of the Stage', *Newsweek*, 15 August 1977

Penelope Mortimer, 'Tom Stoppard: Funny, Fast Talking and Our First Playwright', *Cosmopolitan*, January 1978

Margaret Gold, 'Who are the Dadas of *Travesties?*', *Modern Drama*, XXI, March 1978

Philip Roberts, 'Tom Stoppard – Serious Artist or Siren?', *Critical Quarterly*, Autumn 1978

Bart Mills, 'Tom Stoppard moves into Political Writing', *Newsday*, 7 October 1978

Eric Salmon, 'Faith in Mr. Stoppard', *Queens Quarterly*, LXXXVI, 2, 1979

Mary R. Davidson, 'Historical Homonyms: A New Way of Naming in Tom Stoppard's *Jumpers*', *Modern Drama*, XXII, September 1979

Craig Werner, 'Stoppard's Critical Travesty; or Who Vindicates Whom, and Why?', *Arizona Quarterly*, 35, 3, 1979

Atticus, 'Stoppard in Greeneland', *Sunday Times*, 20 January 1980

Joost Kuurman, 'Tom Stoppard', *Dutch Quarterly Review of Anglo-American Letters*, 10, 1980/81

James Morwood, '*Jumpers* Revisited', *Agenda*, 18 iv/19 i, Winter
    1980/Spring 1981
Kenneth Tynan, 'Withdrawing with Style from the Chaos' excerpts
    from a profile which originally appeared in *The New Yorker
    Magazine*, 19 December 1977, and has subsequently been
    reprinted in full in *Show People* (see above, section c); Tim
    Brassell, '*Jumpers:* a happy marriage?'; Douglas McMillan,
    'Dropping the other Boot'; Judy Simons, '*Night and Day*'; 'Trad
    Tom Pops in' (interview with David Gollob and David Roper) –
    all in *Gambit*, X, 37, 1981 ('Tom Stoppard Issue')
Michael Owen, 'Is this for real, Tom?', *Standard*, 15 October
    1982
Anon, 'Juggler to the British stage', *Observer*, 14 November 1982
Roger Scruton, 'The Real Stoppard', *Encounter*, February 1983

*Note:* all sections are arranged in chronological order. Place of
    publication unless otherwise stated is London.

# Index